WAITING FOR RAIN

Life and Development in Mali, West Africa

D1523316

WAITING FOR RAIN
Life and Development in Mali, West Africa

by Lewis Lucke

Founded 1910
THE CHRISTOPHER PUBLISHING HOUSE
HANOVER, MASSACHUSETTS 02339

PRINTED IN THE UNITED STATES OF AMERICA

Table of Contents

Mali

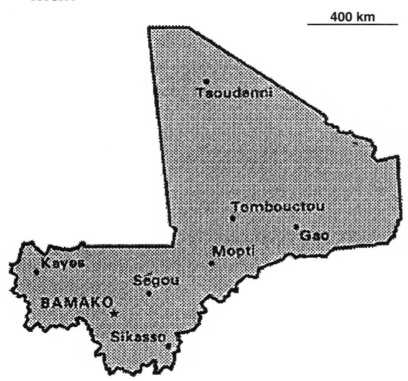

400 km

Tsoudenni

Tombouctou

Gao

Mopti

Kayes

Ségou

BAMAKO

Sikasso

Preface

I have spent the past eighteen years working on economic development programs and living in some of the poorer countries of the world. My first two countries — Mali and Senegal — were in West Africa and had economies firmly established near the very bottom of the pile. Following seven years in Africa, I moved to what seemed virtually like a different planet: to Costa Rica in Central America, and then eventually on to Tunisia where I was caught up in the build-up to the Persian Gulf War. I ended up back in Latin America once again, this time in Bolivia in the heart of South America, and after five immensely satisfying years there finally moved on to Jordan in the heart of the Middle East.

The approaches to development we tried in Latin America, and especially in lovely and relatively prosperous Costa Rica, were far different from the strategies we employed in West Africa. The development problems in Costa Rica involved economic stabilization and structural reform toward a market economy, banking reform, the reorientation of the economy in favor of exports and the like.

The problems of West Africa at the time were far more basic — reestablishing agricultural production in the wake of a devastating drought, increasing the country's ability to provide food security and greater self-sufficiency in agricultural production for its people, improving abysmal health conditions, and so forth.

This is a story about my first developing country: Mali, one of the absolute dirt-poorest countries on the planet. Mali, located in the landlocked heart of West Africa, is representative of the struggle of a country that finally evolved away from an early unholy post-independence alliance of drought and Marxism to where it is today — with a democratically-elected government and reformed market-oriented policies — that, combined with the return of fickle seasonal rains, has become self-sufficient in grain production and a net exporter of food to its neighbors.

Mali is still very poor and still beset by enormous problems but the changes in its ability to better feed itself and its economic philosophy, compared to the more inward, backward and gasping Mali I experienced, are remarkable. Though the partial turnabout in Mali's fortunes do not yet make it a true economic success story — and may have as much to do with the return of sufficient rainfall than anything else — it is indicative of a country that is making progress despite great odds against it.

The story involves the plight of a poor, distant country trying to survive a drought and reform its economy, but is at the same time the story of a well-meaning, somewhat naive and inexperienced aid worker who is out of the developed world for almost the first time, yet trying to learn his trade, his new country, and figure how to make a small difference in carrying out a set of development programs developed in response to still another period of intensive Sahelian drought. The question posed, after all is said and done, is "What have we wrought?"

Mali is still an intensely genuine African country of the Sahel, dependent on the Niger River, unreliable rainfall, and agriculture to survive. Mali and its capital of Bamako are still very far away from the bright lights of Abidjan, Dakar, or certainly Nairobi or Johannesburg.

Africa can be a violent, brutal and frightening place with some of the most intractable economic problems imaginable. One observer of West Africa would be correct in perceiving rampant corruption, deceit, incompetence and sometimes overwhelming misery. But at the same time, it is just as accurately a place of great natural beauty, humor, happiness, and human richness on such a scale that can captivate and move the foreigner who somehow ends up there. At the end of my years in West Africa and particularly those spent in Mali, it is the latter set of qualities that has remained my most indelible memory and meaningful impression.

I am grateful to the Malians who enriched my stay there and this story. I was also privileged to have worked with a dedicated group of professional development colleagues, most possessing a necessary prerequisite for life and work in West Africa — a highly developed sense of humor — and most having come to Mali on their own free will, determined to make their best contribution under often very trying conditions to Mali and its people's development.

Many of these colleagues appear here, but some do not for reasons of space and story line. Notwithstanding, all were part of the human stew that enriched my and my spouse's own lives there.

All of the events and characters that appear here are true. I have changed only a couple of names where this was appropriate, and a few minor details may be off where my notes and memory have failed me.

I am particularly indebted to Dr. Gerald Cashion of Rabat, Morocco, whom I met on my first day in Mali, was my friend and colleague during my entire stay there, and whose knowledge and insights about Mali taught me volumes at the time. Dr. Cashion, who is identified only as Jerry in the book and is still my friend and professional colleague, provided a review of my text for factual and anthropological errors and for that I am very grateful.

I also owe an acknowledgement of gratitude and thanks to Alex Newton, originally from Madison, Georgia and presently residing in Almaty, Khazakstan, who provided me permission to use material from his excellent, definitive travel book on West Africa, *West Africa*, published by Lonely Planet. Alex Newton is the Alex of my book and I am fortunate to have had such a unique and generous development colleague for the past eighteen years.

I would be remiss to not mention my employer, the Agency for International Development, where despite the occasional rise and fall in its organizational fortunes and credibility, I have always been proud to work. AID is composed of dedicated and hardworking people, Americans as well as its vital international staff, and carries out development projects and programs in over seventy countries around the world. I have seen the results of AID's many good works overseas over the years, and despite political perceptions that have made the future of "foreign aid" very uncertain, in my view the U.S. taxpayers can be very proud of AID as having had positive impact in helping to develop the world's neediest countries. I feel the work carried out by AID is representative of the very best in American values. I am especially grateful for the assistance of AID's Center for Development Information and Evaluation in providing ample documentation on the Mali development program without which I would have been unable to complete this book. The opinions expressed in the book are personal and do not represent the views or policy of the Agency for International Development.

I dedicate this book to two people. The first is Farhad Vakil, better know as Mickey, who got sick in Bamako on a day that the planes didn't fly to Paris, and so died after a series of mishaps and errors — far too young and leaving behind a young widow and a three-year-old child. The other is to my wife, Joy, who has been with me throughout all of my now six developing countries, who accompanied me to Mali as a fellow new experiencer of Africa, and who has made her own important contributions to economic development in both Africa and Latin America.

Amman, Jordan
November, 1996

1
Getting Ready

"Mali" is the word for hippopotamus in Bambara, that country's most widely spoken language. The rivers of Mali, especially portions of the vast Niger and its tributaries, still abound in hippos. They can be aggressive and territorial, zealous in protecting their young, capable of devastating farmers' fields in a single feeding, and sometimes dangerous to humans.

Despite its meaning in Bambara, the name of the country originated with the Mande people of West Africa who founded the Mali Empire in the thirteenth century. The Mali Empire grew in richness due to taxes on gold and ivory, and from profits coming from trans-Saharan caravan trade routes. The city of Timbuktu, a real place, flourished during this period, eventually becoming a center of learning with two universities and over 100,000 inhabitants. The greatest leader of the Mali Empire, Kankan Moussa, who undertook a pilgrimage to Mecca in 1324, was said to have been accompanied by an entourage of 60,000 people and vast quantities of gold. Kankan Moussa's lavish gifts of gold made in route in Egypt are said to have destroyed the value of the Egyptian currency for several years.

I liked that the name of the country where I spent almost four years meant hippopotamus. This added some more of a comfortable, inscrutable quality to Mali that I liked and that I came to expect about the place.

There was a lot about Mali I came to know well and love, and amid immense poverty, there was a human richness that was and is my most lasting impression. There was also a lot about the country that was hidden and that I could not hope to understand in my years there. The Westerner in a country like Mali tends to be a relative short-termer who arrives, works for a prescribed period of time and leaves. Though his stay can be intense and even passionate, he inevitably moves on. The Malians remain.

When I left the United States for the West African country of Mali, I had virtually no clue of what I was getting into. I knew flat zero about the lives of the people there. The whole idea of West Africa was an open book in my mind and most of the pages were blank.

The plan, if there was one, was to move with my new wife of less than a year from the shores of the comfortable U.S. to work in one of the most unknown and remote countries of Africa, at least to Americans and most other Westerners. It was also one of the poorest countries in the world, poor even by African standards, with a per capita income of about $120 a year.

At the time, moving to Mali sounded like a true adventure and a lot of fun. What the heck, we were pretty young — I was twenty-seven and my wife was twenty-five — and we had both decided that economic development in the third world was what we wanted to do with our professional lives.

I had turned down a couple of job offers from U.S. banks after graduate school studies in international business to follow my first choice of a career in overseas "international development." My new Texas father-in-law's not altogether inappropriate question of such a prospect and his daughter's role in the whole affair was, "But why don't you look for a real job?" His vision of us working at respectable jobs in Houston or Dallas and returning to our happy home in a comfortable suburb was soon to vanish like dew in the desert. The question though, I was to find, would persist in the mind of my respectable and otherwise reasonable father-in-law for a number of years to come, and never seemed to be particularly well answered to his satisfaction.

The matter of choosing "international development" as a career, however inadequate this description, seemed like an interesting, challenging, and valuable profession. There was the chance to have an intellectually stimulating profession, live overseas, experience out-of-the-ordinary cultures, and hopefully contribute something to their economic development. I also figured too that by living overseas in poorer countries I might be able to avoid big-city commuting, sitting in traffic stalled on some freeway — the idea of which I hated.

However important the matter of that career was to me, I knew it was insignificant compared to the big picture — the struggle of poor countries to reform their economies and undertake change that would provide better lives for their people. Early on I was intrigued with the complexities of how the poorest countries can develop economically. How do you make progress in implementing a free market economy? How can you help some of the world's absolute incredibly poorest countries, often corrupt and devoid of basic resources, implement programs that impact on real people living in extreme poverty and actually improve their lives, or at least insure that they stay alive awhile longer? How, in the face of misery, bureaucratic lethargy, corruption, and the case of far too much need chasing far too inadequate development funds, can progress be made?

This was pretty heavy stuff and such weighty questions would have to wait. The first task was to get a job. I was eventually hired by a U.S.-based development organization that had worldwide responsibilities. One of its priorities at the time was to gear up to provide economic assistance in response to one of the periodic droughts that seemed increasingly prone to hit the part of Africa known as the Sahel.

The Sahel — sahel means "plain" in Arabic — forms the vast and mostly savannah and grassland area between the Sahara desert to the north and the more geographically fortunate higher rainfall African countries to the south. The Sahel is also thought of, when it is thought of at all, as the dividing area and transitional zone between the Arabs of North Africa and the blacks of the Sub-Sahara.

The Sahel stretches from Senegal on the extreme western edge of Africa all the way to Chad some 2,000 miles away and encompassing an area about the size of the U.S. west of the Mississippi River. The Sahel includes all or parts of seven countries with a population of over 40 million people.

I was fortunate to get the job I had. Many of my competitors for this job and in the entire development field had Ph.D's in some technical field, had more extensive international experience, and many had been former Peace Corps volunteers to boot, which I figured gave them a big leg up on producing results in tough overseas settings.

A few years before I had turned in my Peace Corps application — in fact I did it twice — but never heard back from them. I was even told by the Peace Corps recruiter back in Chapel Hill to which county I would likely be assigned — Senegal — and the type of work I would be doing for the next two years — community development — whatever that was. After waiting patiently several months for the wheels of the Peace Corps bureaucracy to turn, I gave up and called them. They had never heard of me. I completed the entire application process again and after a decent interval called them. The answer was exactly the same — we can't seem to find your papers and who are you again?

H.L. Mencken once said about the South that "divine inspiration was as common as hookworm", and therefore it seemed inadvisable to ignore potentially divinely inspired signs of any sort. This would not do. So, it was clear enough that God did not wish me to be a Peace Corps volunteer. In fact I felt lucky to have a junior-level professional job in development. And given the state of the U.S. economy at the time, I felt lucky to have a job at all, much less one in my chosen field.

I thought my main aces in the hole job-wise were that I had a relevant graduate degree and that I could speak French. I was wrong about the graduate degree — everybody had one.

French was a different story. I had started studying French in the eighth grade at home in North Carolina — that well-known hot-bed of Francophonia — and had kept it up all the way through a year abroad program at the University of Lyon in France. I had become inspired about French for a couple of reasons: one, I had lusted in my heart after one of my high school French teachers and therefore took the course more seriously than others. Two, on the way back from my first overseas jaunt as a seventeen year old, I had stopped over at Orly airport in Paris. To paraphrase Mark Twain's *Innocents Abroad*, it was there I first realized that there really were people out there who ate frog's legs and spoke and actually thought in French as their native honest-to-goodness first language.

That made quite an impression on me, and though at the time I could basically do no better in French than order from a menu and badly at that, it was a start and I was motivated.

The most substantive reason I took French seriously as a subject of study had occurred a few weeks earlier on the same trip as the stopover at Orly. I had accompanied a group of amateur archaeologists to Israel on a summer dig of a Solomonic-era temple site, excavating the temple ruins by day and living in a tent at a nearby kibbutz by night.

While on the way back to our kibbutz from Tel Aviv, the bus reached its nearest point to our destination and disgorged two friends and myself for some unknown reason in the middle of nowhere. We took off walking toward the lights of a village twinkling off in the distance, as it was quite dark and we were still a good ways from our kibbutz destination. After having walked several kilometers along the highway, we saw several tough-looking Israeli soldiers walking towards us. The fact that their rifles were leveled at us reinforced my strong impression that this was not the movies and that I was a long way from home. The head soldier addressed us in Hebrew. Soon realizing we were foreigners and seeing our bewilderment, he immediately switched to what I assumed was the only other language he knew — French.

After more than a couple of repetitions and a few impassioned explanations from us in English that we were Americans and therefore obviously harmless, I pieced together that we were in an area where curfew was due to be imposed in a few minutes and that if we were still on the road when that happened, we could be challenged by the next patrol and possibly shot. He said *shot*.

Our next move was to get off the road and walk faster with a true sense of purpose to the village, where, it being too small to have a hostel or cheap hotel, we were offered overnight accommodations in the local jail where the jailer was kind enough to leave the cell doors open. That was my first and last night spent in any jail, at least so far, I am happy to report.

Morning saw us on the first bus back to the kibbutz, happy to be back on familiar ground and happy that I had had enough comprehension of French to understand the soldier's warning.

Definitely this was a language worth knowing. After all, even at such a tender age, it had already helped save my skin.

My "Year Abroad" program at the University of Lyon cemented my love of France and my ability to decipher the *passé composé* tense and sometimes even the subjunctive. The fact that the French university system was on strike practically the entire school year didn't effect the fact that I learned more about the language — albeit to my enduring delight and satisfaction — far from the classroom in the more pleasant surroundings of Provence, Gard, the Massif Central, the Cote d'Azur, and the Beaujolais region.

I was to soon find that it really was no big deal for Americans to speak a foreign language, as long as that language was Spanish. Being from North Carolina, I found it impressive that any American could get by in any foreign language at all. In North Carolina, foreigners were even rarer than Catholics. We occasionally had trouble understanding folks from New York much less from a real bona fide foreign country. Americans who could speak good French were few and far between, however, and the fact I could do passably well early in my career was an advantage.

My job was based in Washington, D.C. My employer had projects all over the developing world, and my first duty was to help find American experts in specialized technical fields to work overseas on a host of different development projects. At this same time a prolonged drought in the Sahel was starting to have serious consequences on people of the region. The seasonal rains had failed again and agricultural and livestock production were devastated. People were starving.

Significantly, the plight of the Sahel had been discovered by the Western media and the image of starving children and emaciated cattle on the barren wind-whipped landscape of the Sahel was a strong though brief fixture on the nightly news. North Americans and Europeans responded typically with concern and generosity, and though the focus was only too brief, the attention allowed us to begin to design a program aimed at alleviating the immediate suffering caused by the Sahel drought and to begin to think of how we could assist the people there to reestablish a means of sustainable development — particularly in food production — once the initial crisis had passed.

My job became focussed uniquely on the Sahel drought, trying to help figure out which projects we were proposing made the most economic sense. My job also was to help the Sahel governments themselves assemble their own portfolio of the most feasible projects for presentation to the international donors — mostly the Europeans, Canadians and Americans — for financing.

It was while doing this latter chore that I traveled twice to France, including once to beautiful Montpellier in the south, to help shape and polish this project presentation that the Sahel countries would eventually make. My wife, Joy, left in a small basement apartment near Dupont Circle in Washington, D.C., was forced in my absence to dig her way out of a three-foot snowfall that had completely paralyzed D.C. and had temporarily trapped her underground. I returned to seeing the end of the melting snow where days before cross-country skiers had the streets of D.C. mostly to themselves. My happy stories of the warmth and beauty of southern France were received by her with less than unbridled enthusiasm as I returned to a still paralyzed and melting Washington.

Joy, working away at a job with Georgetown University while I worked on the Sahel, had of course wondered where my job would lead us. Discussions had been progressing at the office on the possibility of a long-term Sahel assignment, but my wife, like me only months before, still had only a vague idea of where the likes of Chad, Senegal or Mali actually were on the globe.

My employer was starting to get serious about an overseas assignment to Mali. I took the news home.

"Well, they're talking about sending us to Mali in March."

"Maui?" I think I saw visions of beaches and surfboards flash across her mind.

"No, Mali."

"Bali?" Visions of sleek Indonesian dancers, hands gesturing, briefly appeared and quickly vanished.

"Ah, no, it's Mali, you know, one of the countries in the Sahel. The capital is called Bamako. That's where we would be living."

I saw no vision cross her mind. Zip, none at all.

It was time to get down the atlas.

But first, I had to deal with an office glitch. Someone in command had now decided I should be assigned to Latin America instead of Africa.

Latin America? This made no sense. I spoke only a few words of Spanish, and my only experience with the region had been to drive over the border a couple of times from Texas into Nuevo Laredo. I wasn't particularly interested in the region, at least compared to Africa, and besides, I had already been working on the Sahel drought relief program and I spoke French. What was going on? This sounded more like something that the military would do.

I went to see the person in charge of overseas personnel assignments. It didn't take us long to get down to business.

"We're sending you to Latin America and you want to go to the Sahel instead? And to Mali? That's the end of the road. That place is terrible."

He looked at his papers

"It says here you already speak French. And you can go soon?"

He looked up at me.

"We normally can't find people to go to Mali. And you want to go there?" he repeated to make sure such a thing could be true.

"Wait here. I'll be right back."

Five minutes later he reentered the room.

"OK. You want to go to Mali? Well, great, it's all set."

Your normal American learns very little about Africa in school. African geography, economics, culture and most everything else about Africa are almost completely ignored in the non-specialist curriculum of U.S. high schools and universities. Even most African-Americans know little or nothing about the vast continent of their ancestors — twice as big as the continental United States in area and the home of some forty-four separate countries.

One recent exception is of course the anti-apartheid fight in South Africa and the odyssey of Nelson Mandela from political prisoner to president. That and the democratic elections in South Africa were widely reported. For a while.

One African country alone, Nigeria, contains over eighty million people and is the world's tenth largest producer of OPEC petroleum. Africa, where most anthropologists agree man originated, the site of epic twentieth century struggles for independence from the colonial powers, for majority rule in South Africa, and for freedom from hunger and disease, is largely off the screens of the American public.

Of course there are a few exceptions that briefly command our attention. We are from time to time riveted by scenes of starvation and human disaster in Biafra, Rwanda, Ethiopia, Somalia, Sudan or the Sahel. It is not good for the media to hit the airwaves with too many African disasters at a time, as compassion can be generated and attention devoted for only for short periods and preferably in only one place at a time. Compassion burnout over African disasters is a real phenomenon.

Media focus and attention on Africa is generally rare. During my stay there, only three U.S. newspapers bothered to have full time correspondents based in Africa — *The Washington Post*, the *New York Times*, and the *Los Angeles Times*. There were and still are few media correspondents to cover over forty countries in a land area twice as large as the United States.

The first portions of the ethnic genocide sweeping the East African country of Rwanda in 1994, where an estimated 500,000 people were massacred over a two month period, was reported in the United States but barely so. When perhaps a million mainly Hutu refugees fled across the border into neighboring Zaire amid a cholera epidemic, the scope of the human tragedy was too great to ignore. The world responded for a while with help and sympathy to this overwhelming disaster, but then the TV cameras moved on to the next world hot-spot and the Rwandan refugees, still struggling to survive from one day to the next, faded from Western view and consciousness.

It is tempting to compare the lack of media coverage and Western outrage of African disasters with that of the more familiar European variety such as Bosnia. In Somalia, the 1992-93 drought was reported on U.S. television and was a major factor in mobilizing U.S. aid and intervention in that country. But little or no coverage went to a similar drought at the same time in the Sudan, to continued warfare in Angola, to election strife in Madagascar and Nigeria, to a monumental refugee problem in Burundi and other countries surrounding Rwanda, to continued mayhem in the virtual ex-American colony of Liberia, or Zaire, to the impact of AIDS on East Africa, to post-civil war reconciliation in Mozambique, and a host of other problem places on the African continent.

It is much too easy but understandable for us to concentrate on one digestible though disagreeable disaster at a time, such as Somalia, and not bother about the rest. Or concentrate instead on the nasty or near-comic African villains that pop up from time to time, Idi Amin or self-declared Emperor Bokassa of the Central African Empire being the best examples. The good news too — and there is some — is similarly ignored by the media but this of course is not unique to Africa.

Anyway, we got down the atlas and the encyclopedia and looked up Mali.

Mali was in the center of West Africa, landlocked and bordered by Senegal, Mauritania, Guinea, Upper Volta (later to change it's name to Burkina Faso, or simply called Burkina by those in the know), Niger, Ivory Coast, and finally Algeria to the north. The fabled city of Timbuktu really existed and was located within Mali's borders. The size of the country was greater than Texas and California combined, a fact that got the attention of my Texas in-laws who had never heard of the place. It was also the largest country in West Africa.

Almost sixty percent of the land area of Mali was the Sahara Desert, mostly the northern portion of the country. The southern-most region of the country near the Ivory Coast and Guinea had the most rainfall which was usually sufficient for good agricultural production. It was the 200 to 800mm of rainfall zone in between that was properly known as the Sahel, which was more heavily populated, and where variable rainfall created drought and so many problems. The population of Mali was about eight million with one of the highest population growth rates in the world. Most of the people were concentrated, sensibly, in the Sahelian and southern portions of the country.

There were only 14 people per square kilometer of arable land and the populated land area was often in bad shape due to erosion and overgrazing. There were two major and underutilized river systems in the country — the Niger and the Senegal — which had potential for energy production, irrigation and transport. Originating in the highlands of Guinea, the Niger was one of the great rivers of Africa, winding its way through Mali and the cities of Bamako, Segou, Mopti, Djenne, Timbuktu, and Gao on its way down to Nigeria and the Atlantic Ocean.

Over the next few weeks we learned many other details about Mali, but it was such an unknown destination I got the feeling that the information from books would hardly seem relevant once we actually arrived there.

It certainly seemed like we would get the chance to find out about Mali for ourselves. My assignment to Mali for a minimum of two years and a maximum of four years had been approved. We were to depart Washington in several weeks and proceed directly to our office in Mali's capital city of Bamako.

My official job would be to help design new development projects and evaluate on-going or terminating projects. The project portfolio was then about $12 million a year. This amount, while not insignificant, was certainly not on the scale of several other donors in Mali, and particularly of the World Bank. The World Bank in Mali, as in many other developing countries, was the largest international development agency in terms of the amounts of money loaned and they had their own particular approach to carrying out development programs. The World Bank, being a bank, normally designed and financed assistance programs as loans rather than grants, though some of the loans to the poorest countries like Mali tended to be offered at concessional terms. And though Bank projects were extensively designed in great detail, once approved, the Bank passed the money to the government in question, and let it implement the project, generally with outside technical assistance.

Our approach was a bit different. We had less money than the World Bank, but in the poorest countries like Mali, our assistance almost always was in the form of grants. We had a more extensive in-country presence than the Bank and usually a much more hands-on approach to project implementation. The belief was that this assistance, hopefully well-conceived and closely monitored and implemented by our field staff, could turn a relatively modest financial investment into significant development impact, thereby in the case of Mali helping address the immediate effects of the drought and hopefully nurturing a process of more sustainable economic development.

The next few weeks were full of preparations for departure, each day's list of things to do being crossed off in turn. There were shots to get, health cards to fill out, forwarding addresses to send, good-byes to make to friends and family, visas to get, furniture to store, household possessions to be divided into storage or freight, bills to pay, a car to buy and ship (shipping our old beat-up Fiat to the wilds of Africa didn't seem a particularly good idea) and a host of other things that kept us in a whirl until the last moment.

Living near the Malian Embassy in Washington, D.C., I decided to take our passports over myself to obtain our Malian visas. I took all the required forms and photos with me. The Malian Embassy was and still is located in a fine old rowhouse on R Street, Northwest, not far from Massachusetts Avenue where many of the more economically-endowed countries maintain their Embassies on so-called Embassy Row. This was February and it was bitter cold in D.C., the wind blasting me as I approached the Malian Embassy entrance. The red, yellow and green Malian flag, frayed, dirty, and half wrapped-around its flagpole, whipped in the cold breeze as I stepped inside.

Once inside, I had a shock. The place was badly in need of a paint job. More to the point, it was freezing. In fact there seemed to be no heat inside at all. Since the Embassy was totally quiet and seemed quite deserted, I proceeded up the narrow stairs looking for a living soul. I poked my head into one large office and saw there an African-looking gentlemen sitting at a desk, shivering from the cold and just as clearly miserable, who proved to be the Malian Charge d'Affaires, the Acting Ambassador. He was dressed for the temperature in a battered, out-of-style winter coat. There was a wool cap on his head.

He leaned forward from his old, metal swivel chair that looked as if it had come from a yard sale and greeted me in French.

"*Ca va?*" How's it going?

His breath was visible in the cold air as he stood up and we shook hands. As he stamped our passports with the visas he explained quite honestly that there simply was no money in his budget to pay for heat. He nodded silently and looked me in the eye with no further comment when I told him we were moving to Mali, perhaps for four years, to work on development projects there.

He handed me back our passports and simply said in French, "*Bon sejour au Mali.*" Have a nice stay in Mali.

Let's hope so, I thought.

As I tramped my way home avoiding patches of ice on the sidewalk, I realized I had had my first insight on Mali. If the Malian Embassy was any yardstick to judge by, the place must be major poor.

2
Bamako, Mali

Air Afrique flight 109 disgorged a small eclectic group of passengers onto the blistering tarmac of Bamako's international airport, including us. We had arrived in the middle of the hot season and it was my twenty-eighth birthday. I had lived in Phoenix for a time and knew what hot was. This was hot.

The Air Afrique flight which had arrived directly from Dakar, Senegal, didn't tarry in Bamako, and as we claimed our six suitcases and my guitar case, took off to continue the remainder of its milk run through the Sahel — to Ouagadougou and Niamey, then returning in succession eventually back to Dakar.

Our first night in West Africa had been spent in Dakar the previous evening, where we had landed after flying in on Pan Am from New York. I had noticed the name painted on the fuselage of the Pan Am 747. It was Maid of the Seas. This was the same plane that would be blown up over Lockerbee, Scotland as Pan Am flight 103 some years later.

We had arrived in Dakar an hour ahead of schedule just before dawn, and having no CFA — the currency for many of the former French colonies in West Africa — could not avoid getting ripped off by the taxi driver who demanded and got the sum of $28 to take us into downtown Dakar. We had reserved a hotel room in advance from Washington. I was prepared to lower my expectations and I had seen worse than this, but Joy was having a harder time with the Hotel Atlantide. Located on a side street in the center of Dakar, it was dilapidated, hot and dirty, but mostly just dirty.

This was the place that had been recommended by a friend? Some friend. Joy and I both wanted to be flexible and adapt well to our new environment, but flexibility in this case did not require her to put a bare foot on the floor or take off her clothes. We slept deeply the sleep of the jet-lagged and sleep deprived, and in my wife's case, fully clothed. I imagine we were the first and last people to actually make a reservation for the likes of the Hotel Atlantide all the way from the U.S.

I was worried about how my new, young wife would react to Africa. She had traveled overseas before, but only on first class college girl tours of the great cities of Europe, where all arrangements had been meticulously planned in advance. Traveling to and living in the Sahel would not be comparable to that, that much I knew. I had heard lots of stories about colleagues set on an overseas career whose spouses had freaked out once they realized they were expected to survive at the very margins of civilization. Such marriages didn't tend to last very long. Though Joy seemed to share my enthusiasm for moving to the Sahel and had professional economic development aspirations of her own, one just never knew how other people would react. I would have to keep my fingers crossed and hope for the best.

Once we awoke around noon, still jet-lagged but full of optimism, we walked around the streets of Dakar to get our first glimpse and smells of Africa. We bought good croissants and strong French coffee on Avenue Ponty and watched the human parade go by. By this time of day the sun was radiating heat from buildings, mixing with an array of cooking and other more earthy smells of West Africa. The tall and distinguished-looking Senegalese women, most in traditional flowing robes but some in European dress, made the greatest impression. With the new smells, the heat, the open markets with African art and clothes on display, and the everyday bustle of a completely different culture, it all seemed very exotic.

In the afternoon we met a friend from Washington who was doing a short consultancy in Dakar for the U.S. Agency for International Development. Together we found the ferry for Goree, an island in the Dakar harbor that had no cars or bicycles, had old colonial homes with wrought-iron balconies, a colonial town hall, and peaceful views across the water back towards Dakar.

Goree was also the site of the Slave House, built by the Dutch in 1776, and used as the departure point for captured African slaves on their way to the Americas or the West Indies. A visit to this place was a sobering affair. Looking through the Slave House door to the sea that had been the passageway on to the slave ships, and the last door from the African homeland to slavery or death in a strange land, one only had to be human to feel the pain that had been long ago inflicted in this now dark and silent place.

We were to return to Dakar after a year in Mali and walk down the same streets. How had I ever, ever considered Dakar to be strange or exotic? You could get cafe au lait and croissants there. There were beautiful beaches and a whole ocean. There were grass lawns, leafy trees and grocery stores full of the culinary finery of France. After Bamako, it was Paris come to Africa!

Our Air Afrique flight left for Bamako and the other Sahelian capitals the next morning at 8 A.M. Armed this time with CFA and renewed confidence, we headed back to the airport and paid the proper taxi fare of less than half of what we had been forced to pay the previous morning. It was a warm beautiful day and the strong breeze was off the ocean. The plane was waiting on the tarmac and on time. Joy had not taken the first plane back to the States and had not complained about anything other than the Atlantide. Things were looking up or at least not recognizably disintegrating.

As our flight approached Bamako, the sky was crystal clear and parts of the city and the surrounding countryside were visible below. There were large patches of green here and there but much vaster expanses of what seemed like sun-baked dirt interspersed with adobe-looking houses and villages built in clusters. The African villages became thicker as they approached both sides of a large river — the Niger — and became a huge disorganized hodge-podge of a large town — our first glimpse of Bamako. The plane's air conditioning didn't fool me either. It looked hot down there.

A Malian soldier stamped our passports without comment and we gathered our bags together. Our office in Bamako had been contacted by cable with our arrival time and flight number and we knew that the standard procedure for new arrivals was to be met and assisted at the airport.

Or so we thought. The few passengers with whom we had arrived had already disappeared, and the spartan, concrete Bamako airport, built with financial and technical assistance from the Soviet Union, was quiet and nearly deserted. We were still feeling optimistic but this was not good. We could possibly find a taxi to take us into town but once again we had no Malian Francs and no idea where our house, if there even was one, was located. Would a taxi driver, assuming there were taxis here, know where my office was?

Our questions were superseded by the appearance of an American-looking man, bearded and seemingly in his mid-thirties, purchasing the international edition of *Time* magazine from an airport vendor. Seeing our lost appearance he introduced himself as Jerry and asked if he could help. Well, yes, we had just arrived and had not been picked up, I supposed I should go straight to the office, did he have a car, did he have room for us?

Jerry said, "Oh, it's you! We'll be working in the same office. I heard you were coming but the administrative office always makes arrangements for a driver to come out and expedite you through the airport. I just was out here because I thought I could find a *Time* magazine. I can't believe they didn't meet you."

All's well that ends well. We piled our suitcases and my guitar case high in Jerry's open-air orange Jeep and hung on to the roll bar as we headed into Bamako. I was to later discover that it was a supreme faux-pas to not meet new arrivals at the airport, especially those arriving in Africa for the first time. Arriving for the first time in a profoundly under-developed country, it is important to start off on the right foot.

Being met by Jerry was a plus, however, and was the start of what would prove to be a long and close friendship. Jerry said he and his wife had been in Mali already for six years. They were budding anthropologists who had come to Mali to do their doctoral research for Indiana University. The Chicago-born son of a jazz musician, Jerry had been a stock broker before going back to school to become an anthropologist and moving to Mali. I was to discover no one in the course of my years in Mali who could compare to Jerry in his profound knowledge and appreciation of Mali and its culture. This was the one right guy to run into first.

Being nearly broke after living for three years in rural Mali, Jerry and his wife Barbara had become development consultants, Jerry now working full time as an anthropologist and project evaluator in my employer's Bamako office. Both he and his wife spoke fluent Bambara, the most widely spoken local language in Mali. Though French was fine for dealing with folks in the government and the capital city, I would find that even a small knowledge of Bambara was a great plus for working effectively in the rural areas.

The Bamako airport proved to be in the countryside some seven miles from the center of town. I would later come to know the airport intimately because of my frequent travel around the country and because of the tradition of seeing friends off, especially when they departed the country for good.

The two lane paved road into Bamako was in pretty good shape. We soon began to pass both numerous low mud buildings and what seemed to be entire villages of rounded huts along the way. The villages became more dense and eventually merged into neighborhoods of one story, concrete villas surrounded by whitewashed fences where, Jerry pointed out, many expatriates lived, including the deputy chief of our Bamako operation.

It was nearly noon and while it was a work day, Jerry drove us to George's house to see if anyone there knew what to do with us. To our surprise, George, a tall middle-aged man with reddish hair, skin suited for Ireland and one of my many new bosses, was there along with his wife Helen and a small group of my new colleagues from the office. It seems we were expected for lunch as guests of honor, despite the lack of an airport pickup. The other guests included David, a bearded, youngish member of the agriculture office, Alex, a wild-looking ex-Peace Corps Volunteer and non-practicing lawyer also in my office, and Kent, the head of the administrative office who looked sheepish when Jerry explained that he had found us at the airport lost and unmet. It was a very casually dressed group and the conversation about work and Mali was positive.

Finally, we felt welcomed and a bit more at ease, and somehow Helen had found out it was my birthday and presented me with a cupcake and candle for dessert. Afterwards, my colleagues returned to the office for the afternoon work period. The Malians had adopted the French workday — 7:30 A.M. to 12:30 with a two hour break for lunch where everyone hurried home for a hot lunch — followed by a return to work until 5:30 P.M. I knew I didn't much like to commute, but with this schedule we could all do two complete round trips to the office per day instead of one.

Feeling good now about our arrival and it being time for my new friends to go back to work, we could proceed to be delivered to our new house. Helen drove us in her white Peugeot 504 station wagon with our bags and the guitar piled in the back. We crossed the Niger River on a long bridge that, Helen explained, was Bamako's only one and which had been built with financing from the People's Republic of China.

On the other side of the bridge we were in Bamako proper or *"centre ville"* as the French would say. Large mango trees on both sides of the large avenue provided shade as we passed the French Embassy, which as past colonial master still provided budget support, technical assistance and did its best to provide continued cultural inspiration for their African ex-charges — Rimbaud and Voltaire for the downtrodden.

The broad street quickly narrowed to a chaos of small shops and stores as we inched our way through a throng of vehicles, especially mobylettes, and busy Malians going about their daily business. We passed the "Grand Mosque" with its tall minaret on the right — a gift of the Malian's Islamic brothers in Saudi Arabia — and turned right. The Koulikoro Road led east along some railroad tracks away from the center of town.

Helen was talking to us but we largely ignored her. We were too busy gawking at the sights — women, perhaps less stately than the ones we had seen in Senegal but impressive in their own right — balancing baskets, firewood, buckets, and what have you on their heads, often with a small baby bundled on her back in a cloth tied around her shoulders. The womens' outfits were of printed wrap-around cloth in a variety of colorful designs — there were no European dresses here. The men were less immediately striking than the women, but bustling about in profusion, some walking, some riding in the back of Peugeot pickup trucks called *"bachees"*, Helen said, others riding mobylettes, others sitting behind small stalls selling God knows what. Some of the men wore white knitted skull caps and a good number seemed to be wearing wool ski caps — suitable for the Alps but for the life of me seemingly inappropriate for the heat of the Sahel. We also noticed that some of both men and women were walking around with small sticks protruding from their mouths.

"Chew sticks," explained Helen. "It's the Malian toothbrush."

Joy, wide-eyed, turned to me. "It's so African."

Our new home was in the new Bamako suburb of Korofina. The locals called Korofina the "neighborhood of the drought." This was because evidently some of the Mali drought-relief money had ended up in the hands of local entrepreneurs who had constructed scores of comfortable villas. The villas would then be rented at high prices to expatriates, almost all working for various development agencies or western Embassies.

The house was new and seemed more than adequate for just two people. It was certainly much larger and finer than the basement rowhouse apartment in Washington we had just left. There was even an empty swimming pool in the small front garden. Incredible, I thought, our own swimming pool.

The driveway gate to our house had been hurriedly opened by a Malian man on duty who looked to be in his forties and whose bald head glistened in the sun. This was our temporary gardener, Helen explained, whom we could keep or replace as we saw fit. The gardener was friendly and seemed very eager to please. He greeted me with, *"Bonjour, patron."*

Patron? A twenty-eight year old being addressed as "Patron," essentially the French word for "boss," by a guy over forty was a little strange and would definitely take some getting used to. The gardener introduced himself as Samba.

Helen was obviously seeing the house for the first time herself. She had brought along a basket of some basic canned goods, fruit, juice and some cleaning products that she said we could replace once we got established in the house and could do some shopping of our own. We all noticed at the same time that there was very little furniture in the house, though at least there was a bed. A "welcome kit" which contained sheets and some kitchenware was there which we could use until our air freight and household effects arrived.

We asked Helen what the concrete pad was in the front corner of the garden. She said, "Oh, your generator will go there. How strange that it's not installed. You have to have a generator here because the electricity is so unreliable."

I tried a light switch. Nothing. I opened the refrigerator. It seemed brand new but without electricity it was of little use. Next I tried the faucet. There was no water.

"Oh, yes," said Helen, "I understand that water's a real problem here in Korofina. So many new houses have been built that the utilities haven't been able to keep up. It may come on later. We don't have this problem where we live over in Badalabougou. Well, I have to run, welcome again. Remember an office car will be here tomorrow morning at seven to pick you up."

Joy and I looked at each other as Helen's Peugeot disappeared out the front gate. We guessed that everything would be fine eventually but how long would we be expected to live in an almost empty, unfinished house without power and water? This was going to be interesting. I had put a flashlight in a suitcase which would do temporarily for light, but I didn't know what to do about water. The combined living room, dining room had two air conditioners built into the wall but of course there was no current. The house, a low concrete box built to please European tastes, was not a native design constructed for the elements. Instead, the house acted as a very efficient absorber and storer of heat. And heat seemed to be one commodity not in short supply.

It was hard to sleep in the heat. I got up in the middle of the night and tried the water. It was on. We ran around and filled up the sink, the tub and even ran some water into the swimming pool. Lord knows how long this water would have to last us. When we finished, Joy soaked a sheet in the water and tried to sleep with it around her, hoping that the evaporation would be cooling. She would later try to sleep in the partially-filled bathtub but nixed that because she feared she would slide down into the water and drown. It was also none too comfortable.

It was going to be hard to make a powerfully positive impression at the new job. I needed sleep in order to even try to be impressive.

Joy accompanied me into town in the office car. The driver seemed genuinely friendly and acted glad we were in town. There were lots of "Ca va's" all around. Back we went into Bamako, down the Koulikora Road and through throngs of milling Malians and a cacophony of cars, bachees and mobylettes in the streets, to my new office located not far from the Niger River bridge we had crossed for the first time the day before.

While I got the lay of the land in the office, Joy would get some money changed, shop for basics, and try to find someone who could give her information about the scores of things we needed to know in order to survive our entry into Mali. Temporary salvation appeared in the persona of Jerry's wife Barbara, who was visiting the office and took Joy in tow.

Our Bamako headquarters was a rented, whitewashed two-story structure arranged halfway around a courtyard that served as a parking lot for private vehicles and the motor pool. Another smaller two-story building in the corner was the administrative headquarters. The building was located near the impressive-sounding Malian Development Bank near the city side of the Niger River bridge not far from the French Embassy. Several government ministries were nearby and the neighborhood gradually transformed from business and government buildings to a residential area of once grander but now slightly decaying homes and beautiful trees, mostly large stately mangoes.

Our office building was old and a bit dilapidated, but seemed functional, especially with its fresh coat of white paint. Large mango trees well-draped with unripe green fruit provided shade and a little shelter from the heat. A huge backup generator sat at the far end of the courtyard that seemed capable of lighting up a good portion of Bamako. Generators, I was finding out, were your friend.

Outside our compound beside the red laterite road was a row of tables and benches of vendors selling French-looking baguettes and Nescafe instant coffee in the morning to a host of customers, giving way to grilled meat on sticks — brochettes — near noon. There was a restaurant called the *"Bonbonniere,"* meaning Candy Maker in English, down the street a bit, but Jerry said its most consistent presentation was food poisoning and that the wise choice would be to avoid the place at all times.

I tried to meet as many of my new colleagues as possible the first day. There were twenty Americans in the office and a much larger Malian staff, including professionals, secretaries, drivers, janitors, and so forth. Everyone seemed genuinely friendly and happy to see us.

It was not until mid-afternoon that I met the director of our Mali operation. Tales of Ron Levin abounded but we had met only once and very briefly in Washington. He was known to possess very strong opinions and size up new staff very quickly. You were soon evaluated as an asset or a major liability, and being a liability was not a happy fate. One story circulated and was often repeated that Levin had waited until two non-performers had departed on U.S. vacations, then had their household effects packed up and shipped back to the States. A cable soon followed telling the employees not to bother returning to Mali. Levin, fond of good Cuban cigars that he would use to point at the object of his attention or scorn, also insisted that his staff work on Saturdays.

A graduate of Harvard Law School and the Sorbonne, Levin spoke flawless French and reasonably expected his American staff to be proficient in its use. After all, speaking English professionally in Mali was neither polite nor possible. Virtually no one understood nor spoke English.

The story went that Levin had the practice of inviting new arrivals to his house for dinner, and in the presence of Malian guests — usually a Minister or other high official which meant the language used was uniquely French — would turn to the new American and ask a question to get them into the conversation. This was called being put on the spot and the point was to test your French. The story eventually proved to be absolutely true, and in my own case I was pleased and immensely relieved to have evidently passed the test.

I passed Levin climbing the steps of our building as he returned from an official reception. He looked hot and miserable in his gray suit and tie, understandable given the temperature over 100 degrees fahrenheit and similar humidity.

"I hate having to dress up in this place," he said, greeting me warmly. "It's just too hot here to wear a suit. How was your arrival? I know it's a shock when people arrive here for the first time. Mali is very, very underdeveloped."

Ogre reputation notwithstanding, we got along well and I never had any trouble with Levin.

I was impressed with my Malian colleagues. One, Omar Dia, was tall and regal in bearing, and dressed in his traditional robe called a boubou, looked the epitome of wisdom and good counsel. Another, Boubacar N'Dao, was gregarious, experienced in the ways of Mali and Americans, and was the office's institutional memory and gadfly. Another, Moktar Diakite, looked a lot like O.J. Simpson in a boubou and was clearly highly competent and intelligent. He was in charge of all procurement for our entire Malian operation. I also met some more of the drivers, a few secretaries and the memorable head janitor, Vieux Diallo — "Old Diallo" — and his son in the communications section, Petit Diallo, "Little Diallo."

Among the Americans, I saw Alex and David from the day before and chatted briefly with George. Alex's southern lilt had been honestly acquired in a small Georgia town and though he did not quite look the part now, he had graduated from Duke Law School and worked as an attorney on Wall Street. George's pale white skin was splotched with red and he obviously suffered perpetually from the heat.

I also met Magda, a large, friendly black-American woman dressed in a tie-dyed shift who was one of the office's few U.S. secretaries. Magda would prove to be a bit of a hard luck case with a heart of pure gold who had lived and worked all over Africa and had somehow ended up in Mali. Magda told us she had had a fire at her house the night before and had lost many of her possessions, but greeted us warmly and promised to come over soon with information and advice.

Next there was George Thompson, our engineer and a true aficionado of Mali. This second George was decidedly friendly, disheveled, dressed in a Malian tie-dyed shirt open on the sides, and had long hair, a scruffy beard and crooked wire-rimmed glasses. I had thought engineers tended towards conservatism with lots of pens in their button-down shirt pocket. Not George.

Tom was in charge of our health portfolio, totally committed to his work in a country with terrible health conditions, and possessing a keen appreciation of the local female population. Lance was a pipe smoking aggie in charge of the agriculture office. Ernest was a slow-talking and distinguished controller in charge of financial operations. Jon was much younger than the others — in his late twenties like me — managed an energy project, and had a Malian girlfriend. He had been hired in Mali after having completed his service as a Peace Corps volunteer. Gail was from New York City, about my age, and had arrived in country with her husband only about a month previously. She shattered my stereotype of Yankees by having studied agricultural economics at Cornell and then moving like the rest of us to the Sahel.

It was an out-going and eclectic group, certainly an interesting bunch, and I was mostly impressed. I could work with these folks and maybe would enjoy getting to know them.

Meanwhile, Joy had disappeared under the protective custody of Barbara, hitting the outdoor produce and meat markets for the first time. She was soon to have her favorite markets and market women and be able to haggle proficiently in French to get the best deals, but to start with there was no better teacher than the experienced and Bambara-speaking Barbara.

At the end of the work day, I ran into Kent who I now understood had been responsible for our not being met at the airport. Kent turned out to be our neighbor in Korofina and offered to drop me at home. We pulled up in his green Peugeot 305 wagon and I invited him to come in to see the house.

It was clear that it was his first look inside the house and I could tell he was surprised that there was so little furniture and that the generator was uninstalled. He promised that he would get his people working on the generator tomorrow and would see if we could get some more furniture from our warehouse. He also said that if it was too hot to sleep, we could just walk over to his place and use his air-conditioned guest room.

That night, awake and perspiring again in the heat, we did just that, beginning what would be a several-time-a-week ritual of putting our pillows under our arms and walking down the hot, dusty side roads of Korofina to Kent's house and his spare, cool bedroom.

The generator eventually got installed, though it immediately burned out and had to be replaced. This took about another month but we were slowly learning it was wrong-headed and unrealistic to apply the same standards of the U.S. or Europe to this part of Africa.

Things broke and fell apart in Africa with great frequency, and when they did they could be hard to fix. A part was missing and had to be ordered from France. If it came by air, you could have it in several weeks maybe, assuming it didn't get lost and it could be freed from customs and if God willed it to happen. There were a lot of variables you couldn't ignore or take for granted. Sometimes it was a choice of maintaining perspective and staying calm or simply going nuts. The former was the preferred and saner alternative. The French had a good applicable expression, *"L'Afrique, c'est le professeur de la patience."*

Africa teaches patience.

The water situation was improving too. I discovered that the water would come on almost every night around two in the morning. While there was rarely sufficient water pressure to run into the house, the pool faucet was at ground level and by leaving this faucet on, we could actually fill the pool.

Kent arranged to have metal barrels installed on the roof of the house and a hand pump and hose was provided. Samba, the gardener who I decided I liked and could not do without, would pump the water from the pool into barrels on the ground, and then pump the water in turn to the roof tanks which could be released when needed to run through the house's water pipes to wash dishes, flush toilets, and take a quick shower. We soon discovered that bathing was easier and more reliable in the pool and soon we just left the soap and shampoo outside. Later, we could actually use the pool as a real pool, but for the present the pool was in reality our "emergency water reservoir."

About that time, the columnist Jack Anderson wrote a column back home accusing U.S aid workers in Mali of living in the lap of luxury as evidenced by our swimming pools. Actually it was almost impossible to rent any villa or any recently constructed house in Bamako that did not have a pool — that's the way they came — but more to the point, without our water reservoir cum pool which was used for everything from bathing to washing dishes, we would have been much harder pressed to survive. The Peace Corps Director in Mali, dutiful soul that he was, rented his own villa with the normal accompanying swimming pool but proceeded to have it immediately filled in with dirt so as to not give the wrong impression to outsiders or volunteers who would occasionally visit Bamako from their assigned villages.

The consensus among my colleagues was that Jack Anderson was welcome to come on out and see the situation for himself. And please bring his own water.

We were getting the feel of our new city. It was like no place we had ever seen on earth but it was a whole new incredibly interesting world:

National Geographic come to life right outside your door. The job was interesting and I studied hard to learn about the country and projects we were implementing and starting to design.

Joy was also content. After only three days Kent offered her a job as his assistant, a function we had privately agreed that he desperately needed. After only ten weeks of formal training in French back in Washington, Joy was employed and actually working and communicating in French, combining her Texas accent with a Malian-French one that while perhaps not exactly beautiful was very functional.

A little further down the Korofina side road from Kent's house lived a couple with the U.S. Embassy named Dan and Ann. We had met Dan very soon after our arrival and, being neighbors, they had kindly invited us over for Sunday lunch to meet a few of their friends and swim in their pool. The other guests for lunch included the CARE director — an entertaining British fellow named Felix — and the CARE deputy director and his wife, Chris and Elizabeth.

As proof that the world was indeed a small place, I realized that I had met Elizabeth previously. She was from the next town over from mine back in North Carolina, and we had attended the same university and had even taken a course together. Elizabeth had gone to the same exchange program at the University of Lyon in France the year before me and we had several good mutual French and American friends. It amazed me to run into her again in Bamako, Mali of all places, and she and Joy hit it off immediately.

Joy and I were brand new to town and this group of people, but Chris, Dan and Felix were obviously good friends and we immediately felt at home. But we were not prepared for the brand of humor on display from Dan and Chris: leper jokes. I had never been a particular fan of political correctness, but leprosy — a common enough sight in Bamako I was finding out — was a horrible affliction and not exactly my idea of joke material. Chris and Dan went back and forth with their leper jokes, however, and excepting us, the entire group roared with laughter. Joy in fact looked wide-eyed and shocked. Maybe, I thought, this is how one stays sane in one of the poorest and unhealthy cities in Africa, but I was too new to know for sure.

Bamako was more a huge amalgamation of traditional African villages grown together than a proper "city" in the western sense. Before we left the States, Joy's mother in Texas had asked her Bamako's population.

Joy replied "Around seven hundred thousand, I think."

Joy's mother exclaimed, "Seven hundred thousand! For a city that big you're going to need a new pair of heels!"

I didn't quite get the connection but a new pair of flip-flops would have been far more appropriate.

And the Junior League was a profound disappointment as well.

There was a small mostly congested downtown area in Bamako of small stores, shops, seedy bars, and a few unpretentious mostly African style restaurants. There were even several traffic lights, though most had broken faces and they only seemed to work part-time. Government buildings were interspersed with more stores and shops moving away from the city center, with an occasional Embassy compound or development agency thrown in.

Directly in the center of town were the two "supermarkets" of Bamako — Somiex and Malimag — directly catty-corner from each other.

Malimag and Somiex were living examples of non-functional state enterprises which operated more as employment agencies for friends and relatives than real markets. Somiex, the state-enterprise with exclusive responsibility for Mali's external trade, had the barest counters of the two.

Along the aisles of this large store one could usually count on finding canned Chinese mushrooms, Chinese jam, some small blue boxes of sugar cubes, and cans of instant Nescafe coffee. The other shelves were mostly empty. Malimag was under more progressive management and one could expand the selection to include bottled water, cooking gas, and a few more canned goods. Not nearly Wal-Mart but better than Somiex.

Moving out from the center of town were a series of open markets, most impressive being the *Grand Marché*, the Great Market, constructed in distinctive Malian Soudanese architecture and full of passages and mazes where small shops sold fabric, mud cloth, jewelry, spices, trade beads, hardware and much more.

Malian merchants in the *Grand Marché* and elsewhere had no problem with letting even the most obvious tourist or foreigner browse unbothered through the stalls — they could take "no thanks" for an answer, unlike many of the merchants of Senegal who were much more persistent and aggressive. The *Grand Marché* had the overall pleasing smell of a conglomeration of new fabric as well as spices and dyes that were displayed for sale in open bags and in piles throughout the market, mixed with a few other strange odors, some strong and some faint, and one of them being a distinct hint of urine.

The gold market, formally called *La Maison des Artisans*, was near the Grand Mosquee where you could also find a traditional healer or backyard dentist. The gold market sold a variety of gold jewelry or gold in bulk, the jewelry being sold exactly at the prevailing world price for gold with nothing extra for the exquisite artistry. You could tell when you were near the gold market — it was right behind the largest *"Defense d'Uriner"* (Urinating Forbidden) sign in Bamako.

This entire area of down-town center Bamako was a crowded beehive of activity as the residents of Bamako made their way on foot, in bachees, or in donkey carts, with buying and selling going on all around of seemingly every necessary item or commodity for life in a large African village.

As one headed out away from the city center and the Grand Marche toward the Koulikoro Road, you passed the National Museum with excellent displays of masks, jewelry, weapons and wonderful tapestries and wedding blankets from the Mopti region.

The large permanent meat and vegetable markets were near the office but daily or weekly markets existed in almost every neighborhood, selling everything from live sheep and huge sacks of rice and millet to small piles of peanuts, okra and hot Scotch Bonnet peppers displayed on low wooded shelves or on plastic sheets or other coverings directly on the ground. Hardware and tools were sold in separate markets and shops not far from the *Grand Marché*, near stall upon stall of male tailors, many of whom were skilled enough to copy almost any garment if they had a picture or another original garment to work from.

Across the dirt plaza and boulevard from my office and down the road not far from the river was Bamako's one modern hotel, Hotel de l'Amitié, built with assistance of Nasser-era Egyptians of all things. The Amitié had suffered through inept Malian government management in the sixties and seventies until the French were again ceded control. There were two restaurants, a nice bar, a huge outdoor pool, and even an air-conditioned movie theater.

There were other hotels in Bamako — Les Hirondelles, the Grand, and the Majestique, which was anything but. However stories abounded of cockroaches of neolithic proportions in these places and the western aid consultants and assorted visiting business people tended to avoid these like the plague and stay at the Amitié instead. There was a decent hotel a few kilometers outside of town to the west along the railroad tracks called the Lido that was pleasant with a big pool and even a pizzeria.

From the Bamako train station one could travel — in packed discomfort — to western Mali and ultimately Dakar, though the trains were antiquated and would break down frequently and the trip would often take twice as long as advertised. If you had to go to Senegal and couldn't afford to fly, it was still better to take the train. The road to Senegal was impassable in places much of the year and the train at least would get you there, hot and tired and sometimes beaten and bruised, but generally alive.

Up the hill from the train station was the National Zoo, but it was not much of an attraction. Many of the animals were apparently always near the point of starvation, and visitors reported that there was not much to see. The scavenging hyenas seemed healthy but that was about it.

The paved road toward the airport branched outside of town — the left fork leading to Segou, Mopti and eventually Gao near the border with the country of Niger and near where the Niger River turns south away from the desert. The right fork headed south to the town of Bougouni, then either east toward Burkina Faso or further south toward Guinea or Cote d'Ivoire, though the pavement soon petered out on the Guinea portion and developed major pot holes and fractures on the Cote d'Ivoire piece.

The road to Kati led up a steep incline out of Bamako past the hospital at Point G and on towards the west and Senegal through Bafoulabe and Kayes, the capital of Mali's First Region and better known in Mali as the hottest continually inhabited city on earth. I met three young American female Peace Corps Volunteers who had lived in Kayes for two years and had, they claimed, perfected the art of bathing with only one cup of water. These roads, however, like many things in Africa, tended to fall apart or disappear in the rainy season or, once constructed, never be maintained.

Whatever the condition of the road, most Malians traveled in-country by bush taxi, usually a white Peugeot 504 station wagon that departed at odd hours stuffed with people and possessions and with a roof rack crammed to the sky with more baggage and odds and ends of all kinds including an occasional bound-up sheep or clucking chicken.

My most familiar road in Mali was the Koulikora Road, the road from town and the office to Korofina and home. This road was a constant chaos of trucks, bachees, mobylettes, pedestrians, sheep, goats and chickens — all seemingly crossing the road at once and moving down it willy-nilly. Along the road was a string of vendors selling mangoes, papayas, roasted chickens and what have you, plus stand upon stand of the Malian 7-Eleven equivalent, the *tabel-tiggi.*

Your friendly road-side *tabel-tiggi* was a portable wooden crate manned by a single vendor offering a wide array of goods for the discriminating shopper: candy, matches, mints, cigarettes, batteries, lantern parts, bar soap, and more. The *tabel-tiggi* also offered the helpful service of selling individual cigarettes from the open pack, either the locally made Malian Liberté brand or French Gaulloises which were the choice of the local elite.

The Koulikoro Road was always interesting and never boring. To drive it at night trying to avoid trucks with no lights, bachees stopped in the middle of the road, and pedestrians dashing across, all obscured by dust and smoke from cooking fires, was a challenge not for the feeble of spirit or the weak of heart. Sometimes an occasional traffic policeman tried to control traffic and lecture offenders, but in Mali the police were too poor to have cars — they only had whistles — and the normal reaction of a driver to the policeman's whistle was to put pedal to the metal.

The Malian government, aided by the Germans, was doing its best to transform the Koulikoro Road from two lanes to four. Each year the work would restart and the construction crews would further impede the flow of traffic. Then the government would run out of money and construction would grind to a halt. Next the rainy season would hit and the work done to date would be almost completely washed away. Then the rains would stop — but there was no money to restart the work. Then the next year's work would recommence just in time for the next rainy season and the entire cycle would be repeated.

In our nearly four years in Bamako, this happened four times. When we left for good, the Koulikoro Road appeared almost the same as when we arrived — two lanes of busy chaos with the other two lanes still under perpetual construction.

I wondered if the saga of the Koulikoro Road was analogous to other development activities in Mali.

Bamako had been a small village, insignificant in comparison to more historically important Malian cities such as Segou, Djenne or Timbuktu, until the late nineteenth century when the French completed their conquest of the Western Soudan, as the area was called then, and turned it into a regional administrative capital, connecting it by rail to Dakar. The original plan was to connect Dakar by railway all the way to Niamey in present day Niger, but that never happened. The tracks still spanned some 1200 km from Dakar to end some 25 kilometers past Bamako at the town of Koulikoro, making it the longest rail link in West Africa.

Dakar served as the capital for the French Soudan from 1883 until the region became independent from France in 1960 and eventually broke into the present national configuration in 1961. During the colonial period, France had been primarily interested in developing a source of cheaper exports back home, particularly rice and cotton.

By independence Bamako numbered some 350,000 people but the population had almost doubled by 1976. Both the population of Bamako and the second largest city, Segou, continued to grow at high rates, thanks to a high birth rate and rural drought that had made rural village life more tenuous. When we arrived there, Bamako's population had grown to over 10% of Mali's total population of more than seven million and was still rapidly expanding.

By far the most predominant ethnic group in Mali was the Bambara, comprising around a quarter of the total population. The Bambara were descended from the Mande people of the ancient Mali Empire and lived mostly in the area around Bamako and to the south and east and dominated most of the high government posts. Their art, particularly their woodcarvings, is highly regarded. The Bambara language is virtually the same as Djoula, the market or commercial language spoken throughout West Africa.

The Foulani, sometimes called the Foulbe or Peul — tall and handsome traditional cattle herders — were the second largest group. Other Malian ethnic groups of note include the unlikely named Bozo, traditional fishermen along the Niger and other rivers; the Touareg, the "blue men of the desert"; the Songhai, the former rulers of a great Islamic empire in the sixteenth century living in the remote region of Gao; and the Dogon. The Bozos do not have wild red hair, fake noses and wear grease paint.

The Dogon are perhaps the most fascinating Malian ethic group, numbering no more than 300,000 and inhabiting the Bandiagara escarpment in a barren area some 100 kilometers from the city of Mopti. The Dogon have long intrigued western ethnographers and anthropologists because of their highly developed animist religious traditions, their knowledge of astronomy, and their unique artistic traditions of dance and wood sculpture. They fled to their plateau and the slopes below in the fifteenth century to escape pressure to convert to Islam and even today are primarily animist in belief, only 30% or so adhering to Islam.

The Dogon displaced an earlier people, now disappeared, called the Tellem whose old burial caves and granaries can still be seen on the high cliffs, and whose unique religious art came to influence the Dogon. Today the Dogon are industrious farmers of millet and unique small onions originally introduced by the French that are sold throughout the country and even exported to Europe.

Religion is integrated into the life of the Dogon, down to the design of their villages and compounds. Dogon villages are built in the shape of a man, stretching from north to south. The head is an open-sided men's shelter built of eight wooden posts and covered with millet stalks. The eight posts represent the eight original Dogon ancestors, or the first four men and four women created by their god Amma. Women are banned from the shelter. The men spend their time there lounging, joking, staying cool, talking and solving village problems. The hands of the "man" are formed by two special houses for women where they are supposed to stay during menstruation. Village compounds, themselves designed in the shape of a man, form the central area of the body.

Dogon villages are reminiscent of those of cliff-dwelling Indians in the southwest United States. Some of the most spectacular Dogon villages are built high up steep slopes or atop towering cliffs and the houses are of mud with flat roofs instead of the conical huts of other peoples. The granaries remain the traditional shape with the conical roof, however, and are assembled on the ground then hoisted up. Some of the houses have elaborately carved wooden doors less than a meter high that are adorned with religious symbols and are highly prized by art collectors.

When a Dogon dies, masked dances are held in a procession that follows the body of the deceased as it is paraded head-high through the village. The body is then lifted by ropes to a cave high up on the cliffs by a young Dogon man that has earlier made his own perilous ascent up the rope. The burial cave could have been in use since the time of the earlier Tellem people.

Dogon dances and ceremonies are elaborate and full of religious significance. Masked Dogon stilt dancers from the town of Bandiagara outside Mopti put on one of the most incredible performances to be seen on the entire African continent.

The Touareg inhabited the northern regions of the country, especially around Timbuktu. They are a fierce people and proud of their Caucasian origins. Traditionally nomads, the Touareg's way of life has been seriously effected by the droughts which much reduced their herds of camels, sheep, and goats, and have forced many to become farmers or even city dwellers. This transition has been hard for the proud Touareg, some of whom have been forced to live in makeshift camps outside of Timbuktu that grow in size when droughts hit and shrink when they don't, depending on donated food to live.

The Touareg are famous for their fighting prowess and art, particularly swords and other metal objects. During my stay in Mali, relations between the Touareg and other ethnic groups would only rarely flare into violence, but this would become a far more serious problem a few years into the future.

Except for these occasional flare-ups with the Touaregs, Mali's ethnic diversity had not translated into ethnic tensions, particularly in comparison to such intractable tensions in other parts of Africa. Overall, relations between Mali's ethnic groups were not a problem and a plus in terms of the country's development potential, though future relations with the Touaregs were certainly unpredictable.

Mali was also approximately 85% Moslem, having been converted from animism between the sixteenth and eighteenth centuries, with influence from Arab traders and various waves of Islamic invaders. Only the Dogons had successfully resisted conversion to Islam on a large scale, aided by their isolation on the Dogon Plateau.

Islam played and still plays a large role in the lives of Malian and surely affected the way they acted and thought. God's will was a significant force to be reckoned with. While the Malians revered Allah and dreamed of making the "haj" to Mecca like all good Moslems, these Malian Moslems were more flexible and understanding in their thinking about other cultures and religions than some of their cousins in other parts of the Islamic world. Christianity had made fewer inroads in Mali than in the Ivory Coast and Senegal, for example, though many Catholic orders and Protestant missionaries scattered throughout Mali provided health and other services to the population and of course kept up the never-ending struggle for souls and converts.

Mali's main economic activity was agriculture with millet, rice, sorghum being the principal cereal crops and a variety of vegetable crops being produced as well. Cotton was the primary agricultural export and foreign exchange earner, mostly grown in the southern part of the country where rainfall was the highest. Cotton cultivation and textiles were the charge of a mixed public and private enterprise run jointly by the Malian government and a group of French businessmen whose importance to the national economy could not be overemphasized. Phosphates and gold were the primary minerals, gold being produced in modest but important quantities in the southern part of the westernmost First Region of the country. Western prospectors were always looking for oil in the remote northern desert regions as well as deposits of other precious metals and uranium which had already been discovered in the desert regions of neighboring Niger.

There were three seasons in Mali: The "cold" season from November to about mid-March which was the time to grow vegetables and other temperate crops. Malians seemed to actually suffer from the cold, particularly at night, though to me the temperature never seemed to drop below the upper-seventies or low eighties fahrenheit. The wool caps and heavy jackets would come out and be worn, notwithstanding. The sand-laden Harmattan winds off the Sahara would also peak during this period.

From March to May was the "hot" season, and that was appropriately named. No rain would fall but the Harmattan could also blow, depending on whether the overall climactic cycle leaned toward rainfall or drought. This period was adverse to most crops.

From June to October there was a transition period, also with very high temperatures. Depending on the area of the country, this period more or less corresponded with the rainy season, though rains — if they began at all — could begin considerably later and stop sooner. The rainy season was not the rainy season of a more humid tropical zone, however. I would later see rainy season in Central America and understand a new definition of rainy season. In Mali, rainy season meant it was theoretically possible for it to rain, and during my stay there at least, occasionally it did.

New arrivals in a place where Americans were few were expected to be introduced around the U.S. Embassy and have a brief introductory meeting with the Ambassador. I had my meeting with the Ambassador, a distinguished and experienced career diplomat in her fifties named Patricia Byrnes.

Ambassador Byrnes proved herself to be a trooper who would frequently go on field trips to the bush of Mali, where comforts were almost non-existent and even an Ambassador could not be pampered. I took my first field trip in Mali in the company of Ambassador Byrnes and Ron Levin.

It was fascinating to visit the Dogon plateau and the isolated villages with the Ambassador. Bringing our parade of vehicles into the larger Dogon town of Bandiagara at dusk, it began to rain hard. Rain was a significant event at any time to the Dogons, but evidently when coinciding with a visit by high level foreigners, it was an event of mystical and religious proportions. The receiving delegation and all the assembled villagers went wild — clapping, chanting and dancing, hands raised towards the heavens and the descending deluge.

We were a big hit. Timing is everything.

The Ambassador went everywhere and ate everything and had a wonderful time, humor and grace never failing. The only time she looked a bit unsure of herself, and she was not alone, was when the village elders of a waiting village far in the bush seemed to be readying a volley of ancient-looking muskets and rifles to be fired in our honor. The problem was that they were aiming the rifles directly at us.

The delegation spent that night in a large rounded banco hut, broken up into individual rooms along the sides. The heat was stifling and the mosquito nets in the rooms were in shreds. Joy, who was on the trip in her new official capacity as deputy of the administrative office, noticed one other thing she didn't like: cockroaches, big ones, as long as your hand.

Our host for the trip was the Governor of the Fifth Region, Governor Donfaga. Donfaga was a military man who had a reputation for dealing violently with the occasionally rebellious Touareg village, and would later become the chief of the Bamako police. Donfaga looked not to suffer fools lightly. He was the perfect charming host, however, and every morning of the trip had posed us the normal polite question that anyone who has spent more than a second in the French-speaking world asks and responds to unthinkingly.

"Vous avez bien dormi?" Have you slept well?

The question is best expressed in proper French by posing the question in sing-song, with the lilt rising abruptly at the end of the sentence.

We never saw the Ambassador emerge from her room, but Levin came out of his room, chest bare and perspiring.

"Just make it to morning," he ordered, cigar nowhere in sight.

Joy insisted we make it to morning somewhere other than that room, as far away from the heat and neolithic cockroaches as possible. We proceeded outdoors and found a narrow metal table sitting outside the hut under the stars. We tried our best to make room for two on the table and threw ourselves down to try to sleep.

"Huh. Just let that guy ask if we've 'bien dormi'ed in the morning. I'll tell him exactly what I think," said Joy as she tried unsuccessfully to get comfortable on the metal table.

Governor did just that, the lilting French perfect in every respect.

We all smiled sweetly and in unison replied, *"Oui, Monsieur le Gouverneur, merci, et vous?"* You bet we did, how about you, and thanks for asking.

Ambassador Byrne's tour in Mali soon ended and she was assigned to another post in Asia, far away from Mali. Her replacement was to be a female political appointee from Atlanta. The newly arrived Ambassador made her rounds and soon came over to our office to be introduced. Tom, the chief of the health office, graciously introduced himself and the assembled group and Malian and American workers in the office.

"What should we call you?," Tom asked.

It was important to know whether to be formal or informal in how one addresses the Ambassador. In London, Paris, Mexico City or a host of other important cities, the Ambassador is "Mister Ambassador" or "Madame Ambassador." But Bamako was in the Sahel, and it was hot and we were all out near the end of the road together. Mali was no place for being overly formal.

Further, at that particular period, there was virtually no electricity in town and the temperature at mid-day could reach 115 degrees or more. The dress code demanded sandals, and though shorts were unacceptable for work, polo shirts and the lightest-weight khaki pants were *de rigueur.* In my entire stay in Mali I put on socks and endured the torture of wearing a tie exactly twice a year, for the Ambassador's official Fourth of July reception and the U.S. Marine Corps Ball, the annual dinner dance put on by the Marine security guards from over at the U.S. Embassy.

The Fourth of July reception was always held at the Ambassador's residence in the old part of town not too far from our office. Near sunset — the time of the reception — scores of fruit bats swarmed high above the tall mango trees near the Ambassador's house, inevitably leaving a pungent calling card on the suit or tie you had just dug out and had pressed for the occasion. The bats were just trying to tell us we were ridiculously and inappropriately dressed for the climate. Formal, Mali was not.

The new Ambassador replied to Tom, "Oh, call me Madame Ambassador."

Our hearts sank.

The new Madame Ambassador had less than a smooth entry into Mali, aided and abetted by the rough side of Ron Levin. At a dedication ceremony for the start-up of a new project in an agricultural area southeast of Bamako, Levin made a speech in his Sorbonne-perfected French to the assembled entourage of high Malian government officials. He then turned, introduced the Ambassador and asked her to step forward and make impromptu remarks. She was horrified as she was not on the program, had no speech prepared and spoke only basic French to begin with. The "speech" was an unqualified disaster and our relations with this Ambassador were forever sullied.

She didn't last long however. Soon after bouncing so many personal checks at her own Embassy that her check cashing rights were revoked, a change of administrations in the U.S. took place and the Ambassador was quickly removed.

The third and final U.S. Ambassador of our stay arrived a couple of months after the political appointee departed. We understood that his last name was Borg and he was a career diplomat but that was all we knew. During his first week in Mali, Ambassador Borg invited a group of my colleagues over to his house to meet him and swim in his large pool.

With trepidation we approached the Ambassador's residence. We remembered what the former Ambassador had been like. Ambassador Borg himself answered the door. He looked to be in his early forties and was wearing cut-off jeans and an old t-shirt. In one hand was a large liter-sized bottle of beer.

We relaxed. This was much more like it.

Ambassador Borg was a friendly, effective Ambassador and good for morale of the Americans with whom he came into contact. Unlike many Ambassadors I had met and would continue to meet in the future, he also had a bent for not taking himself too seriously: he was known to give his chauffeur the night off, put on the chauffeur's hat, and drive groups of delighted Peace Corps Volunteers around town, they sitting contentedly in the back of the big official black limousine where the Ambassador was supposed to be, probably marveling at their good fortune.

Our neighborhood of Korofina was a mixture of traditional low banco houses and buildings with several short streets of expatriate housing like ours. The much more extensive traditional Malian neighborhoods soon turned into round huts that ran for several miles in every direction, eventually fading away as the bush began. The expatriate housing may have been luxurious by comparison, but the traditional area of Korofina was one of many Bamako *"quartiers"* or neighborhoods where new arrivals from the countryside — unable to make a go of agriculture at home and looking for the opportunities of the big city — moved and eventually put up their house and, if they could afford it, their compound.

It was in these areas of Korofina I would go for my near-daily jog or bike ride. Our air freight had finally arrived after three months of living out of suitcases, and though we still would wait months longer for our other effects and car to arrive, I had put my bike in the air freight and, after a fashion, I had wheels.

Not many Caucasian joggers or bike riders ever went into the far reaches of Korofina, but that was where I preferred to go. This was the real West Africa and the real Mali, seemingly not much effected by modern civilization, and, for the most part, totally traditional. Groups of women would gather in small groups pounding millet into flour and telling stories and laughing, clapping their hands between blows. Old men dressed in boubous and skull caps congregated in the shade of the occasional big tree, shielding themselves from the sun and the heat, telling jokes or solving neighborhood problems. As I jogged past them, I would wave and greet them with one of the ritual Bambara greetings I was trying to learn. This area of town was far more interesting, not to mention safer than the main road which had trucks, cars and too much dust.

I soon became popular with the locals as I flashed down the red laterite roads on my yellow Raleigh 10 speed, or in my running shorts when I jogged. Crowds of young boys and little girls would pile out of their huts and compounds to throng the side of the road to watch me go by, clapping and laughing at such a strange and exotic sight.

Their chant was always the same.

"Tou-ba-bou! Tou-ba-bou! Tou-ba-bou! Tou-ba-bou!"

Toubab was a word that originated with an old French word for medic, "toubibe." It had started out symbolizing medical help administered by the early French colonists and had come just to mean white man.

The little children were chanting at me the equivalent of, in a friendly kind of way of course, "Honky, honky, honky." I would smile and greet them in Bambara.

I later learned a little more about the use of the word "toubob." It literally had meant "white person" but in the eyes of the Malians it had come to more mean "stranger" or "foreigner."

This was explained to me by Charles, a black Peace Corps Volunteer from Washington, D.C., who would later become a friend and professional colleague.

Charles said, "Now look. You're a toubob, but I'm a black toubob. A Malian looks at me and he doesn't think 'Here's a fellow black or better yet, here's an African-American.' No way. He's thinking, here's another foreigner who happens to be black."

"You mean they're thinking something like, 'There goes a black white guy?'," I asked, grasping for cultural enlightenment.

Charles smiled. "Sort of like that. It was a real shock when I understood how they really thought of me."

I was later to hear other black Americans talk about similar experiences in West Africa. Some at the time were tourists who came as a result of interest in their African ancestry and culture spurred by Alex Haley's book *Roots* and the subsequent television dramatization. Some were shocked to find that most Africans considered them Americans first, and obvious foreigners, color being more or less incidental. Some of the returning black Americans had expected something more resembling a homecoming.

For most if not all of my black American colleagues in development, such distinctions as foreigners or whatever didn't matter at all. They were there to do a job and contribute what they could to Africa and its development, and that's what they did, period.

I began taking Bambara lessons. Greetings were a good place to start as they are an important African ritual that offer cultural insights as to how the group looks at the world, as well as giving a prescription to start a conversation.

The morning greeting would start with "Hello" or "Good morning" and be acknowledged with a different response depending on whether it was a male or female doing the answering. Then a whole chain of polite questions would follow in sequence.

How's the family? How's the wife? How are the children? How's the compound? How's your health? How's the day going?

The responses always began with the gender identifier of *"mba"* if you were a male and *"nze"* if you were female, both meaning "All's well" or "Everything is OK."

Then it was entirely normal to start the whole process over and run all the greetings by again. The greetings would change as the day progressed to represent different descriptions of the light rather than just shifting literally from "good morning" to "good afternoon." The whole process could go on for five minutes or more and was an integral part of the Malian day.

Malian colleagues thought Americans strange and overly blunt to begin the day with only a *"Bonjour,"* or even worse, to do the unthinkable of simply starting the day talking about work with no polite greeting at all. When this happened, the Malian would invariably stop and begin again for the underpolite American.

"*Bonjour,*" they would say in proper admonishment.

Malians would be blown away and honored for a foreigner to speak Bambara, even only a few words or just the greetings.

We should have been so lucky with the French.

3
West Africa Wins Again

After three months of living out of our suitcases we began to suspect that our sea freight had been sent to Malawi instead of Mali. After Kent sent a flurry of cables back to Washington, however, the sea freight which represented most of our modest worldly goods finally showed up, and after another wait to get liberated from Malian customs we had a few possessions. Not long afterwards, I received a cable from the Peugeot people in France saying that our car had been delivered to the port down in Abidjan, Ivory Coast.

Maiga, one of our favorite office drivers, went down to the big city of Abidjan and drove our car back for us, which, to our relief and near amazement arrived unscathed.

It was good to have full-time transportation again. The household stuff was nice too, but since we really didn't own all that much anyway, and after living for six months with very little, I had sort of forgotten about a lot of it. As far as possessions, I was getting by with my guitar and shortwave radio.

The shortwave was our one electronic connection to the outside world. The U.S. Congress was still funding the shortwave service of the Armed Forces Radio and Television Service at the time, broadcast from Germany, and we could get news and sports and somewhat keep up with what was going on in the States. If I wanted to listen, I could sometimes pick up a Sunday NFL football game from the U.S. starting about seven o'clock at night. Without the shortwave radio, we would have felt much more isolated and cut off from the world.

We occasionally saw the *Herald Tribune* which was printed in Paris, though these tended to be rare and at least a week old. We had a subscription to the Washington Post at the office, but it was generally a month out of date and by that time interesting only for historical content.

We had a telephone at the office but it was generally impossible to get through to the U.S. When you did get through, you had to be careful to wait to say "over" at the end of your sentence because an interruption in mid-conversation would cut the transmission at least for several seconds. The phone was a very unreliable form of communication and we didn't even have one at home. There was a seven hour difference between Mali and the East Coast of the U.S. so we rarely spoke to the main office back in Washington anyway. I never saw a Malian phone book and doubt that such a thing existed. In Mali one used messengers instead of telephones for local business.

Joy and I had heard a lot of talk about WAWA. It stood for West Africa Wins Again.

WAWA was when your flight decided not to stop in Bamako for some reason and kept on flying to Dakar without you. WAWA was when you had boarded your flight yet were kicked off the plane because some high government official decided to put thirty religious pilgrims on their way to Mecca in your place. WAWA was when you went on a field trip to far-flung Gao via the one Air Mali jet, only to find once you arrived there that the President had absconded with the plane to Paris and it would not be coming back to pick you up for the return trip.

WAWA was when the spare part you needed to fix your generator was sent to Monrovia instead, or your life insurance policy was canceled because your mail kept ending up in Malawi instead of Mali. WAWA was when you showed up for a flight and the plane was there, but you couldn't leave because the flight attendants never appeared. WAWA was when your maid completely forgot how to make apple pie even though she had made it every week for the past three years. WAWA was when your new car arrives at the port unscathed and between then and its delivery, lost three of its tires, the spare, the jack, the windshield wipers, and most of its paint.

WAWA was when you had a chair made by a local carpenter and forgot and gave the dimensions in inches instead of centimeters, and the chair came back fit only for Shaquille O'Neal. WAWA was when the government ran out of foreign exchange to import diesel fuel to generate electricity and the expensive new dam the donors have financed seemed to be silting up a lot quicker than anyone thought possible. WAWA was when a policeman confiscated your camera for national security reasons for taking a picture of a local parading Boy Scout troop. WAWA was when you waited nine months for your four new project vehicles to arrive from the United States, finally got them released from customs, and found that three weeks later only one of them is functional as two have been wrecked beyond all repair and the third needs a part that can't be found except at the factory back in Detroit. But don't worry, the part can be ordered — and if it doesn't get missent to Bolivia or get trapped in an African customs house — you may have it in a few months.

That's WAWA. You soon came to know WAWA well. It was as real as hookworm and as endemic as malaria.

Mali was desperately poor, but despite this the Malians had a well deserved reputation in West Africa for being open, uncomplicated and friendly. There was no chip on their shoulder about anything. Though some Malians' occasional shyness in dealing with foreigners could seem a bit uncomfortably like deference, we found the Malians more richly human and kind than any other nationality we had known before or since.

There were over three hundred U.S. citizens in Mali, including a large Peace Corps Volunteer contingent of about seventy. The rest included the Embassy staff, a very few private sector people, missionaries, and scores of aid and development workers like ourselves. All the main U.S. and other development organizations were represented — AID, Care, Save the Children, Planned Parenthood, Plan International, World Vision, Lutheran Relief, Catholic Relief, etc. The large majority of Americans were in Bamako, excepting the volunteers and missionaries who were scattered even to the remotest corners of the country.

As an ex-French possession and still French-speaking country at least at the upper echelons, Mali was still under the direct economic and political influence of France. The French were the largest bilateral donor, provided Mali essential direct budget support and guaranteed the convertibility of the Malian Franc. There were many more French citizens in Mali than Americans, including many more private sector types, such as the Renault representatives or the Elf petroleum folks, plus many technical advisors to the Malian government, diplomats, and even a few ex-colonial era types who had stayed on.

My theory about the ex-colonial nationals living in their ex-colonies is that they can occasionally tend toward insularity, thinly disguised superiority and sometimes arrogance. Get them out of their ex-colony however, say move the French to ex-British Gambia, or the British to ex-French Senegal or Mali for example, and you have an entirely different situation. The French will be outgoing and friendly in the Gambia, yet more snobby and arrogant next door in Senegal or in Mali. Same is true for the Brits: lots of fun in Senegal but much harder to get to know in The Gambia.

Add the French insistence that foreigners speak their language correctly if not perfectly, and the situation could be a bit strained. I loved France, had lived there, had gone to school there, still had good French friends from those days, and in many ways felt it to be my second country. Folks in the French countryside and small towns reminded me of country people everywhere — generous, warm, friendly and helpful.

The French in their ex-colonies however could be a more distinct breed. In social situations with them, I saw French people literally recoil when confronted with Americans trying their best to communicate in their fractured French. This variety of Frenchman had a well-used reply: *"Je n'ai rien compris."* I haven't understood a thing, even though they generally did. This was often said with a look of indignation and horror, best expressed with elbows bent and palms uplifted and away, eyebrows arched, and mouth turned down.

Most of the Americans really tried hard to learn French and many did fine, but most people agree it is a harder language to learn as an adult than, say, Spanish.

Marilyn, the American wife of a livestock specialist working on one of our projects, had a particularly poignant experience. While driving down the Koulikoro road in her Peugeot, she sideswiped a moped, knocking the driver over on the side of the road, fortunately only injuring him slightly. Marilyn jumped out of her car and ran to aid the poor still-prone young man.

" Oh, *merci beaucoup!"* she cried. *"Merci beaucoup! Merci beaucoup!"*

This surely mystified the injured Malian, but saying "Thank you very much" was all the French that poor Marilyn could muster under the circumstances, but maybe he understood from her tone of voice that all she really wanted to know was if he were all right.

The French were all around town but a large group congregated at the Tennis Club in town near the railroad station. There were only four courts and two of them were in pretty sad shape, but it served as the Bamako equivalent of French social center and country club rolled into one.

The French and other expatriates alike could join the club, but something about its official status in the eyes of the Malian government did not permit Malians to be members, a fact I thought strange. The even modest dues however would have served to exclude all but a very few Malians anyway, had they been interested in joining. All the expatriate tennis players belonged as these were, at the time, the only courts in town, except for one in terrible condition at the Hotel l'Amitié.

The governing board of the Tennis Club tended to act at times like an extension of the French Ministry of Culture and a local surrogate for the Academie Francaise, keeping the French-speaking world pure and free of too many evil foreign — particularly American — influences. Accordingly, even in a place like Bamako, there were lots of rules at the Club: certain times when you could play doubles, times for singles, times when children were not allowed, times for lessons and times when lessons were forbidden, and of course another set of rules governing the club rankings and challenges to be able to move up the ladder. As at Wimbledon, tennis costumes should be white, of course. Some of the members liked to congregate and watch others play, speaking authoritatively about what "La France" thought about this or that international issue and what the country should do about it. At the Tennis Club, many members were evidently of the distinct belief that French power and glory were still at their zenith.

If you were French and were ambulatory you could join the club. For foreigners, including Americans, Canadians — even French Canadians and the like — you had to have a try-out with one of the board members to see if you were a good enough player to make the grade for admission. I thought that was a strange policy, but I had my tryout and they decided to let me in.

I was ranked at the bottom of the "A" players, the strongest group, and was expected to challenge my way up from there. I played challenges occasionally, and slowly over the months climbed my way up the "A" group. There were three or four consistently strong players then — the Commercial Officer from the American Embassy, a young French guy of about twenty who had grown up in Bamako and had a beautiful game, and a Malian teenager named Ibrahima.

Ibrahima wasn't allowed in the club as a member and was too poor to pay dues anyway so he was therefore unranked. He was a kid off the street who got to play because he gave lessons to club members and because he was so obviously talented a player. He told me he had started as a ball-boy at the club earning less than twenty-five cents an hour, and had learned to play with a racket some member had thrown away, using the court when no member was playing. He also told me he had played barefoot for years before being given an old pair of sneakers. I began to pass him balls, old shoes, and an occasional racket. This wasn't entirely altruistic. The more I helped him out the more he would feel obliged to hit with me.

During my stay in Mali, I eventually made it to the number two ranking. This happened because the Commercial Officer at the U.S. Embassy finally departed Mali for good and because Ibrahima wasn't officially in the rankings. This gave me license to say modestly at any given future date when asked about my tennis ability, "Oh, I used to be ranked number two in the country, but well, you know, that was a while ago..."

I certainly wouldn't tell them which country unless they thought to ask.

The United States had a medium-sized though complete Embassy and staff in Bamako. The official Americans were well known for bringing in a core American staff then hiring a large group of locals to complement them. Local salaries were relatively good and the work was steady, so the Embassy was able to attract motivated and qualified workers. This policy was in marked contrast to other Embassies, such as the Chinese and the Soviets, who would never hire locals for security reasons and therefore brought everyone from the home country down to the drivers, masons, clerks, and janitors.

The French also had a good-sized Embassy. Other European governments like the Dutch, British, Belgians, etc. for the most part had their Ambassadors for several West African countries, including Mali, based in Dakar or Abidjan. The Canadians let the director of their assistance program act as their official representative and had a large group of their citizens in Mali, mostly a fun-loving bunch of French-speaking Quebecois.

There was a small but diverse group of embassies in Bamako however. The North Koreans were there, along with huge embassies from the Soviet Union and the Peoples Republic of China. The Libyans, always up to some mischief, had an Embassy near the old hippodrome next door to the Marine House. The Cubans, also predisposed to international intrigue at the time, were represented by a full embassy in my neighborhood of Korofina. I wondered what the Cubans and North Koreans spent their time doing in Mali. Perhaps they gave each other alternating cocktail parties.

The Soviet Union's embassy was located near our softball field and the Peace Corps office. We had no idea what the Soviets were up to behind those massive walls. We were told by the U.S. Embassy to be cautious about the Soviets — their people were evidently under strict orders to avoid any kind of interaction with westerners. The ones who approached you therefore were probably working for the KGB. The advice was "Be careful."

I figured I had nothing of much interest to share with the Soviets anyway. What could I give them anyway except information on our development assistance program? This was public information to boot. I even used to find pages of our project documents being used to wrap the brochettes sold at the outdoor food stands near the office, so if the Soviets had asked, we would have been glad to tell them what we were up to. Or just go talk to the brochette man.

The Soviets you did see were for the most part a pretty raggedy-looking group. They would arrive in *"centre-ville,"* downtown Bamako, on one rickety Russian-built bus with clothes color-coordinated by Ray Charles and obviously on a shopping expedition. They seemed to marvel at the wares and selection of items available — even Somiex impressed them with its shelves of Chinese jam and mushrooms — and the great array of tools, pots, clothes and hardware in the open-air market must have seemed a virtual consumer cornucopia.

They bought little but seemed fascinated by the African scene, and walking kindergarten-like in a tight, somber group, were soon herded back into the bus to disappear once again behind the Soviet Embassy walls.

I thought this was a sad way to treat people but it conformed to what we'd been told to expect about the Soviets overseas. I talked only to one Soviet my whole time in Mali, the Aeroflot representative, and it was widely assumed that his real job was with the KGB. There was one Aeroflot flight to Bamako a week from Moscow via Romania, I assumed mostly to ferry students back and forth.

The Soviets had an extensive scholarship program throughout the developing world. I had met more than a few Malians who had studied at Patrice Lumumba University and some were neutral about the experience — it was an education. The rest strongly shared the same sentiment: there was no better advertisement for the West and capitalism in the entire world than attending school in the Soviet Union.

The Aeroflot-KGB fellow, Alexi, was a friendly sort who spoke some English and played tennis at the French tennis club. He told me if we wanted to fly Aeroflot to Moscow and then connect on to Western Europe, the fare structure was "flexible." With Aeroflot you could go in and make your best deal.

A Malian friend, Mamadou, explained another Soviet activity. There was a gold mine in the remote southern part of the First Region near Kalana. Gold, along with phosphate, was one of the few minerals that Mali exported in any quantity.

"The government of Mali owes a lot of money to the Soviets for past weapons sales," said Mamadou. "The Russians manage the Kalana mine and take most of the gold directly back to the Soviet Union. Mali doesn't really know how much is being mined or how much the Soviets get. It's a really bad deal for Mali."

The Chinese had another large compound on the Koulikoro road beside Jerry and Barbara's place. We rarely saw the Chinese at all and from the road the Embassy compound seemed quiet and totally devoid of activity. Perhaps, we thought, there was really no one inside, or perhaps they just never came out.

In Mali, the Chinese had financed construction of several manufacturing plants — a tannery, rice mill, textile mill, cigarette plant, and match factory — and still provided Chinese technicians to help in their operation. They were also in the process of constructing Mali's first pharmaceutical plant.

Later in our stay in Mali during one of the periodic warming periods of China's relationship with the U.S., the American Ambassador was invited to come over one Saturday afternoon and bring several friends to play ping-pong. I was invited to go. There really were Chinese people inside the Embassy compound. We were given paddles and paired off against our Chinese hosts. Before we began to play, one young Chinese diplomat made some brief remarks in heavily accented French. The games were dedicated to *"l'amitié,"* to friendship, he said. When I tried my spin serve on my Chinese partner, he smiled — ah, so this guy thinks he can play — and soon thoroughly and completely crushed me to the point of helplessness. After every point won, he smiled and slightly bowed saying again, "This is for friendship." Losing didn't bother me. I was just contributing in my own small way to international friendship and understanding.

The North Koreans were the most unknown group of all. They would not associate at all with any Americans or as far as I knew any Westerners. I knew they operated a large rice perimeter outside of Bamako. Otherwise we knew nothing about them except that they were starting to build a bizarre socialist-looking "cultural center" over in Badalabougou dedicated to eternal friendship between the people of Mali and the Koreans of the Democratic People's Republic, which sounded to me a bit like a dubious proposition.

Part of our adaptation process to life in the poorest reaches of the so-called Third World was the discovery that we could afford to hire help. Most Americans are not immediately comfortable with servants or the idea of having servants and some even feel guilty about having them, at least at first. One couple from California, more politically correct than most I suppose, pointedly referred to their servants as "helpers." This would make our French friends, more experienced in the ways of expatriate Africa, delirious with laughter. "You Americans," they would say. "Next you'll be asking the cook to sit down with you at the dinner table. Ha, ha, ha."

Development projects tended to be longer-term in nature and one was not always around to see their eventual impact on people. With servants, though, you had their entire extended family to help support, like it or not, as part of your indirect responsibility and your impact on these people was more often than not direct, immediate and visible.

With our three servants, I estimated we directly supported at least fifty people when you included children, cousins, parents, uncles, aunts, nieces, etc. It was the African way. When one person had a paying job, the extended family shared in the wealth. When no one had a job, everyone suffered until someone in the family figured out how to get one. It was therefore our duty to give or advance money to finance purchases of sheep for the Moslem holiday of Tabaski — the feast at the end of Ramadan — plus other holidays, for baptisms, for home renovations or purchases, funerals, bicycles, and you name it.

I loved Samba the gardener right from the start. He was bright and cheerful, could fix anything, and he worked hard every day pumping the water from the pool to the roof tanks so we could have running water or filling up the washing machine with a garden hose since there was never enough pressure for the water to enter on its own. A chew-stick, the Malian substitute for a toothbrush, was constantly in his mouth. I gave him clothes and tennis shoes and money for Moslem holidays though he never asked. His good cheer never seemed to fail him. How could he seem to so sincerely love his job? Didn't he know he was dirt poor?

In addition to Samba, the office employed us a night guard named Yaya Samake. Yaya would come about six in the evening and stay until six in the morning, supposedly awake and on the alert for robbers. Mali had very little in the way of violent crime, but petty theft was always a possibility and the guards were mostly provided as a deterrent.

Yaya would wait until dark then pull out our lawn chair and fall fast asleep. When the electricity would fail at night, as it invariably did during that period, Yaya's job was to start the generator. Yaya however slept like a log and could not be wakened once he fell asleep. I would struggle with the generator crank myself while Yaya snored peacefully away. I began to call him Yoyo to myself and once out of frustration following an attempt to crank the generator at three in the morning, tied the comatose Yaya to his lawn chair with a couple of bungee cords. Neither he nor I ever mentioned the incident.

Joy and I advanced or gave Yaya money to finance two marriages, two baptisms, a new roof, a bicycle, a concrete floor, and numerous *"fetes"* or religious holidays, which we considered our duty.

I awoke once late at night to hear a noise outside the house. I peered out my window to see a young man with a crowbar trying to force open my louvered metal kitchen door. As I knew Yaya was asleep, I reacted as any unarmed person would do when confronted out of a deep sleep by a robber: I gave him a primal scream of the first order telling him, in essence, to please remove himself from the premises but in a tone of voice to shock him out of ten years growth and for me to lose my voice for three days. I watched him vault my wall with the speed and grace of a deer and be forever gone.

This turn of events upset Yaya, and as his French was weak, he went and paid for a scribe to have his thoughts and a proposal to me put into proper written French. The note began with the somewhat archaic flowers of the written, formal French language which was still used in French-speaking Africa: "Distinguished and most worthy and generous patron..." and ended with the formal "please accept this, distinguished sir, as a sign of my most respectful consideration."

In the middle of the note Yaya got down to business. He wanted me to buy him a gun so he could *"bien proteger la maison,"* i.e. protect the house.

This was a non-starter. "Yaya," I said, "first you will shoot me by mistake and then you'll shoot yourself. Why don't you just try staying awake?"

The next night the ever-sleepy Yaya was on his station, but this time with a Bambara bow and a quiver of arrows at his feet. Yaya slept less, or at least less fitfully, and we never had another robbery attempt.

Badji, in her mid-forties, was our indoor worker who did the cleaning, the laundry, boiled and filtered the huge pots of water we needed each day, soaked the vegetables in iodine and occasionally cooked. We had inherited Badji from our friend Linda who had worked for a Texas A&M livestock project and had recently departed Mali for the U.S.

Before we found Badji, we had hired a tiny man named Khalifa to be our inside man. Khalifa showed up at our door when we first arrived, looking for a job. His letters of reference had been washed in his clothes by his wife, he said, but he had worked as a houseboy many times before and knew the routine about soaking all the vegetables in iodine and boiling and filtering water. Khalifa seemed all right and even invited us to his house to meet his wife and children, and we sat and sipped strong hot, very sweet tea with him that he prepared over a little charcoal stove. We were touched by this gesture to totally green newcomers like ourselves.

We felt good about the relationship until I started noticing that money I kept in my briefcase for travel expenses was disappearing. We had our suspicions but kept quiet — we had no proof — and we were so rich anyway compared to Khalifa. We hoped that it wasn't true and were certainly far too cautious or guilty to confront him with our suspicions.

All doubts were finally erased when a travel advance worth a couple hundred dollars I had received in preparation for a trip down to Abidjan totally disappeared from my briefcase. I had told Khalifa about the coming trip and then had left the briefcase alone with him in the house. When he didn't show up for work again, I went to see the local police.

Dealing with the Bamako police was to be a valuable lesson in the ways of my new African environment. There were no telephones to call the police station so I drove there.

"We'd be glad to pick up the suspect," said the Bamako gendarme, "but I have no transport so you will have to drive me to his house."

The policeman got in my little Peugeot and off we went.

I remembered where Khalifa's little rough-and-tumble mud compound was located and we found him at home. Khalifa greeted me with a sullen, *"Bonjour, patron,"* looking straight down at the floor and avoiding my gaze. He didn't deny stealing the money and went quietly with us, me driving everyone back to the police station and waiting for the wheels of Malian justice to start turning.

"How much money was stolen?" asked the policeman.

I knew exactly. "It was 47,000 CFA," I replied. I had heard that severe beatings by the police were commonplace and I didn't wish that on Khalifa.

"Look, Khalifa," I told him, "just give the money back and we'll forget about the police. You can't work for us anymore, but let's make it easy on everyone. Just give me back the money."

The policeman listened silently. Khalifa replied, "I am sorry, *monsieur*, I have already spent it."

Next I made a big mistake. I said I'd leave then and check back the next day to see if Khalifa had changed his mind. Of course when I arrived back the next day and asked the police about Khalifa, they replied, "Oh, he has been released."

Naive foreigner that I was, I hadn't realized that situations like this were the bread and butter of the barely paid police. Khalifa had simply made a better deal with the police than the one I had offered the day before, using my money of course, and had been released. I had not until then understood the rules of the game.

Khalifa's replacement Badji was a considerable improvement — honest, friendly and hard-working. Badji, like most rural women in West Africa, cared not a whit about exposing her breasts for all to see, but would never be caught dead in shorts or with legs otherwise exposed.

Badji had a habit of doing the housework topless. I didn't want to interfere with the long-established customs of the host country but Badji's breasts had long ceased to be functional anatomical parts and sagged in smallish flaps in the direction of terra firma. Perhaps sensing our discomfort at such a display, Badji shifted from toplessness to wearing the size C cup brassiere that Linda, a big woman from Texas, had left her. Badji could not come even close to filling the C cup, and the attempt was futility personified.

I was far from home.

Badji was an interesting woman who had actually lived for a while in New York City as the cook to the Malian Ambassador to the United Nations. She had spent two years there while managing to learn only a few words of English. New York must have been a bit much for Badji. She would only go outside with a pre-printed card informing the New York police of her name, address and situation so they could deliver her, totally lost once again, back to the Malian Ambassador's residence.

Badji was kind and reliable, and spent her free time caring for her teenage daughter and trying to build her own small house on a piece of land that she had purchased on the outskirts of Bamako. Like in the more developed world, Badji spent a lot of time and money on lawyers to arrange the necessary permits and titles. We worried that she was being taking advantage of.

Badji did tend to have occasional lapses in her thinking. We came home once to discover that she had enlisted Samba in hauling our living room carpet outside for a good cleaning, which involved hosing it down and hanging it over the bushes to dry. I also one day returned, fortunately in time, to discover her preparing to wash my record collection with soap, water — and steel wool.

In the sixties, Mali, like many other newly independent African countries, had decided that it needed a national airline of its own. Thus Air Mali, a true non-money making, money-burning third-world state enterprise turkey was born. It was not long before Air Mali was rechristened Air Maybe by its clientele. Some of the French used the same expression, "Air Peut-etre."

Schedules were established and then completely ignored. Air Mali offices were built but not manned. Planes existed but didn't show up.

I was later to learn the interesting story of another Sahelian airline, Gambia Airways. Gambia Airways operated in stark contrast to Air Mali — it had offices and sold tickets only on other airlines. Gambia Airways itself possessed no aircraft!

Air Mali flew a small motley collection of aged Anotov thirty-seater passenger planes that had been inherited from the Soviets, and one U.S.-built Boeing 727 that was the pride of the fleet. It was this plane that was at the beckon call of the President, and when he wanted to use the plane to go to Paris, to Paris he went and to heck with the passengers stranded at the far reaches of the country with no way to return to Bamako.

Stories abounded about Air Mali. Once, unable to pay for back fuel bills at Paris' Charles DeGaulle airport, the French blocked the plane at the departure gate with a fuel truck until the Malians made good on the bill. Another time when the airline could not pay for enough fuel for the 727 to fly the entire distance to Bamako, they went half way to Algiers instead. Once in Algiers, the surprised passengers were asked to pay for fuel by attendants who plied the aisles with an open bag to receive the contributions.

Air Mali at one time had a maintenance agreement with the Irish carrier Aer Lingus, but the Malians soon ran out of funds to refinance the contract. I had met one of the Irish technicians at a party, and even **he** would refuse to fly Air Mali. None of this inspired confidence and no one flew Air Mali if it could be avoided.

I flew it several times, both Anotov's as well as the 727 when I felt I had no choice. After about a year in country, I had to go to Gao to evaluate one of our projects. Instead of the tough two day drive, part of which was through desert where you could find yourself navigating by compass, I decided to risk going by Air Mali. The 727 was on the runway in

Bamako, and eventually the flight attendants arrived and off we went. I noticed that the two attendants didn't bother to sit down during take off.

Upon landing in Gao, and long before the plane rolled to a stop, the other passengers pushed by me and a newly arrived colleague, Dick, and stood beating on the door trying to get out. We thought this was odd behavior until I noticed an aged fire truck chasing us down the tarmac. Only then did I realize that black smoke was billowing from a small fire in the rear of the aircraft. The fire was put out by the fire truck, we left the plane, and it eventually took off again for Bamako. As it turned out, it did not return for us: the President had decided to go to Paris — WAWA — and we were therefore left to our own devices to make our way back to Bamako over a thousand kilometers.

Just as well. I really didn't want to get on that plane again anyway.

Flying the aged Air Mali Anatov was an even more harrowing experience. After making the desert run from Gao to Timbuktu, the Anatov would land on a desert strip at Goundam before heading down to Mopti and then back to Bamako. Landing at Goundam, the passengers had to leave the sweltering plane and seek shade under the wings while waiting to depart. From my spot under the wing, I inspected the tires. They were so bald the cord in the tires showed completely through.

I got the attention of the pilot who was also standing under the wing.

"Have you seen these tires? How can we take off and land with tires in this condition?"

The pilot looked at me like I was crazy and gave a shrug.

"Ehhh. I think we can make it."

We did, fortunately, but the same plane was to crash in the desert two years later trying to leave Timbuktu, killing everyone on board. That seminal event proved to be the end of Air Mali as the airline was abolished soon after.

In a wonderfully creative adventure novel by Clive Cussler, *Sahara*, the author describes several scenes where flights of ultramodern Malian Air Force jets sweep the skies in pursuit of the heroes, the Malian Air Force being controlled by an evil genius Malian official with unlimited technological resources at his disposal. The stark reality was 180 degrees to the contrary. The Mali Air Force of my time there possessed a couple of Russian-built C-130-like troop planes plus two antique and frequently broken down Korean War-era MIG-17 relics in its entire fleet. One of the MIGs crashed while I was in Mali, leaving only a sole fighter plane available.

Later in my Mali stay I was to experience another close call on a plane. Having been dropped off by a chartered twin-engine Twin Otter at a remote dirt strip east of Mopti, I had joined a group of Malian and American technicians mapping Mali's land-use resources. We had finally emerged from the bush over a week later — and later than we had planned — ending up in Mopti. Our French pilot had been waiting for us near the Mopti airport in Sevare the entire time to fly us back to Bamako.

He was going crazy from boredom and in a hurry to leave. I and two other colleagues piled in the plane and we immediately took off.

Scant seconds later, the plane was completely surrounded by an angry red sandstorm — the Harmattan — blowing in from the Sahara. Suddenly we had virtually no visibility and except for the instruments, couldn't tell up from down. The pilot radioed to Bamako and discovered that the Bamako airport was closed due to the same storm. The trick now was to figure how to get back to the Mopti airport in one piece.

We eventually made it back, me helping to look for the ground while the pilot flew by compass and as close to the ground as he dared. I caught a glimpse of the runway below that we were crossing at an incorrect angle, but with one turnaround the pilot put us down safely.

My colleagues and I proceeded back to Bamako by road, leaving the poor pilot to wait some more, this time for the Harmattan to subside and the skies to clear.

My worst experience flying, however, was not on Air Mali at all, but rather on the private French-owned charter service, Mali Air Service. We had rented their single-engine Cherokee to fly to Kayes on a field trip, me to visit several sites where we were going to begin designing a road project in that region, and others to work in Kayes before returning on the same plane to Bamako later in the day.

Our little group of four had assembled at the Mali Air Service hanger off to one side of the Bamako airport. The pilot was late but we waited patiently. He eventually showed up, somewhat perturbed, but after the preliminary checks we were off.

I should have figured we would have trouble with the pilot. He was newly arrived from France, he said, did not know Mali at all, and told us that in fact this was his first flight in a Cherokee.

More ominous were his clothes. He was dressed totally in black. Black shirt, black slacks, black leather jacket in his arms, and strangest of all, a black ascot around his neck. Meet your pilot, Dr. Death.

Kayes was about an hour and a half flight from Bamako. I sat in the far rear of the five seater, while my colleague Lance sat up front beside Dr. Death. With less than thirty minutes to go in the flight, a curious thing happened. The engine stopped. We were at about five thousand feet and suddenly the only sound was the propeller turning motorless in the wind.

I refused to believe this was happening. There must be an explanation. If there was, the pilot was having trouble explaining it. He was frantically playing with the dials and looking panicked. This too did not inspire confidence. Where was that reassuring Chuck Yeager-like voice affected by every American airline pilot on earth?

I couldn't help but notice that we were also descending toward the ground at a good clip, gliding just fine, but after a few minutes of this getting uncomfortably close to terra firma.

The pilot turned on his radio.

"Mayday! Mayday!" he shouted. Chuck Yeager this was not.

He turned to Lance. "We're out of gas. Where around here can we crash land?"

Out of gas? Crash land? This was getting serious. I had my doubts about crash landing and so did Lance.

Lance replied, "Crash land? I don't think that's going to work. Look down there. It looks like a cross between the Grand Canyon and the moon." It was true, the rocky and uneven terrain of the First Region was no place to freelance a landing.

I was still having trouble believing this was happening.

"Lance, what's wrong with the plane?" said I very nervously from the rear seat.

Lance looked at me over his shoulder with his pipe clinched in his teeth and protruding outward, replied in words I would never forget.

"My friend, we are going down."

I had understood that when in life threatening situations your whole life could flash before you. This didn't happen to me. I think that twenty-eight was too early to have accumulated sufficient quality replay material.

In any event we were getting down pretty close to the ground, I would estimate a bit less than a thousand feet. However this was going to be resolved, it was going to happen soon. The pilot, sweat streaming down his face onto his idiotic black ascot, was still playing with the controls.

Suddenly, he reached over and turned a lever in the middle of the control panel. The engine roared to life and we immediately began to pull up away from disaster.

The pilot had forgotten to switch his fuel tanks. He had not known that the Cherokee had tanks in both wings that had to be manually switched. This little detail had almost been the end of us.

Ten minutes later we arrived in Kayes and landed without further incident. I was wondering how I should react. Should I say something nasty to the pilot about the improbable legitimacy of his birth, should I look for a bar in Kayes, should I kiss the ground?

I decided to be cool. I was too relieved at being alive to say anything to the pilot, and besides, I wasn't planning to return to Bamako in the plane anyway. I walked away from the Cherokee sitting on the Kayes tarmac and didn't look back.

I found out later upon my return to Bamako a week later that Lance, who did return later that day in the same plane, was to have still more fun. The plane hit a storm on the return trip and was bounced all over the sky. My day was bad but Lance's was worse.

After this experience and my experiences with Air Mali, I decided I would do my best to travel in Mali by vehicle, no matter how bad the roads were and how much extra time it took. On airplanes, I was beginning to feel very vulnerable.

Air Mali's feats in the air were nearly matched in performance by its brother state-owned utility company, Energie du Mali, better known by expatriates and Malians alike as "Energie du Mal" — "Bad Energy."

In many ways, Energie du Mali's troubles were understandable. They were trying to provide a twentieth century service in a non-twentieth century setting in one of the poorest countries on earth. People were crowding into Bamako creating more demand than the utility could meet. Limited funds kept capital investment low on energy infrastructure for hydropower that would have met Bamako's power needs, and foreign exchange needed to import diesel and equipment for the traditional generating equipment was always inadequate.

The utility responded by a series of blackouts by neighborhood and though there may have been some organization to which *"quartier"* was blacked out and when, it was never discernible.

Mostly my neighborhood was out. If we had only had a few government ministers or a couple of ambassadors from important countries, we may have been spared. But we did have the generator. I was not a great mechanic but I came to understand the inner workings of my generator and took better care of it than many people do their first-born. Being good neighbors, we ran electrical cables from our house to our French next door neighbors to run their refrigerator, and another line to our Malian neighbors behind us to run their lights. Besides, I figured they could better tolerate the generator's noise if they were all benefitting from it.

Energie du Mali's billing and collection policy was haphazard at best. There were no meters, certainly none at our residences, and the amount you paid seemed to be based not on actual use, but on your ability to pay. Our administrative office had a monthly marathon negotiation session with Energie de Mali to arrive at an acceptable figure that included our staff's home consumption.

After being in Mali more than a year, my office received a $7,000 electricity bill for the month of May. This was just for the office and included no residential use. There was one main thing wrong with the bill. During that period, we had been exclusively on the generator and had received not the first drop of current from the utility company. Energie du Mali had been out the entire month. Kent sent his team back to negotiate.

Energie du Mali was always hard pressed to perform, but the month of May was a new low. First, it was the end of the hot season and demand was the highest. Then three of the four diesel generators at the main Bamako generating plant broke down and the Malians could neither fix them nor pay to import the necessary parts. They were down to one diesel generator for the entire city, supplemented only by a small hydroelectric plant at Sotuba outside of town.

The power went off at our house in Korofina with a sense of finality. We were not to have a drop of power for another two months. You could not run your generator for more than a few hours at night, first, to preserve the life of the generator, and second, diesel fuel was becoming hard to find.

This meant reacquaintance with serious heat. We had just measured the temperature inside our house. With two air conditioners and two ceiling fans going full blast, the temperature was 95 degrees. Not being able to use the generator meant we had to deal with temperatures well into triple figures. To make matters worse, Bamako also ran out of cooking gas at the same time.

The office responded well to the gas problem. They issued us a bag of charcoal for cooking, and a little metal grill to heat it in. Badji picked up some straw fans in the local market to use on the charcoal.

This worked fine for actual cooking but it was a very inadequate process for boiling the large pots of water that we had to do every day in order to make it safe for drinking. The office also dispatched a truck to Bobo Diolosso in neighboring Burkina Faso to buy diesel and cooking gas, and we all survived.

My sister picked this time to visit us from the States, and though it was well over 110 degrees during the day for the entire length of her stay, she too survived and had a genuine African experience. Her most vivid memories were of us all bailing out of a well-planned picnic in the country because of the heat, and watching the hippos play in the Niger River from a respectful distance and the vantage point of a small boat.

It is impossible for a developing country's formal economy to progress in a meaningful way without a reliable source of electrical power. Despite the troubles of Energie du Mali, hope was around the corner. The country had obtained loans from the Islamic Development Bank and European Community to finance the construction of an impoundment dam south of Bamako at Selingue. Construction had been underway for a few years. The nay-sayers said that the distribution system could never handle the increased load, but when the day came to pull the switch and turn on Selingue, it all worked perfectly. Finally we had a reliable source of electricity and the home generators could now be neglected for a while.

Joy and I had settled in to Bamako, made friends, and both found jobs in our field that were challenging and totally absorbing. Despite living at what our parents would have described as the end of the earth, we were the fortunate ones who were trying in our own small ways to make a contribution to development.

My friendship with Jerry had grown. I spent all day long working with Jerry in the office, much of it spent picking his brain about Mali, its people, its problems, and its culture. We also had fun together outside the office, and more than a few times we ended evenings with friends at Jerry's house, I playing guitar and Jerry singing old heart-felt blues songs using an inverted empty beer bottle as his microphone. "Smokey Joe's Cafe" was his personal favorite.

We also had gone together on numerous field trips into the "bush," including villages where Jerry was well known from his days of gathering research material for his doctoral dissertation.

One of these villages was Keyla, in the High Valley area about two hours southwest from Bamako outside the community of Kangaba. Kangaba was an important cultural center of the Mande and the home of a sacred house whose roof was reputed to magically fly, unaided, off its walls every seven years to be soon rebuilt by the local populace.

This was an area of the country where the rainfall was considerably higher than many, and after the rainy season with the crops coming up and the general greenery surrounding the traditional conical hut villages, it was easy to idealize and admire this peaceful existence and almost see it as idyllic. To have scratched the surface a bit would have revealed poor health and sanitation conditions at a minimum, but at this time of year these villages and the surrounding countryside were beautiful.

We had stopped by Keyla on the way back from a visit to a agricultural research station in the High Valley. We were greeted by the village chief, Yakuba Diakite, and invited to eat with his family and spend the night. Keyla was a griot village and Yakuba, as village chief, was the chief griot. Griots in West Africa were the historians and story-tellers of the clan, their job being able to recite family lineages far back into the past, as well as recall and explain the most significant events in the life of the village. Each seven years on the day the roof flew off the sacred house eleven kilometers away in Kangaba, Yakuba led the Keyla griots on a walk into Kangaba, where they chanted the stories of the Mande people all night. It was clear that Jerry's and Yakuba's relationship went a ways back.

Before the sun set, we visited village notables and exchanged greetings with women in Yakuba's compound as they ground the millet into flour and cooked. They laughed and clapped their hands together between pounds of their millet grinder and by all appearances were succeeding in making hard work as pleasant as possible.

Women, I knew, did much of the manual labor in West Africa, including cooking, cleaning, child care, hauling water and firewood, some agricultural field work, and cultivation of gardens. Depending on the village's location, hauling water and firewood alone could be back-breaking work. Men's work was in the fields, or with the cattle, and though this did not imply a life of leisure, it was clear that the women's lot was a very hard one with work never-ending.

Yakuba introduced us to several of his fellow griots in the village and to the local *"forgeron,"* the blacksmith, who showed us his workshop and tools. The blacksmith, in his simple round hut, had fashioned bellows that worked with foot power and was sufficient, to our surprise, for him to fashion shotguns from scratch. We admired one of his finished products that he proudly held out for our inspection.

We sat around Yakuba's compound that night and talked. He talked quietly and articulately about the price of rice and millet, the cost of fertilizer, and the need for agricultural price reform. We fell asleep under the stars in his compound on our cots with their mosquito nets stretched above us.

When we left Keyla the next day to return to Bamako, we made one more stop — to visit the town of Djoliba just beside the main road leading back to Bamako. In the 1960s, Djoliba had been selected by the Malian government as its first "model village" and with a loan and technical assistance from the United States government, set out to construct 130 new houses of American design using village-wide collective work teams. Traditional round huts with thatched roofs and family compounds were torn down and in their place had been built cement houses with tin roofs. A high American official had come from Washington to dedicate the modernized Djoliba and the Americans made further plans to develop a diverse set of "small industries" in the village.

Our inspection of Djoliba showed the cement houses to be still in place for the most part, but now used mainly for storage and for keeping animals. No people inhabited the houses — they had moved back into reconstructed traditional huts as the "modern" houses designed and built by the Americans were simply too hot, with the kitchen poorly designed and far too near the bathroom. Except for the sheep and goats that now inhabited the "model village," Djoliba stood before us as a silent reminder of how the good intentions and efforts of a development agency could ultimately prove to be pure folly. I discovered as well that the loan provided by the Americans for Djoliba was never repaid by the Malian Government.

Two days after our return, Jerry fell ill. I hardly saw him for three weeks and even the normally nonplussed Barbara, now six months pregnant, was starting to show concern. The eventual diagnosis was dengue fever. When we checked our mosquito nets we discovered one of them had a big tear, undoubtedly the one Jerry had used. He eventually recovered after about a month, emaciated but alive and finally on the mend.

Jerry always had a constant stream of Malians in his office and at his home. Some were trying to sell him Malian wood carvings such as the magnificent stylized wooded gazelles called *"chi-wara,"* others were there seeking advice, and others asking for loans.

Later it would dawn on me what was happening. Jerry had totally crossed the cultural divide and, Bambara-speaking hot-shot that he was, was holding court in the traditional African style. Supplicants came and gathered around him the way they would with a traditional village chief or wise man, counsel was offered in return, and then the supplicant retired, apparently satisfied. Jerry seemed as happy with and energized by the arrangement as anyone.

Inspired by Jerry's example, I decided to try to learn about Malian art. Malian wood sculpture and traditional blankets were among the best in West Africa, encompassing several ethnic groups — the Bambara, the Dogon, and the Soninke among others. My favorite were the wooden *"chi-wara,"* that the Bambara used mounted on baskets and tied to the head for dances and ceremonies, and that we had seen in art galleries in the U.S.

So-called Fulani "wedding blankets," complex, earthen-tone blankets made in seven separate panels sewn together, were made by weavers commissioned by the parents of the bride. Wedding blankets could take up to two years of work to complete, though as a result of the various Sahel droughts and resulting hard economic times, most families could no longer afford the luxury of hiring a weaver for so giant an undertaking.

To acquire such items, you just put out the word to a few Malian friends, and soon vendors would appear at the door, wood sculptures, carved wooden door locks or whatever stashed in burlap bags on the ground awaiting your inspection. The art vendors would assure that all of their pieces were authentic and old. Even a non-expert like me could tell that this wasn't true, the patina of the piece — the shine on the object which came from years of human handling — being the best indication of authenticity. When the brown shoe polish covering a mask came off on your hand, you could fairly reliably determine its life to be measurable in weeks rather than years.

The problem with the Malian masks was that they seemed to be almost as popular with termites as they were with aficionados of African art. You could tell if the termites were present because they tended to leave little tell-tale piles of fine sawdust on the object. You dealt with this in various ways: our friends from the Texas A&M livestock project left their collections in a shed with a powerful insecticide overnight. My personal favorite was to put the masks in the freezer for a day or so which worked fine, size being the only limiting factor.

We were not just discovered by the African art vendors. There were the jewelry vendors, the vegetable lady, the egg man, and the frog seller. The frog seller was the most interesting and my personal favorite. He arrived at the door, smiling, with a living, writhing burlap sack of live frogs on his back. He sold by the dozen. After putting in your order, the frog man would proceed down our sidewalk and commence to hammer the frogs, with a clearly audible splat, head first down on the concrete. Once skinned and cleaned, the finished product was then delivered to the door where Badji went to work with the garlic, parsley and olive oil.

The same frog seller would also occasionally bring live rabbits, something the French generally prized more than the Americans. One look at the bunnies in the bag, noses twitching unsuspectingly, and Joy put her foot down.

"No way we're eating the Easter Bunny," she said, and so we didn't.

Joy and I were beginning to get to know the Iranian couple, Mickey and Ellie, who had arrived to work on an AID project. Mickey was the son of a former Iranian Ambassador to the United Nations under the Shah. His real name was Farhad but his mother had early on started calling him Mickey because she thought as a three year old he looked like Mickey Mouse. He had grown up in New York City rather than Iran, had gone to college in California, and as near as I could tell was totally Americanized. Before Iran fell to the Ayatollah, Mickey had worked for the Iranian embassy in Washington, living by his accounts a very merry bachelor existence and rubbing elbows with the Washington, D.C. social elite. With his sharp wit, sense of humor and social connections, it was no wonder that Mickey had loved his life in the U.S.

Mickey had returned to Iran after the Shah fell, partly to get to know his own country and partly to learn his native language, Farsi, a bit better. Under an Islamic fundamentalist regime, however, Mickey and Ellie had to flee Iran, and in the case of Mickey, flee for his life. Having an Iranian passport, he was at that time unable to reenter the U.S. or France, and upon fleeing Iran was able to obtain only a short temporary visa for Switzerland where his parents resided in their own exile. After bouncing around for a time he applied for and was offered a development job as a credit specialist in Mali with a U.S. firm working on contract with an AID project. Mali had become an unlikely refuge for Mickey. He was otherwise a man without a country at least until the political situation changed.

Ellie and Mickey had been married for a year when they landed in Mali, much like Joy and me. Ellie, schooled in England, sophisticated and used to comfort, was shocked by Mali and we privately wondered if she would be able to adapt. The problem was that if she didn't, there was no place to go. Joy and Barbara immediately liked Ellie and took her on as a personal project.

During one of Bamako's worst periods of heat, no electricity and no water, Mickey and Ellie and Joy and I had decided to go for a long weekend to Bobo-Diolosso, the second largest city in Burkina Faso and connected to Bamako by a mostly paved road. Burkina was just as desperately poor as Mali and it was a sign of our own near desperation that we chose Bobo as a vacation destination.

But Bobo did have an air-conditioned French-run hotel with a nice pool and real Paris-like croissants, and supposedly a couple of nice restaurants. We went to one our first night in Bobo, called the *Eau Vive* (Living Water), run by an order of Catholic nuns. I though it was infinitely civilized to be served a bottle of chilled white wine by the nuns and then at nine o'clock having them treat us all to a singing presentation of "Ave Maria." Then it was back to serving the wine and running the restaurant.

We had tried from the start to make friends with as many Malians as possible. This was their country and if one didn't know the real folks, how effective could you really hope to be at the job? We were not ones to want to spend all our time with expatriates, and certainly not just Americans.

Our attempts at inviting Malian friends and colleagues to our home proved more complicated than we had thought. While it was easy to meet a male Malian colleague for lunch or a beer after work, inviting the same person to your home with his wife, we soon understood, presented the Malians with a terrible quandary. For economic reasons, they knew that they could not reciprocate in any comparable way to your invitation to them, though we would not have expected nor wanted any lavish treatment.

Also, what to do about the non-French speaking Malian spouse, or spouses since there could be multiple of these? This would be very uncomfortable for the invitee. But how could they be impolite and refuse your invitations? We sadly concluded that we would make our ties during the day, at lunch, or after work, not make our Malian friends and colleagues uncomfortable with a home dinner invitation. To our surprise and disappointment, a wide economic and cultural gap was there and hard to overcome. This would not be the case in any other country, including other countries in Africa where we would later work.

If work and the daily grind were consuming and sometimes hard, there was still another side of life. With our expatriate friends — Americans, French, Canadians, Dutch and Italians — we could always entertain each other with dinners, put on plays, play softball and tennis, and see an occasional movie.

The Marine Security Guards at the U.S. Embassy had an open house every Tuesday night at their residence to show mostly old, poor quality films projected on their courtyard wall. They sold popcorn and big beers and you watched the movie under the African sky. The Libyan Embassy sat silently next door and I figured that the Libyans were probably unamused by the sounds of the Grade B American movies making the rounds of the U.S. military circuit in West Africa.

My friend and colleague Alex was the mover behind amateur plays. Though some later arrivals would eventually form a real theater group that had elaborate sets and a real stage and actually memorize parts, Alex knew that most of his friends would enjoy just reading their lines, in costume of course, and with an impromptu stage beside someone's swimming pool.

Thus it was Alex who decided we would perform Woody Allen's play, "Oh God." The night for the performance arrived and most of the English speaking community of Bamako crowded through Alex's front gate. Alex met them there distributing leafy heads of lettuce and an occasional tomato from a cardboard box. The idea was to pelt the actors whenever the audience got the urge, à la Shakespeare and the Globe Theater.

I had found that distributing vegetables to pelt one's actor friends was typical Newtonian behavior. A few weeks before, late on All Saints Day evening, Alex and David had loaded David's upright piano into the back of a Peace Corps Land Rover and had traversed the neighborhoods and back streets of Bamako, Alex seated at the piano pounding out "As the Saints Go Marching In" while David and the their friend Dague — the assistance director of the Peace Corps — singing the lyrics at the top of their lungs.

For play props, Jerry and George Thompson had found the skeleton of a small burned-out airplane in the bush — it wasn't Mali Air Service's Cherokee I quickly verified, and God only knows how the plane got there — and hauled it with ropes up to Alex's roof to await the play's climactic scene.

The play was excellent. No one could have cared less that the actor's lines were being read. In my role as Diogenes, I tried to keep my bedsheet toga out of my way so I could read and walk at the same time around the make-shift stage without falling into Alex's pool.

The play built to a climax. On cue, Alex's stagehands, now on his roof, pushed the airplane to the precipice of the roof where George, dressed in toga, mounted it with arms raised in triumph for the concluding act. As the crowd applauded wildly, George and the plane were meticulously lowered by rope off the roof and slowly down to the ground below, coming to rest beside Alex's swimming pool.

This was high drama for Bamako. The plane had provided a real special effect and the crowd's cheers peaked as George stepped from the shell of the plane, arms raised in triumph. The play now over, stagehands pushed the plane into the pool to make room for the big party that followed.

George soon, however, tried to transform comedy into tragedy. Fueled by far too much of the local beer, George forgot about the plane in the pool and dove head first into the water. His head soon reemerged bleeding profusely. We pulled him out of the water while George repeatedly apologized for having acted stupid. Bjorn, a medical doctor from a Harvard project health team, took charge. He bandaged George's head then rushed him off to the Embassy clinic to be sewn up. The play, through to its very final act, had been a smash.

I left early the next morning on a field trip to the area around Segou and then to Mali's Fifth Region, the area around Mopti. I was to accompany Phil who worked on an ICRISAT project that we were financing. ICRISAT, home office in India, stood for International Crop Research Institute for the Semi-Arid Tropics.

The ICRISAT project was supposed to provide genetically improved varieties of millet and sorghum so that they would be more resistant to the dry and drought conditions of Mali and therefore more productive, increasing food security and self-sufficiency for the masses of Malians who ate millet as their basic food.

Phil was an American with a reddish-blond beard from the Midwest who had played college football at Knox College in Illinois and had wanted to be a lawyer until a stint in the Peace Corps had changed his mind in favor of agronomy and economic development. He was presently sporting a large cast on his left leg from where an unfriendly cow had kicked him at one of the ICRISAT research stations.

Since we were planning to redesign the project and extend its life by five years, and I was to do most of the writing and defending, I needed to understand the project.

ICRISAT had three small research stations in different rainfall zones of Mali to test the improved millet varieties under different climatic conditions. The first was further down the Koulikoro road from my house at a village called Sotuba where Phil had had his unfortunate encounter with the cow. The second was outside Segou, 250 kilometers from Bamako, and the third up in the Fifth Region, in the Seno area on the so-called Dogon plateau some 100 kilometers from Mopti.

Besides developing better varieties of millet, ICRISAT was also working to test new agricultural technologies on millet such as crop rotation,
intercropping millet with other crops, fertilizer use, and experimenting
with different planting dates during the cropping cycle.

The road to Segou was newly paved and we zipped along in Phil's
new yellow Toyota pickup with the ICRISAT emblem on the doors.

I took up the conversation.

"Phil how long does it take to turn research like you're doing into a
product that will actually benefit the people here?"

Phil looked at me askance.

"God, chef, it takes time. If we have good results in Mali it'll be
because we do the research right and take the time required. We're in a
very tricky rainfall zone, as in sometimes it just doesn't rain. It gets very
complicated. If all goes well we might be able to have real improved
varieties and better ways to plant them in, say, five to six years. It'll
take longer than that for farmers to have access to them on a large
scale though."

Six years or more. I pondered that for a while. ICRISAT had undertak-
en their first trials at Sotuba, but was just beginning in Segou and the
Dogon country.

"Has the government been involved?"

"Have they ever. It's really their project. We have an agreement with
the Ministry of Agriculture and the government owns the station land.
They participate in and approve all the planning which means I spend a
lot of time in meetings with the Minister and his people. Sometimes I feel
more like a bureaucrat than a technician."

Phil went on.

"The problem is not the research time or the science involved. With a
little luck, we'll be able to manage that. The real problem with agriculture here is that farmers are supposed to sell cereal crops like rice and
millet at fixed prices to the cereals marketing board, OPAM. The prices
are set artificially low by the government, in theory to stop price gouging
by middlemen, but the real reason is to keep food prices down for people
in the cities, especially the government bureaucrats and the military."

"This acts as a disincentive for farmers to produce for the market, and,
really, only about 10% of millet production is actually commercialized.
Farmers aren't stupid. They can usually sell excess production to a paral-
lel market at about two times the OPAM price, but OPAM still acts as a
disincentive to grow food. So the government feels it can't raise consumer prices, farmers produce less, more food has to be imported, and
foreign exchange Mali doesn't have flows out. To make matters worse for
the farmer, when millet yields increase, say by 10%, this increases the

marketed surplus of millet by about 100% which drives prices down even more and the farmer takes it on the chin again."

Phil took a deep breath and continued.

"What impact can we really have if we have improved, more drought resistant millet varieties, if the farmers won't produce them because the price structure is so screwed up? OPAM needs to go or at least be reformed. The donors are starting to actually talk about the need to reform OPAM, but since the government isn't on board, we're probably a long ways off from that."

We spent the night in the outskirts of Segou, sleeping on cots under the stars in the compound of a local ICRISAT employee. Segou was Mali's second largest city with a population of 50,000 with a more glorious past as former capital of the Bambara culture. With its broad avenues and big trees beside the Niger, it had the feel of age and faded past glories. The Niger River was nearby off to our left.

In the morning, the little kids in the compound shyly approached us as we folded up our cots, staring at the spectacle of the strange-looking white foreigners who had appeared in the night. One very little girl grinned shyly at us wide-eyed as she cowered behind the legs of her older sister for protection.

There was not much to see at the Segou research station. These are the boundaries of the station. This is where the first trials will go. This is where we will put the office. The generator will go over there.

Between Segou and Mopti the road worsened and was patchy but mostly still paved. Phil pointed out a turnoff from the main highway.

"Down there is the old 'Office du Niger.' This used to be a huge irrigation scheme mostly for rice as well as for cotton, sugar cane, and citrus fruits, though rice was and is the major crop by far. The 'Office' was begun by the French in the 1930's and had the potential to irrigate nearly a million hectares. It had its problems under the French but it did help make Mali self-sufficient in food and the breadbasket of West Africa."

Phil explained that while ICRISAT's work in Mali concentrated on rain-fed agriculture, the recession agriculture, or plantings carried out as the seasonal flood from the Niger basin receded, was how most rice and wheat was grown in Mali. Irrigated rice schemes in the Niger flood basin could be effective, but far more expensive to build and maintain.

"The flood doesn't necessarily originate with rains in Mali, though that certainly helps. It mainly comes from heavy rains up-river in the highlands of Guinea near the source of the Niger. During a normal rainy season, an area about the size of Massachusetts is flooded in Mali, basically the area between Segou and Timbuktu. This can be prime productive agricultural land, especially for rice grown as the flood recedes."

I asked what happened to the "Office du Niger."

"Well, the French mostly left after independence. Maintenance of the dikes and other infrastructure wasn't kept up by the Malians basically because it was just too expensive — that and the fact that the state tried to convert the *'Office'* to a giant collective farm for a while and was a terrible manager."

"Also, in order to really increase yields of irrigated rice, you need to transplant the young rice plants before the river rises enough to bring in the irrigation water. Here in Mali, there's usually not enough labor available to do transplanting correctly, so the yields can be low. The irony is that those farmers who don't transplant rice because of labor shortages can't properly weed the non-transplanted rice for exactly the same reason and the yields suffer again."

Phil went on. "There were other problems, too. Poor drainage kept cotton and sugar-cane yields low, and some of the rice polders were poorly designed and constructed. Also, the *'Office'* could never get enough functioning tractors and other machines to the right place at the right time during the growing season and the harvest. So far anyway, the *"Office du Niger"* for the most part just hasn't been well executed nor has it made a lot of economic sense."

"The *'Office'* has shrunk to about 50,000 hectares, but the yields barely cover its operating expenses. The World Bank, French, and Chinese are trying to help upgrade the *'Office'* but there's a long way to go. Man, talk about wasted potential."

We spent the next night at the Motel de Mopti in Sevare at the end of a long causeway leading into town through rice fields. I stared at the incredible Sudanese-style mud mosque of inner Mopti, distinctive and graceful.

We watched sunset from the Bar Bozo at the last point of land sticking into the Niger. Huge canoes called pinasses, some with outboard motors but most without, plied up and down the river, some entering the little harbor beside us. There was a very strong smell of drying fish and fertile mud that permeated the atmosphere.

Phil and I drank a tall cool beer and watched the Bozo fishermen and their boats out on the river. Hordes of flies tried to commit suicide en masse by flying into our open beer bottles. Soon we learned to replace the bottle cap on top of the open bottle and remove it only to drink. The national bird of Mali, Phil explained, was the fly.

This reminded Phil of a joke.

"Hey, chef, do you know how you can tell how long a Peace Corps Volunteer has been in Mali?" I didn't.

"Well, the first year volunteer gets a fly in his beer and he throws the whole thing out. The second year volunteer dredges out the fly and keeps drinking. The third year volunteer squeezes out the fly, drinks the beer and pops down the fly as a protein supplement."

Phil leaned back in his chair, took a swig of his big beer, and smiled contentedly. It was time to order dinner.

To get to the Dogon plateau station was a much tougher trip. The pavement ended in Mopti and the road past Bandiagara soon turned into a bone-jarring downhill rocky track that at times transformed itself into deep sand. We started to see the small conical huts of the Dogon perched on cliff sides and hilltops. Amazingly, Dogon women would balance large loads on their heads while at the same time climbing up home-made ladders and hand-holds in the rock to get to some of the more inaccessible villages.

A huge rock was perched at the top of the cliff above the women climbers. Phil said that the Dogon believed that if the rock ever fell into the abyss below, it would signal the coming of a great Dogon king, bringing about a new, glorious age for the Dogon. For the moment anyway the rock seemed firmly in place and the Dogon renaissance would probably have to wait.

As we passed through small Dogon villages, women would stop pounding their millet to stare at our vehicle while little kids in turn ran waving and yelling after us. Cars in this part of the world were rare and their passing was obviously a big event.

Outside one village we stopped the car by the side of the road to admire a young princely-looking Dogon man on a beautiful white horse, while at the same time he stopped to stare at us. He was adorned in a red fez hat with black tassel in the middle, fancy long brown boubou, and wrap-around sunglasses. The horse's mane was adorned with hanging amulets and mirrors. He nodded wisely at us as Phil started the Toyota once again down the road.

After being beat-up on the rocky track for several hours, we entered a flat area with many millet fields and Dogon huts on the plain, unlike those on the cliffs we had seen earlier in the day. In the distance groups of women stood or pounded millet in the open. Many carried the distinctive baskets the Dogon made. There were not many trees but from time to time groups of baobabs would appear as we drove past. The baobob is a sacred tree to many in West Africa where it is believed that the souls of the ancestors congregate and wait to be consulted for earthly advise. I had heard that baobabs looked like a tree grown upside-down, roots in the sky, and I could understand the analogy.

We arrived at the Seno station after dark, located near the little Dogon village of Koporo-Keniepe. The guard helped us haul out our cots and we set them up beside a round hut. Something that looked like a scorpion with wings ran across my shoe. The guard passed us a hollowed gourd of warm millet beer called *kojo*. Millet beer may be better cold but somehow I didn't think the Dogon got much opportunity to ice it down.

We lay awake and listened to the eery silence of the Dogon plateau for a while before we finally fell asleep. This was a strange and almost mystical place and I felt a very long way from home.

Phil spent the morning with Seydou, the Seno station manager, planning the millet and sorghum trials for the coming agricultural season. I watched and listened and absorbed what I could.

Phil explained that the rainfall on the Dogon plateau was normally less and more sporadic than the other zones around Bamako and Segou. The big drought of a few years before had struck hard here, decimating livestock and crop production, and the area had not yet completely recovered. Each year after the first rainfall, assuming there was one, the Dogon would decide whether the first rain was an isolated event or the real beginning of the rainy season. If it was the rainy season, the Dogon headed en masse to the fields to plant, their *dabas* (short-handled hoes), in hand.

Driving into Bamako with Phil was an experience in applied relativity. I felt like I was emerging from another century and suddenly arriving in New York City.

The following evening, Saturday, Joy and I went with Magda and Alex to a concert. I had never heard of a real Western-style concert before in Bamako, and as concerts here were few and far between, this would turn out to be both our first and last. Miriam Makeba, the exiled South African singer and song-writer, formerly married to trumpet player Hugh Masakela, was in town. She even had a band with her.

This sounded too good to be true. There just wasn't any quality live music in Bamako that I knew about or performers coming here, even any of the interesting local music, at least on a large scale. Bamako was not a normal destination of any known musical group, of that I was sure.

While going to see Mariam Makeba may not have been of much significance at all if we had been in the States, for Mali this was the moral equivalent of going to see the Rolling Stones on tour.

I had heard Makeba's music and was intrigued by the distinctive sound. I had also admired her too as a victim of and fighter against apartheid. It was amazing that she would end up having a gig in Bamako, but I was not complaining.

The concert was in Bamako's Sports Palace, an indoor coliseum that I was told had been financed by the Soviets soon after Mali's independence. Beside it was an outdoor stadium that was used for important soccer matches. The audience was much more male than female, and most of the attendees were dressed in their *"grand boubou's,"* the elegant robes reserved for special occasions. The coliseum was barely lit and dark and I could not help but notice that it was very dirty. The music cranked up and the audience was appreciative but no one got up and boogied like people would have probably done in the States.

I was keeping my fingers crossed that Energie du Mali would perform past expectations. I didn't want to get caught in that coliseum with thousands milling around for the exits in the dark and I didn't want the music to stop.

Makeba sang a couple of her best known songs and the crowd came to life. She introduced her band and her songs in simple but understandable English-accented French.

"Please excuse my French," she said, "I was colonized by the English."

Several young female accompanists sang back-up and crowded around the microphones while swaying like African versions of the Vandellas. As the song reached a climax, one backup singer slightly bent over and turned her well-shaped posterior end to the audience and, well, gyrated in time to the music, though this description is pitifully inadequate and the moral equivalent of describing the Grand Canyon as "big."

Magda explained, "That's called *'le ventilateur'*." The fan.

"Wow," said Joy and I, wide-eyed.

The men in the crowd went wild. Boubou'ed figures rose to their feet as one, applauding and yelling. If Energie du Mali could have harnessed the electricity spontaneously produced in that space, power cuts would have joined hooped skirts and buggy whips as obsolete.

I now knew for all time which area of the female anatomy was most admired and appreciated by the African male.

I ran into a colleague from work as we left the concert. John said, "I've invited Miriam over to the house for brunch tomorrow morning. You're all invited."

John was a black American from Virginia who had been with the U.S. Army in a prior career and had a Vietnamese wife. I was grateful for the invitation and the chance to meet Miriam Makeba, but when we arrived and were introduced, I was disappointed. She wasn't friendly. I had the impression that, perhaps very understandably, apartheid had done quite a job on her and that she was not about to make small talk with random, strange white people at someone's brunch. No problem though. Her band was a gas — fun Liberians who had been living with Mekeba in very difficult conditions in the neighboring country of Guinea. We talked music and the lead guitar player told me that Bamako looked pretty fancy compared to Conakry, the capital of abused and socialist Guinea. Everything is truly relative.

The French Canadians and the Americans played softball on Sundays at Pere Michel's field, named after a French religious mission located next door. The huge Embassy of the Soviet Union stood silently across the road from the softball field. The Marine guards from the U.S. Embassy brought the equipment.

Softball was an excuse to be social but the game itself tended to be mostly male and much more serious than I expected. I had the feeling that a lot of pent-up frustrations from jobs and life in the Sahel were vented though the competition of softball. After the games, the Americans and the Quebecers would alternate as hosts for beers for the players and the fans. There was a lot of post-game celebrating and male bonding going on here, but at least once a year with an underlying purpose for the ultimate glory of the sport. To whit, WAIST — the annual West Africa International Softball Tournament — was coming up in Dakar, and who among us should represent Bamako?

WAIST took place every year in mid-February. Teams from Abidjan, Ouagadougou, Nouakchott, Freetown, Bamako, plus several teams from Dakar were usually invited to attend. Most of these teams even had uniforms, which was very impressive to the rag-tag bunch that normally turned up from Bamako. For many of the players and spouses, especially for the likes of those living in Mauritania, Mali, and Burkina Faso, it was a perfect excuse to get out of the Sahel and fly to Dakar for the beaches, the seafood and the complete change of scenery. For us, since Bamako had a long and hallowed tradition of being quickly eliminated from the tournament, softball was more or less incidental, or so we told ourselves.

Tom was a long suffering Bamako veteran from past WAIST's. He reiterated to us relative newcomers that we had never won the double elimination tournament, and in fact never seemed to have made it very far at all, losing games and earning a quick exit being our normal pattern. After all, worse things could happen than losing WAIST. Losing early would probably mean more quality beach time and there were a lot worse things than that.

We assembled our volunteer team for WAIST. We had one French Canadian aggie, a young U.S. Marine from the Embassy who was an amazing physical specimen, another Embassy administrative officer, a half dozen aid workers like myself, and a Peace Corps Volunteer who had access to Daddy's money and could therefore afford to finance such a trip.

The Americans in Dakar organized the entire tournament and kindly found homes to stay in for those who wanted to save hotel money. They even had us a field with real grass on which to play — a French military base's soccer field on the outskirts of Dakar.

Going back to Dakar for Joy and me was a great experience. We had actually thought **this** was really African and exotic at one time. Looking at Dakar with the eyes of someone from Bamako was to see an entirely different city than one we had seen almost a year before.

Joy bought French pastries. I discovered where to buy boxes of frozen shrimp and had even brought my cooler along to haul them back to Bamako in just such an eventuality. Best of all, we went to the beach. Body surfing in the beautiful, beautiful water near Dakar was my personal preferred cure for Bamako. Never had the ocean been so appealing or felt so good.

While sitting in a taxi at a Dakar traffic light near the Place de L'Independance, Joy and I saw a familiar face smiling up into our open window, clutching an empty tomato paste can. It was the leper that normally hung out near my office in Bamako asking and sometimes demanding money. Sympathy was the normal emotion reserved for most lepers but this fellow's modus operandi was to curse me loud and long when I didn't give him money and not thank me particularly warmly when I did.

He however seemed very happy to see us in Dakar. Old friends.

We shelled out again, this time out of amazement. Joy said he probably flew over First Class on Air Afrique.

The only small disappointment had been deep sea fishing. The ocean was rough and most of our group felt a bit seasick. To counter the seasickness several people took doses of dramamine which made them drowsy. We didn't catch or even see any of the sailfish we had been after either, but it didn't matter at all. This was still like being in Disney World.

In preparation for WAIST, I purchased dark blue T-shirts for the team at the open-air Dakar clothing market. Unlike the other teams, many of whom had fancy softball uniforms from the U.S., these would have to do as the Bamako uniforms. I had the team's name printed by hand on the front by a Senegalese tailor — "So-So-Mali-Beaux," suggested by Barbara back in Bamako. Somalibo was the name of one of the two local Bamako beers, served only in large liter-sized bottles. Beaux meant 'good-looking guys' in French. So-so was about how we would have rated our softball prowess. It was a good name.

It was time for the tournament to begin. The teams milled around the field waiting for the first round games to begin and crowds of spectators began to assemble. Tom, our captain, attended all the preliminary organizational games which set the rules and made the team pairings. Some of the other captains and especially the Dakar organizers were insisting that the tournament be fast pitch rather than the normal slow pitch with a ten-foot maximum arch that we played in Bamako. Tom argued against fast pitch. A good fast pitcher could be such an advantage that this player could almost single-handedly control the outcome of the game.

Tom tried to convince them but failed. Fast pitch it was to be. We had done our best to avoid it and our consciences were clear.

The committee had obviously not known about Pat. Pat was our fast pitcher. He was an all around fabulous player and windmill fastball pitcher from hell, but in Bamako since we had seen Pat pitch we had banned the windmill and only played slow pitch. I was the regular slow-pitcher and had expected to pitch for WAIST. Pat rarely threw anything but strikes, and these strikes were so fast that by the time even a good batter had decided to swing, the ball was usually already safe in the catcher's mitt.

Pat was from Phoenix and worked in our controllers office as a financial analyst. The fact that he was probably the best fast pitcher presently standing on the African continent had proven a nice surprise. We had now been forced to unleash him on the other unsuspecting WAIST teams.

I moved from pitcher to second base and we did just that. We won our first game against a team of Dakar-based Canadians 12-0. Pat had pitched a two hit shut-out. The next game we won 22-1 against Free-town, Sierra Leone. Our third game we decimated a team of fellow Sahelians from Ouagaudoudou — traditionally a WAIST powerhouse — 12-2.

Mickey, probably the world's best Iranian shortstop, sparkled. Tom, the left fielder, played a perfect errorless game. Ron, the catcher, was a Ph.D sociologist from Baltimore and an Orioles fanatic. He was a long time softballer and natural athlete who was every bit up to the task of catching for Pat, and was steady at the bat.

Much to our surprise we were rolling.

Since the tournament was double-elimination, the championship game was played against the same Ouagadougou team which had lost its first game against us. Being from another Sahelian capital like Bamako, these guys were fellow troopers and as glad to be in Dakar and were having as much fun there as we were. Following their loss to us in the semi-finals, Ouagadougou was determined not to be humiliated again. We could see them practicing intently at the other end of the soc-cer field, their pitcher throwing to the batter as fast as he could over-handed to simulate Pat's normal underhanded windmill speed.

At game time, Pat did his normal imitation of a machine and we went ahead early. Ouaga played a good game, and even got several long hits off Pat. Pat made the difference, however, and Ouaga could never over-come the advantage he gave us. Tom made a spectacular over-the-shoul-der running catch of a long ball hit deep to left field to end the game and we surrounded him in a big pile-up to celebrate our victory. His suffer-ing as a perpetual WAIST loser was over. At the WAIST banquet that night as he accepted the tournament trophy for Bamako, Tom spoke the truth. The difference had clearly been Pat.

When Air Afrique landed in Bamako the next morning at 9:30, Tom was still holding our trophy. A crowd of our supporters had actually shown up there at the airport to meet us, waving and cheering from the observation deck as we walked toward the terminal. Waiting outside were Ambassador Borg and my new boss, Levin's replacement, David Wilson. Wilson was opening big liter beer bottles and passing them all around. Beer for breakfast in Bamako.

There was only one little glitch. Our Quebec friend, Richard Savard, who had been filming the triumphant entry of the team into the terminal with his hand-held movie camera, was being arrested and led away. He had forgotten that the airport was a high security area where it was absolutely forbidden to take pictures. I suppose some Malian officials thought that the Americans or Soviets or God-knows who else were interested in filming the airport to help plan for an invasion of Mali.

Joy asked the obvious question.

"Why would anyone want to invade Mali?"

Richard was obviously a clever and insidious Canadian spy working in cahoots with the evil Americans. Ambassador Borg had a quiet word with the airport authorities and Richard, immeasurably relieved, headed back to town, camera out of sight.

My new boss, David Wilson, had not been in Bamako very long. He had previously been head of our office in N'Djamena, Chad, a country in the eastern Sahel similarly at the end of the road like Mali, or perhaps even more so. While in Chad, David had become caught literally in the middle of a civil war, his house being in a crossfire between the two warring factions. He had barely escaped with his life leaving all of his accumulated possessions behind. What he missed absolutely the most was his complete Frank Sinatra record collection. The rest he knew he could live without.

I had met David briefly during his Chad days several months before down in Abidjan, Ivory Coast. Like going to WAIST in Dakar, Abidjan was similarly striking. This was a modern looking city that reminded me of France, much more so than even Dakar, and more evidence that Mali was much the far poorer African relation, though one with an infinitely pleasing personality.

Our offices throughout West Africa had an annual planning meeting in Abidjan, with head office people flying in from Washington to attend, to agree on plans for the coming year's new project designs and evaluations and so forth. David was there representing the Chad office. The hotel where we stayed had, of all totally incongruous things for West Africa, a huge ice skating rink.

In his mid-fifties, David had the bearing and physique of a world class athlete. He even still played in a rugby league for middle-aged crazies when back in the States. His immense arms hung far down his side ape-like and he was renowned to be an excellent tennis player. I was later to find out that David seemed to spend the latter part of each March in the U.S. on business. Though he would deny it when I accused him of it, I felt sure it was because this was the time of year that the NCAA college basketball playoffs — his passion — were held. He had told friends that once he retired from development work his goal was to join either the senior professional tennis circuit full-time or the Senior Olympics, neither of which I had ever heard of.

David would prove to be a fierce competitor in all sports — tennis and softball were the main ones in Mali — but also so-called Gala Frisbee, a game invented by ex-Peace Corps volunteers in Chad and named after their local beer.

Gala Frisbee consisted of two players on each side trying to knock down two empty liter-sized beer bottles placed side by side with a frisbee from a distance of about ten meters — four points for two knock-downs, two for one knock-down, and a point for a touch or a leaner. David was a determined and skilled Gala Frisbee player as well, and he set the ground rules — each player had to have an open beer in their empty hand at all times. Sort of like horseshoes for alcoholics.

I had once been a decent tennis player myself and looked forward to a game with David. We made plans to play early the next morning and I took care to get a full night's sleep to be prepared.

David showed up at the court at the appointed time. He looked fine though perhaps just a little bit rocky. He had been up all night, he said, gambling in the hotel casino with friends and drinking Scotch. He had stopped by his room only to change into his tennis clothes and had come directly to the court.

If I couldn't beat a much older guy operating on no sleep and who had been out gambling and drinking whisky all night, there was something badly wrong.

I didn't know David Wilson. We played two sets. I won the first but with him sobering up and warming to the challenge, he clobbered me in the second. Who was this wild-man anyway?

David was a different manager than Levin had been. He was a very bright and capable engineer by training, but with a different philosophy. Where Levin would insist on late hours and Saturday as a normal workday, Wilson would walk through the offices in late afternoon and tell people to get out.

"You have to be well rounded and do something other than work," he said. "Spend some time at home and get some exercise. You'll be better for it."

To me, Wilson would seek me out in my office and say, "I'll meet you on the tennis court in fifteen minutes. Be there."

4
Underdevelopment is a State of Mine

The new boss's different philosophy notwithstanding, we still worked hard. We had fun outside of the job too, but it was impossible to forget for an instant that we were there to carry out a development program in one of the planet's poorest countries. To have thought otherwise would be to ignore the incredible poverty and hardship all around us.

Mali's economy was suffering from years of abuse, some of which was self-inflicted. The situation was complicated by Mali's geographical isolation and the vagaries of the weather.

Mali's first President from 1960 to 1968, Modibo Keita, chose the socialist path to development. He expanded the role and power of government and curbed that of the private sector. The state took over banking and private industries of any size, and with the assistance of the Communist block, set up public companies such as SOMIEX which controlled trade, and OPAM, which controlled cereal marketing.

Keita's idea was that with surpluses from state enterprises and taxes on the rural economy, he could spur industrialization in the cities and at the same time transform traditional agriculture, producing low priced food for urban residents and exporting surplus crops. Accordingly, the government tried to set producer and consumer prices and control grain marketing. It was also Keita who instituted the policy of a guaranteed state job for those Malians completing secondary school.

Keita also tried to organize collective farms, left the West African Monetary Union — adopting the Malian Franc as its currency — and financed its budgeting by borrowing heavily from the Central Bank.

Modibo Keita's socialist path was a disaster. The Malian Franc soon became overvalued and inconvertible. Though Keita had intended that Mali would become self-sufficient in consumer goods, inefficient and monopolistic state industries lacked managerial expertise and market-inspired discipline, and drained state revenues while producing insufficient and shoddy goods that few Malians wanted to buy. Low producer prices inclined farmers toward subsistence agriculture. External debt mounted among growing budget deficits.

Keita finally tried to rescue Mali and himself by signing an agreement with France in 1967 to reschedule his debt, receive French backing for the Malian Franc, and reinstate a measure of monetary discipline.

This was a step in the right direction but proved too late for Keita. He was overthrown by Lieutenant Moussa Traore and a group of followers in a coup d'etat in November, 1968. Traore and his cohorts won control by ambushing Keita's car between the town of Koulikoro, forty miles to the east of Bamako, and the capital following Keita's arrival in Koulikoro from a boat trip on the Niger. Lieutenant Traore was soon to become General Traore without bothering with the intermediate ranks.

Moussa Traore recognized many of the problems he had inherited but was slow to change course. He continued Keita's policy of employing all secondary school graduates until 1983 and created regional development organizations that sopped up more public sector employees. Early reform attempts, such as increasing agricultural producer prices, were overtaken by shocks like the devastating 1972-74 drought and oil price increases. The drought cut agricultural production by 20% and decimated the national livestock herd by 35%.

By the late 1970s, and despite high levels of donor assistance, Mali was in the midst of a crisis. Inefficient state management, negative terms of trade, corruption, misallocation of resources, inflation and counterproductive pricing and tax policies had led Mali to a major fiscal breakdown.

An editorial in *"Le Monde"* from Paris concluded that Mali was *"a bout de souffle,"* out of breath. Another editorial in the local official Bamako paper, *L'Essor*, lamented, "The only thing left to do is to sell Mali to the United States."

I knew and liked Mali a lot, but could conclude with some confidence that whatever the asking price the U.S. probably wasn't interested in buying.

At this low point, the government was, as much out of desperation as anything else, finally ready to make a break with the past and undertake meaningful reform. Though more profound change would come later, at least the government could not deny that the policies of the past had totally failed and that change, though not fully defined, had to come.

The international donors too continued to stand with Mali, offering real assistance in formulating new policies and just as importantly backing them with money. Primary among these influential donors were the IMF, World Bank, France, the United States, and Germany.

This was not a futile effort. Despite everything, there was hope. Mali had a few things going for it: an industrious people which was relatively cohesive with no significant ethnic rivalries; a tradition of private commerce; and physical resources including large areas of still uncultivated land, abundant rainfall in the south, and important river systems and irrigation capacity in various parts of the country.

I saw Moussa Traore many times but hardly ever up close. I was too junior an employee then to be invited to the receptions or other official functions where Traore would be in attendance. Rather, I saw him from the side of the road as his motorcade raced by. I assumed he was going from the airport in the direction of his hilltop office and residence at Koulomba, or vice versa.

Traore's motorcade was led by two helmeted guards riding huge BMW motorcycles, followed by a lead car or two. The black Presidential Mercedes came next followed by a chasecar. The roar of the Presidential motorcade always appeared quickly out of nowhere, reached a rapid crescendo, and just as suddenly was gone. Such a display of quasi-first world speed and efficiency seemed totally out of place in Bamako.

Moussa Traore talked a lot about democracy and democratic participation, but single-party politics was the order of the day. The single party, the National Union of the Malian People, or UNPM, emphasized rural local initiative as its basic tenant for development, yet itself was highly centralized. In reality the UNPM was the vehicle by which Traore consolidated and managed his power.

The single daily government-controlled newspaper in Mali, *L'Essor*, spent most of its space extolling the virtues of the UNPM and describing the activities of its leaders, all in rather archaic French prose. There was no political opposition permitted, and rumors abounded that real or perceived enemies of the state would disappear in the night to the prison at Menaka, or worst horror of all, to the isolated military prison at Taoudeni, over a thousand miles to the north in the far desert corner of the country where Mali, Algeria, and Mauritania came together. No one ever returned from Taoudeni, or so the rumor went.

As exclusive and non-democratic as Mali's government was, it was then mostly gentle and benevolent in comparison to the real African despots, such as Bokassa in the Central African Republic, Macias Nguema in Equitorial Guinea, Sekou Toure in Guinea, or of course Idi Amin in Uganda, among others. Besides, though it would be some time longer before change actually occurred, winds of reform for a more real democracy were starting to blow softly.

You only had to keep your eyes open in Bamako to begin to understand the poverty. Beggars abounded. Lepers still existed and were much in evidence. One leper would daily knock on my ground level office window with the stump of his hand, rousing me out of my concentration as he begged for spare change.

Legions of small boys or even full grown men tried to guard your car or carry bags or do errands for small change that we knew would be a major supplement to the family income.

Conditions in Mali's rural areas, where 80% of the population then lived, were much more difficult.

Malian friends and colleagues alike, like the rest of the population, had to scrape by, not month to month but day to day. Even those who had the advantage of a relatively good job or a fixed income had the disadvantage of having an always growing number of relatives to support, as extended family had to rely on working family members to compensate for those who had no work.

When Abdou, one excellent Malian staff member in our office, was offered a raise, he accepted with regret.

"Thanks," Abdou told his boss, "but with this raise, more of my family will move in with me. I will have less than before."

The average Government of Mali salary at the time was about $100 a month. Salaries had to be kept low in part because of the incredible policy of a government-guaranteed job in the public sector to everyone graduating from secondary school or higher.

The majority of Malian jobs were in, as economists like to call it, the "informal sector" and were invariably far lower than even the public sector or other wage jobs.

Prices were not cheap either. Few Malians could afford electricity, medicine, or products or services other than the most basic. The ingredients too of a healthy diet were locally available yet beyond the price of most. A whole range of vegetables such as lettuce, carrots, cucumbers, cauliflower and the like were considered "toubab food" only, as the Malians simply could not afford them. Most Malians could not hope to buy any of the products in SOMIEX or Malimag, as rudimentary and shoddy these were by our standards.

Rice, the available and staple grain for most West Africans, was also out of the reach of many Malians' budgets, particularly in the rural areas. These ate millet, or when even that was too expensive or unavailable, fonio, another small grassy grain even less exclusive than millet, nicknamed "hungry millet," because when the millet was gone fonio could still sometimes be found.

For these folks, splurging on rice was reserved for Moslem religious holidays or other special occasions, and one had to make do with millet the rest of the time. Malian women spent hours of their day pounding millet into flour that would then be boiled into a mush called *"toh,"* which would be supplemented by sauces made with a few okra or peppers, or a bit of meat. For the Malian poor, and that was the majority, the diet was insufficiently nutritious as well as just insufficient.

Less than 30% of Malians had access to safe drinking water. Rural water from standing water or wells were invariably sources of amoeba at best or even more serious infections like guinea worm. Lack of safe drinking water contributed to a number of illnesses including diarrhea, which was a major cause of child mortality. Urban water supplies in Bamako, Segou, Mopti or other Malian towns were basically untreated, though somewhat less dangerous than rural water supplies.

There were a litany of diseases and afflictions present in Mali, some of which that had been long ago wiped out in the developed world — polio, brucellosis, trichinosis, dengue fever, river blindness, schistosomiasis, sleeping sickness, yellow fever, hepatitis, leprosy and malaria.

Malaria was endemic. Those that could afford it took anti-malarial medicine, but that again was mainly for the foreigner or the fortunate few. If you did not take your malaria medicine, you could almost count on coming down with malaria sooner or later. Malaria was one of the biggest killers in Africa, and in many parts of the developing world, as in Mali, it was rampant. A new strain of cerebral malaria, resistant to the chloroquine drugs prescribed for the more garden variety, had also reportedly appeared in the country.

Malaria was the most common illness in Mali and many Malians suffered from recurring malaria attacks. To me it seemed that the Malians complained about the effects of malaria more than any other disease. Ali would disappear from work for a week. Ba could not be found. When they would eventually stagger back to work, emaciated and trying to get rid of the pain and the shakes, they would shrug it off. Malaria attack. Bad, but it was part of life and happened all the time. This attitude made sense if you survived. Sudden attacks of malaria could and often did kill children and adults alike, and my colleagues told constant stories of family members alive and well one day, and dead from malaria the next.

Average life expectancy in Mali was only forty-three years, or about what it was in Europe in the eighteenth century. The infant mortality rate was 45%, meaning that almost half of the Malian children born would not make it to see their fifth birthdays. There was about one doctor for each 25,000 people.

The principal health problems for children included diarrhea, measles, malaria and respiratory infections. Respiratory infections were very common among children in Bamako resulting from generally unsanitary conditions coupled with dust and wood smoke in the air from cooking fires.

Like other developing countries, Mali's birthrate was very high, with a 2.6% annual population increase. Since Mali's amount of arable land per capita was high, the government did not think that this population rate increase was excessive. The feeling was that with the infant mortality rate so high, a high birthrate was insurance that some of the children would actually make it to adulthood.

Not more than 15% of the population had access to health services and it was not a good idea to become seriously ill in Mali. Mali's health infrastructure consisted of two national and six regional hospitals along with 46 health centers and 400 dispensaries. Urban service was better than rural, but its quality of services was uneven and deteriorating. Drugs and equipment were in chronic short supply. There were a number of health posts in many rural areas but they provided the most rudimentary of services.

Traditional medicine and healers still flourished, as much out of the lack of a modern alternative as belief, both in the cities and rural areas.

Those needing emergency treatment or an operation in Bamako went to one of the two national hospitals, either Point G on the heights above Bamako, or Gabriel Toure in town. Conditions at these local hospitals could best be described as grim and worst as horrific.

Salifa, a colleague from work, had gone into Gabriel Toure Hospital for a routine appendectomy. He died two days later from a post operation infection. The doctor from the American Embassy had visited the hospital and was also horrified by conditions.

I was friendly with several of the French doctors who worked up at Point G doing their alternative military service. My best friend there, Daniel, had just completed his medical studies in Nice and was married to a young Norwegian woman, Anke, who worked in my office.

Daniel's stories about Point G could curl hair. More often than not there was no electricity, no hot water, no bandages, no compresses, no surgical thread, and no attempt at sterilization. Daniel and his French colleagues brought much of their own supplies from France, but the real problem, he said, was not the surgery, but the post surgical infections that would set in and that would have been largely preventable under more hygienic conditions. This is what had been Salifa's undoing.

I had to visit a local hospital as a patient myself only once in my years in Mali. This was to the leper hospital near Bamako and fortunately was not for leprosy, which requires years of exposure to contract or so I was told.

I had climbed the mango tree in my backyard to get at several huge juicy-looking mangos that Badji needed to make mango pie. Whatever economic problems Mali possessed, mango production was not one of them. Mali was to mangos as Saudi Arabia was to oil. They tended to be big, juicy and delicious.

I had not known I was allergic to the toxin on the mango skin. By the time I had scrambled out of the tree with the mangos in my hands, my face had swollen up the size of a basketball and I was covered from head to toe with a nasty red rash. Shirley, the Embassy nurse, took one look at me and drove me straight to the leprosarium. It was clean, efficient and run by an international medical team.

The Belgian doctor knew my symptoms and administered a cortisone shot. The rash soon subsided and my head eventually regained its regular shape. I was impressed that such a facility existed in Bamako, especially since Point G was so horrible, and swore that if we ever had a real medical emergency in Mali and couldn't get on the plane, the leprosarium looked like the place to go.

The international donors were very active in the health field. France, China, the USSR, the United Nations, the U.S. and a host of private NGO's provided surgical teams, medicine, research, vaccinations, family planning and primary health care, although far insufficient for the need. Much more emphasis was needed on primary health care to improve and expand basic coverage and the United States AID Mission was the main mover in this field.

For the foreigner attempting to stay healthy in Mali, it was normally easier that the long list of diseases and horror stories would lead one to believe. If water was boiled and filtered, if anti-malarial medicine was taken regularly, if you watched what you ate and drank, if you had all your shots, and some believed if you took a quarterly gamma globulin shot, you could live in relatively good health and not spend all your time worrying about it.

Peace Corps Volunteers, French *"cooperants"* — the French version of the Peace Corps — and other Western aid workers, mostly living in rural villages, seemed to be the ones most exposed to disease, especially those who "went native" and threw caution to the wind. Some would forget to take their chloroquinine, or some would take it and still come down with malaria. Others would drink untreated milk or water from a well and pay the price.

For the Americans and usually non-Americans working on U.S.-financed projects, there was a policy of evacuating people out of Mali if more than the most routine medical attention was needed. Funds for this eventuality were routinely included in contracts. Medical evacuation would sometimes involve often no more than a trip to a clinic in Dakar, or a trip to Paris or back to the States if the problem were more serious. The Embassy had a full time doctor and an American nurse, the nurse having worked in Mali for more than ten years, and they were the final judges of whether one stayed or was evacuated.

The planes out of Bamako for Dakar and Europe left on Monday, Thursday and Saturday. If you were going to get seriously ill in Bamako, it was best not to get sick on Monday night or Tuesday, we told each other, because you would have to wait until the Air Afrique flight left for Paris late Thursday night to be evacuated.

One "medical" procedure was carried out routinely on both little boys and girls at about the age of nine or ten: circumcision. For the boys, this was a painful undertaking, but was part of the rites of coming of age. Troops of newly circumcised little boys wearing white robes, carefully held so not to rub their wound, would accost foreigners looking for *"cadeaux,"* cash gifts in their honor. Joy thought the little boys were "cute."

For little girls, circumcision was far more traumatic and controversial, at least controversial in the West. Condemned as barbaric and mutilatory in the developed world, female circumcision was and is still routinely carried out throughout many portions of sub-Saharan Africa. The operation is normally performed by a woman who is sometimes part of the family, and involves the removal of the clitoris. In some portions of East Africa such as Somalia and Ethiopia, the operation can be expanded to include the further horror of actually sewing together the young girl's labia to ensure virginity before marriage.

This was one African tradition I could not justify. What was the point? Was this just the rural people that practiced female circumcision? What about the urban or educated Malians?

I posed the question to my Malian colleague, Boubacar N'Ndao, who was educated in the U.S.

"No, almost all the good families do it here. It is something that is just done. I really never thought about not having it done on my daughter."

"Boubacar, you mean you let your own daughter be circumcised?"

"Of course, but we put her in the best clinic to have it done. There's too much risk of infection otherwise."

I figured that if the highly educated and well-traveled of Mali like Boubacar were still sanctioning female circumcision, a lot of it unfortunately must still be going on.

Lack of educational opportunities was another development constraint for Mali. Illiteracy in the rural areas was estimated at a whopping 90% and enrollment rates at schools were actually dropping in the mideighties. The government had decided to emphasize functional literacy programs in national languages rather than French and more of the education budget was directed at primary education. Scholarship programs and technical training were provided by Western and Communist-block countries alike.

It seemed to me that most Western donors in Mali were sincerely interested in helping Mali develop as an independent and economically stable country. Some may have been thinking more about their own self-interest than others, mineral exploitation or future trade and the like, but

Mali's needs were undisguisable and clear for all to see. For all I knew, some of the Communist block interest may have been altruistic too — both the Soviets and Chinese were providing medical teams for example — but I was not in a position to judge clearly.

Mali was also one of the more remote and minor East-West confrontation areas. A tennis partner friend at the U.S. Embassy said he thought in the event of any possible Soviet intervention in other parts of Africa, for example Angola, Mali could serve as a staging area and refueling stop for Soviet military transport planes.

In fact the Soviets had built runways and airports in Mali far in excess of local requirements. They also had their large scholarship program in Mali and Radio Moscow even broadcast for several hours every day in Bambara.

So, the Western democracies kept an eye on the Soviets while they kept an eye on us, but development was in reality the most important, and some would say only, game in town.

The development program I worked on was directed at helping Mali's economy grow by increasing Mali's self-sufficiency in food production which we defined as both as grain production and improvements in livestock.

The drought that had originally brought me to work on Mali back in Washington was over, at least for the moment, so the earlier task of providing immediate disaster assistance to the effected people needed to move to the next stage. It had been decided that this next stage was to assist the Malians in the formidable task of reestablishing agriculture and livestock production. This was already a pretty ambitious undertaking given with the modest funds at our disposal. No matter, we decided that support for improved health care and training were also essential and modest projects in these areas would also be implemented.

The first generation of projects that were designed to implement this strategy were ambitious and scattered throughout the country. I arrived after this first group of projects had been designed but most had been under full implementation for an average of between two and three years. These projects, except for health and training efforts, were essentially intended to grow more rice, millet and wheat, and produce more and better livestock. My first tasks upon arrival had been to help my colleagues see how well or badly this approach was going, and recommend changes accordingly. I would continue to do these evaluations throughout my stay.

We had been in Mali for well over a year and a half now and we felt more and more like seasoned veterans.

Joy was working and was happy with many friends and had survived her first Christmas far away from family. Christmas in fact had been a smashing success. We had had pot-luck Christmas dinner at a colleague's house with some forty other friends, all in great spirits on a bright, sunny, peaceful winter day in Bamako. Winter meant that the temperature may have briefly dipped into the lower eighties.

Frozen turkeys had been special ordered from the States or from a supplier in Denmark, and there were all sorts of Christmas fare and desserts brought by the guests. The highlight of the day had been the singing of "The Twelve Days of Christmas," rewritten *à la Malienne* for the occasion, using humor that normal people in other settings would likely have found totally appalling, but that most of us felt was a healthy reaction to our surroundings and kept things from getting too serious. (...Eight Lepers Leaping, Seven Used Chew-Sticks, Six Beggars Begging, Five Worn Out Shoes, Four Kola Nuts, Three Mangoes, Two Cowrie Shells, and a Case of Warm Somalibo, etc.)

I had my outside interests in tennis, guitar and softball, but felt best of all about my own professional situation. With the help of more experienced friends like Jerry, I was feeling better equipped to contribute to our work.

Phil and I had finished the ICRISAT redesign and the project was moving ahead at full speed. Alex and I had helped redesign a rural development project in the Mopti Region. Jerry and I were making plans to formally evaluate our irrigated rice project in Gao which because of its timing and scope had the potential to be one of the first instructive evaluations of a crop production project designed in the wake of the Sahel drought. I had traveled throughout the remote southern part of the First Region, inspecting village level post-harvest grain processing and storage. I was learning first hand more about the problems of farm-to-market transport, the best way to construct village wells, a little about livestock disease, and a whole lot more about development economics than I had ever learned out of textbooks.

More than ever before, I felt good about my ability to contribute something positive to all this. As jobs went, it had one other important characteristic: it was fun.

Our development program in Mali had food self-sufficiency as underlying premise. It made sense, the argument went at the time, to have fragile countries dependent on agriculture, such as Mali, produce as much food as they needed to consume. This would insure sufficient supply and decrease dependence on unreliable outside food sources that, in addition, would require payment in scarce or non-existent foreign exchange.

The food self-sufficiency argument was appealing in a country like Mali. At the time of independence in 1960, Mali had been a net exporter of food to other countries in the region. Why should Mali have to rely on imports of Thai rice when rice grew and grew well in the Niger flood basin? Why import food when Mali had the land, the people and the water — at least from the seasonal floods of the Niger though not always sufficient rainfall — to produce far more food than it was presently doing? The experience of the old *Office du Niger* had proven that Mali could produce well in excess of present yields.

It is estimated that in 1960, Mali produced 100% of its domestic food grain requirements. By 1975, that percentage had fallen to about only 45%. The food self-sufficiency argument said Mali could and should do better in producing more food for its own use.

Livestock was also important to Mali, and with a herd exceeding over ten million, provided income to half or more of all rural people. We estimated that livestock contributed about 20% to Mali's GDP and generated almost half of the country's export revenues. Most livestock fed on dry rangeland that would otherwise be unproductive, but there was also potential to increase numbers of livestock in the more fertile south and make greater use of animal power in farming.

With all that in mind, we had undertaken projects to produce irrigated and floating rice in the region of Gao, small-scale irrigated wheat in Dire near Timbuktu, a large livestock production project outside Bamako, and two large "integrated" rural development projects, one in the Fifth Region of Mopti, and the other in the Haute Vallee, the High Valley region of higher rainfall southeast of Bamako.

"Integrated" meant that these projects would not concentrate on agricultural production alone but on the whole assembly of needed activities for development — farm-to-market roads, improved technologies such as grain storage, improved seed production and so on, agricultural credit, marketing, and so forth.

We had undertaken economic analyses of all these projects at the design stage. The economic analyses invariably showed that the projects made sense. I was discovering that if the momentum was up to do a project, sometimes overly optimistic economic and then financial assumptions would be used and the design would proceed unencumbered.

The project near Mopti was intended primarily to increase millet production and the Haute Vallee project was intended to concentrate primarily on vegetable and grain production as well as roads, and agricultural credit in the higher rainfall zone south of Bamako.

I had visited our wheat production project in Dire not long after my arrival. I was particularly interested in this project as I had, while still in Washington, done a review of the project's original economic analysis, an exercise I would later realize that when done from a desk in far off Washington, D.C., could hardly hope to reflect reality.

I didn't know much about the progress on implementation but David of the agriculture office, whom I had met my first day in Mali, was the project manager. He was losing his mind, I soon found out, trying to procure and get delivered to Dire small pumps from India that would irrigate the wheat perimeters with water from the Niger. If the pumps didn't arrive in time, an entire planting season would be lost and considerable credibility would be lost with the local farmers.

I flew up to Dire in a rented plane with several colleagues, including David and Alex of Bamako drama fame. It was a rented Mali Air Service Twin-Otter and this time fortunately the flight was uneventful. It was the end of the rainy season and from the air the flooded Niger delta stretched out as far as you could see, villages and other dry areas interspersed with a greater expanse of shallow water. I had never seen so much water in dry Mali before. It looked like the Mekong Delta, said Myron, a senior aggie who had been in Vietnam and had a younger Vietnamese wife.

We landed at the Goundam airstrip located in a desert area not far from the Niger River where we were met by two Dire project vehicles and the two young American project advisors, Charlotte and Dave, who had earlier served in the Peace Corps together in Mali and had been recently married.

Charlotte and Dave struck me as very serious, competent people, dedicated to making the project work. Before going to Dire, we went north on a side trip away from the river toward the village of Gounsao near Lake Faguibine where we had financed construction of a well. This was a very remote and isolated spot with few people. For most of the year, this was the desert. But for a couple of months with the rains and the flood, this area was transformed into a huge expanse of treeless grassland stretching as far as one could see in either direction. The tall grasses moved silently in long waves in time to the wind.

Lake Faguibine was another anomaly. What was this huge reed-lined lake doing in the middle of the Sahara Desert?

The Dire wheat project had been designed two years previously in order to help cut the chronic cereal deficit in the Sixth Region of Mali, the area of Mali with Timbuktu as its capital. The idea was that cereals, mostly wheat, would be produced using farmer-managed pump irrigation using the water from the Niger River.

There was a long standing tradition of small scale wheat production in the Dire region going back to the fifteenth century invasion of the area by Moroccans. With drought conditions prevailing in the mid-seventies and the Malians faced with large cereal import requirements, the government began to focus on maximizing grain production in the region. The French stepped in with financial assistance in 1975 to develop a pilot 300 hectare irrigation system.

With the reestablishment of local wheat production on an even larger scale, Mali could save a couple of million dollars a year in foreign exchange that they presently used to import wheat from France.

The project would operate under the direction of the Malian parastatal organization called *"Action Ble."* *"Ble"* is French for wheat and *"Action"* was a Malian government term for an organization responsible for development within a geographic or crop specific area.

David, the present project manager, had lead the *Action Ble* design team two years before. The project was designed in simplicity — usually a plus to implementation — and total optimism. The project would assist some 2,400 poor farmers increase cereal production by providing small irrigation pumps, which would be purchased on short-term credit by groups of four farmers per pump. The credit would come from a project revolving fund that would also finance fuel, fertilizers, tools and the like.

The pumps would irrigate about four hectares each, taking water from a nearby tributary of the Niger and lifting it into simple, gravity-fed irrigation canals constructed by the farmers themselves.

The project would be implemented under the responsibility and supervision of the *Action Ble* parastatal, and assisted by village and sub-village management units that contained mechanics and extension staff. Despite the fact that the project would be run by a government parastatal, it would be democratic. A group of elected village leaders in each participating village would assist the *Action* with extension and supervision activities and would help assure that land allocation was carried out in a fair way that followed traditional land use patterns. This project would care about the farmers being the owners of the project.

In addition to the pumps, the project was to provide more credit for seeds and fertilizers; training in extension, management and marketing of the cereals; funding for an extended *Action Ble* staff; warehouses and staff housing; a repair shop; project vehicles and two motorized boats; and foreign technical assistance.

By the end of the project five years hence, it was anticipated that there would be more than 9,000 metric tons of wheat and sorghum produced annually. A full 2,200 hectares of wheat would be double-cropped with sorghum and 500 hectares triple-cropped with legumes and forage. Small farmer income would soar as a result of the increased production as well as due to a preplanting agreement that exempted the project from OPAM price controls and guaranteed farmers production incentives. More importantly, as a result of the increased cereal production brought about by the project, the grain deficit in the Sixth Region of Mali would be significantly reduced.

The final good news was that the project would not cost much money. All this for only $2.3 million with a sizable cash and in-kind contribution planned from the Government of Mali.

It seemed like a seductively simple and attractive concept. From Washington and on paper, it had looked like a good idea: using the abundant water of the Niger with simple technology to help farmers, already with a tradition of growing wheat in the zone, produce more cereals for their benefit and that of the region.

Once arriving in Mali, I had begun to hear David complaining about the difficulties of procuring and shipping pumps to Dire. Now, arriving in the area for the first time, I listened to Charlotte and Dave describing their problems as we drove.

Their principal complaint concerned their local Malian counterpart. The Malian director of *Action Ble*, Monsieur Coumare, was not cooperating and seemed to resent the technical advice they offered. More worrisome, he was demanding access to all the project funds in Dire. Further, the director was an outsider to the project zone and did not get along well with the local farmers, whom he treated with condescension. Therefore, the active participation of the farmers in extension and land selection was behind schedule. No training had begun on pump repair or anything else. It was hard enough just getting the pumps delivered and made to work in far-off Dire.

Dire and the reality of the project on the ground looked different than I had visualized it back in Washington. My first impression of Dire was that, in a country that itself was remote and isolated, Dire was in a particularly remote and isolated part of that country.

Dire, located on the north bank of the Niger, was 957 kilometers from Bamako. It was 646 kilometers from Bamako to Mopti by paved road. Upon reaching Mopti, you had to cross the Niger by barge and continue by track — there was no road — another 311 kilometers. Trucks attempting the crossing could be easily stuck in the sand or stymied when trying to cross inundated areas. Dire was another 100 kilometers from Timbuktu, the capital of the Sixth Region, but again there was no real road.

I was still pretty green to development but realized the difficulties of trying to make a project work in such an isolated area. Despite any other difficulties, could a project that depended on outside inputs like pumps, gasoline, fertilizer and transport to market, be made to work? Maybe it could succeed, but from the logistics alone it looked very difficult.

We were received in Dire by the *"Action Ble"* Director, Monsieur Coumare. He was polite and correct but avoided eye contact and lacked the warmth of most of the Malian officials I had previously dealt with.

David, Myron and I arranged ourselves in front of Coumare's small metal desk and settled in low metal framed chairs with yellow plastic tubing. Charlotte and Dave took seats behind us.

Coumare explained his progress in distributing pumps and his difficulty in assuring a supply of diesel fuel for them. Yes, he was concerned about training mechanics in pump repair and this would happen soon. He avoided eye contact with Dave and Charlotte and directed all of his remarks to us.

We proceeded outside of Dire by Land Rover to see the pumps in action. One Songhai farmer stood ready to engage a pump by the river on our right while several others stood nearby by with hoes in their hands. The pump roared to life and water flowed from a hose down the dirt canals that had been dug. With the hoes, the farmers could easily open and close earthen openings from the canals to the waiting fields, where small and immature green shoots of wheat waited.

I was reassured. The technology looked as simple and as feasible as advertised.

David explained that shipments of Indian pumps had arrived from Bamako by truck and boat, but that there were no spare parts yet. Leaving the fields we passed the project warehouse on the outskirts of the village. A large group of pumps that had been provided by the French were now largely useless and lay in pieces in front of the project warehouse. But it wasn't just the old French pumps, Dave and Charlotte pointed out. To my amazement, I noticed that it was also the newly arrived pumps that were there too — uncrated, some whole and some in pieces on the outside of the warehouse — all totally exposed to the elements.

What was going on here?

Charlotte spoke up.

"We've been trying to get the *Action* to store the new pumps in the warehouse for weeks. When they arrived, the *Action* was supposed to have set up the credit fund, and distribute the pumps as the farmers made arrangements with the fund to purchase them. But 'Action Ble' doesn't seem interested in setting up the credit fund — they say they had to get some pumps working or the planting season would be missed. They've just given out some pumps and put the rest here in front of the warehouse."

Dave added, "It's not only that the credit fund that hasn't been set up and the pumps stored correctly. So far anyway, the *Action* doesn't have any inventory control system, and no accounting system I've been able to discover. No training in extension or pump repair or anything else has happened yet."

David, the Bamako project manager, looked pained. I knew David to be a hard-working and conscientious professional, so what was going on?

"Part of the problem is that I've had to spend all of my time on procurement of these pumps, arranging transport to Dire and that kind of thing. Also, the project allows the *Action* to do its own procurement too, it's not just me. Everything is supposed to be coordinated, but the 'Action' just does what it wants. I talk to them about setting up a procurement plan and following procedures and they look at me like I'm nuts."

He went on, "Despite what we agreed in writing about the project, I believe sometimes that the *Action* folks just want us to hand over the money and get out of the way."

I was still pretty new to this kind of thing and asked what I felt sure was a naive question.

"But the Malians have agreed in writing that the project will be implemented in a certain way, including farmer participation, operation of the credit fund, accounting for funds, procurement rules and all that kind of thing. Why don't we insist that the agreement be respected?"

David shook his head.

"It's not that easy. If we start insisting too much, everything will grind to a halt. My boss is hollering at me to move the money and reduce the funding pipeline this year, and if we hold up the project my expenditure rate goes to zero. That will look bad too. I'm between a rock and a hard place. Besides, part of the purpose of working with *Action Ble* is so they can get experience they need on commodity procurement and project management."

What was really happening with the *Action Ble* project seemed in no way to resemble the up-beat project design documents.

We ate our dinner of rice and sauce that night by lantern light at Charlotte and Dave's little banco house in Dire. I had a question for Dave.

"Dave, you live here and you and Charlotte know better than anyone else what needs to be done to get the project on track. You're the technical experts on the project. Why can't you work with the *Action Ble* folks and get some of these problems straightened out?"

Dave grimaced. "Remember in the car this morning I mentioned our problems with the Director? Part of it is personal. Coumare resents us and wants to do as he pleases, and since he has control over some of the funds he can get away with it. When he wants, he just ignores us."

He went on.

"Another part of it is culture and experience. When we talk about inventory systems, accounting procedures, and proper procurement, hardly anyone — particularly *Action Ble* staff here in Dire — has a clue what we're talking about. They've had no training in any of this. The cultural part is that they really see our job as providing the funds and their job at doing whatever they feel is best with them. Project generators are a case in point. The project purchased two large generators, one for the office and the other for the warehouse and repair shop operation. One of the generators is at Coumare's personal residence and the other is still in the crate."

"The other part of it is contractual. Our contracts say that Charlotte and I report both to Coumare as *Action Ble* Director, as well as to David in Bamako. David expects us to be his eyes and ears in Dire, plus implement the project. To implement the project properly I can't be subordinate to Coumare, but that's the way it's set up."

We heard from Charlotte and Dave by radio the next week that Coumare was no longer around. He had fled Dire with the petty cash fund in his project-funded Land Rover. We heard two weeks later that the vehicle had been discovered abandoned miles away across the border in Burkina Faso.

The Ministry of Agriculture assured us that Coumare would be replaced and that the project would continue.

The visit to Dire had been a sobering experience. We had seen wheat growing and pumps pumping, but the flight of Coumare and the sight of project pumps sitting outdoors unused and unstored had been disturbing. The lack of a credit fund and systems for funds control was particularly worrisome.

Jerry listened intently as I explained what I had seen in Dire. Let's give it some time before we panic, we decided. The project is really just getting underway, and those with the responsibility for project implementation have just seen the problems in the field firsthand and can now work to solve them. Also, there will soon be a new Malian Director of *Action Ble* with whom to build a relationship. Let's keep our eyes and ears open and see what happens for a while. We can formally evaluate the project when implementation is a bit further along.

A couple of days later on a Saturday I put *Action Ble*'s problems temporarily out of my mind to attend what friends had described as a major track meet to be held at the Soviet-built stadium, beside the auditorium where Joy and I had heard Mariam Makeba.

I arrived walking as I wanted to inspect the Saturday markets in the neighborhood of Narela, where I had driven through many times but had yet to stop for a close-up inspection. When I arrived at the stadium, I was able to meet my group of European and American friends. We sat near a group of Americans, one of whom I recognized as the Gunnery Sergeant from the Embassy, the head Marine. We were the only white faces in the crowd, the rest of the stadium being nearly filled with happy and enthusiastic Malians out for a treat far outside the normal routine.

The Gunney turned and said, "You're just in time for the 10,000 meters race. Corporal Stevens is running."

I didn't know Corporal Stevens, a Marine guard at the U.S. Embassy, but I had heard of him. He was a serious runner, and in addition to the already demanding fitness program of all the Marines, Corporal Stevens led the other Marines in marathon speed and distance runs throughout the dirt road neighborhoods of Bamako. Corporal Stevens had evidently been practicing and pointing for this particular race for months.

The runners lined up. The six or seven other runners were a pretty motley looking bunch, all skinny as rails, and dressed in a variety of mis-matched costumes probably bought for the equivalent of twenty-five cents in the used clothes market. To my disbelief, one of the Malian run-ners was barefooted. Corporal Stevens on the other hand was dressed as if for the Olympic trials, in silver running shorts and a smart red tank top with serious running shoes.

When the gun sounded and the group took off, it was quickly clear that it was a two man race between Corporal Stevens and the barefoot Malian in the dark blue shorts. After two laps, Stevens and the young Malian had far outdistanced the other runners and several even dropped out to stand panting alongside the track.

The crowd around us was enthusiastically cheering for the Malian runner, but with all the friendly looks in our direction, it was clear that they were happy and proud that a bunch of foreigners had considered their event important enough to attend.

The cheers grew louder and a collective inspiration crossed through the minds of our little group.

"Tou-ba-bou! Tou-ba-bou! Tou-ba-bou!" We stood yelling and clap-ping in unison.

All of the Malians within earshot turned around in shock, then in an instant of realization, broke up into gales of laughter and clapping at the sound of the all familiar little boys' chant about strange white people, this time coming from a group of the same. This was humor they could relate to.

Corporal Stevens was about twenty meters in front of the barefoot Malian as they began the final lap. I couldn't tell if the Malian runner was exhausted or just being savvy, but it seemed clear that the Marine was slowing down. He was visibly tiring and it seemed he was trying to hold on as the race entered its final stages.

The Malian runner spurted with a half lap to go, taking off for the front and with a third of a lap to go passed Corporal Stevens. At the fin-ish line he led by almost thirty meters. The entire crowd, our group included, was on its feet clapping wildly.

We were cheering all the runners, but I was mostly cheering moxie, determination, and bare feet.

5
Going for Gao

I was finding that working on economic development programs was never boring and rarely a simple undertaking. It was intellectually challenging yet demanded practical solutions to complex problems of all sorts. If our work became just an intellectual exercise, the development results we cared most about would not be achieved and we would be wasting our time and money. On the other hand, if one just focussed on the day to day nuts and bolts of implementing a program — say just getting a project commodity delivered on time or contracting with a certain technical specialist — without consideration of the "bigger picture" of the overall economic and policy context, one could similarly miss having either a sound project design or a chance for ultimately successful and sustainable development results.

With this in mind, my interest began to focus in on our stated "big picture" strategy of increasing food self-sufficiency. We had recently begun talking about the aim of "increasing" food self-sufficiency rather that actually reaching it. I suspected this wasn't just because the latter was difficult to achieve. Why the change? Also, I was curious if any policy related to food self-sufficiency really made economic sense in Mali.

With these questions in mind, Jerry and I made plans to begin an evaluation of the Gao rice and sorghum production project which had been under implementation for more than three years. We would start the evaluation and be joined later by specialists from our regional office in Abidjan. The evaluation would be the first assessment of the project and be the key ingredient to judging its progress to date and whether we should continue to fund the project after the first phase of funding ran out in six months.

Leaving Bamako was always an adventure but this time was different. Joy was six months pregnant and would be departing for the States in several weeks to wait it out and give birth at home. I would follow in time for the big event. The airlines would not permit a pregnant woman to fly past the seventh month to lessen the chances she would go into labor at 30,000 feet. Western women normally did not take chances with giving birth in Mali due to inadequate medical facilities if there were complications. Barbara had again blazed the way for Joy, this time on the pregnancy front. She had gone back to Indiana and given birth to their daughter and had recently returned to Bamako.

The pregnancy was going well except Joy had once again come down with amoebic dysentery. This time with the pregnancy, the doctor was afraid to prescribe the normal treatment, Flagyl, which Joy described as poison — effective, but poison all the same. We had written her physician brother in Texas about the problem and he had promised to send a different medicine that would deal with the amoeba — called simply "mebes" by the expatriate legions intimately familiar with the affliction — without hurting the baby. The package had yet to arrive.

So it was with more than a little worry that I made plans to go to Gao with Jerry. I had had enough of flying and Air Mali by this time. We would travel in the brand new Toyota Land Cruiser that the office had purchased and that was far more comfortable than our old Land Rover. I knew it would still be a long, tough trip of some 1000 kilometers as the paved road ended at Mopti, and it being rainy season, roads were always in unpredictable shape.

We were loaded with drinking water, camping equipment, and tools. Our administrative office tried to get us to take military style C-Rations on these trips but having tried them once, Jerry and I decided that we would respectfully decline the honor and make do on the road.

Best of all, we had a secret weapon against all calamities, our Songhai driver Ali Badara. Ali was based in Gao and had driven to Bamako at our request to accompany us back up to Gao.

Jerry had taught me that there was nothing in Mali more important than a good bush driver, and Ali Badara was the best. Ali Badara drove a vehicle through the desert sand like a basketball player who was "in the zone" and couldn't miss a shot. He drove with eyes closed to small slits — snake eyes — feeling the road and shifting cooly with the movement of the vehicle. When we reached the sand portion of the track past Mopti, Ali would stop and wind the long Songhai burnoose around his head and face so that only his eyes would show through the black cloth. Unlike any other desert driver I ever saw, Ali Badara never got lost or stuck in the sand. This guy was no mere driver, he was an artist, and I became convinced that in Ali's hands nothing bad could befall us.

Before we left Bamako, Ali quietly confided to me that he was very glad to hear about my wife's pregnancy. He said that having no children at my advanced age of almost thirty was very strange and that he was happy we had finally done something about it, albeit very late in life.

This had been a topic of conversation for some time among all the office drivers, he told me, and that I had now been somewhat redeemed in their eyes. Well, good, I said, and better late than never.

Between Mopti and Douentza, the roads showed the effects of rainy season. Or they would have shown the effects if they had not been mostly underwater. In the dryer portions of the road, a few trucks stood by stuck in deep mud up to their axles. Water that appeared in large pot holes in the laterite surface could be three inches deep or over three feet, and there was no way to tell for sure without driving through. The scariest part was crossing a large area best described as a huge lake. We could see where the road emerged on the far side of the water, but had no idea how deep it was in the middle.

We had little choice but to go forward. We got deeper and deeper until the water was actually breaking over the hood of the Land Cruiser. This continued for several tense minutes, but Ali kept driving and more importantly the Land Cruiser kept going. I hadn't thought a car could keep running under water with no protection to keep water from entering through the exhaust pipe, but keep running it did. Safe and dry on the other side, I resolved to write a nice letter of thanks to the Toyota Corporation as soon as we returned.

Past Douentza, the landscape changed from Sahelian savannah to dry desert. At Hombori, a distinctive rock formation called Mount Hombori Tondo, reminiscent of Utah, rose some 1,155 meters above the flat plane to meet us. High sand dunes of the desert stood off to the north side of the road.

Jerry, Ali Badara and I stopped to find something to eat outside Hombori. For 100 Malian Francs, or about 20 cents, we bought a bowl of rice from the communal pot and watched the sun set. Two camels carrying blue-clad Touaregs rode out of the desert and descended the dunes toward us. As they got near us, they stopped their camels and stared, saying nothing to us or to each other. Just stared silently at us through the slits in their head cloth.

We kept driving. Other vehicle tracks led off through the sand in different directions in the darkness but Ali Badara seemed to know where he was going. I was glad I wasn't driving. A compass was mounted on the dashboard of the Land Cruiser and Ali glanced at it occasionally.

After several more hours of driving like this, a group of darkened, low banco buildings came into sight. This was the small village of Gossi that appeared on our map. When a lantern light came on at one building, we asked if we could put our cots in their courtyard and sleep. That way we would have water to wash up in the morning and could find something for breakfast before pushing on.

Morning brought a scene far different from Bamako or other areas of Mali I had seen before. This was the real desert and the land of the Songhai and Touareg peoples. It was market day in Gossi and people were appearing in the little village square that served as its tiny open-air market.

I had no idea where these people had come from. Certainly not Gossi itself — it was only a small village with a few banco blockhouses on the dusty track in the middle of nowhere. Off in the distance, where only an occasional tree broke the dry and open landscape where one could see clearly for miles, more people were heading for Gossi. Some walked, some arrived on camelback, coming from where I could not imagine.

Off to the side of the Gossi market square on an old blanket sat a group of young women and girls dressed totally in black. I had never seen people dressed like this in Mali. I asked Jerry who they were.

"These are the Bellah," Jerry replied. "They're a client group to the Songhai and the Touareg."

"Client group?" I had never heard this term before. "What does that mean?"

Jerry didn't pause. "They're slaves."

Jerry went on to explain that, yes, slavery or its near equivalency still existed in a few places in Mali and on an even larger scale in neighboring Mauritania. As a result of lost battles in the far past, accumulated debts or other reasons, a traditional subjugated group had formed. If there was a positive angle on this, it was that the Bellah were not slaves as we in the west normally think about the term. There was no buying and selling of people in this form of slavery, at least in Mali, though it still flourished in Mauritania. But as in the traditional sense of slavery, in return for their servitude the Bellahs were taken care of, fed, clothed, sheltered.

"Could they leave if they wanted?", I asked.

"I think so," said Jerry, "but they probably wouldn't do it. There is comfort and care in the group and this is the only life these people know."

I found the whole notion of the continued existence of slavery, no matter what the anthropological spin, to be shocking and abhorrent. Granted there was no racial angle on this brand of slavery as both the Songhai and the Bellah were black, but the fact remained that for all practical purposes, the Bellah would live their entire lives in servitude to the Songhai, perhaps with no thought or possibility of liberty.

Outside of Gossi, Ali Badara stopped the Land Rover so we could observe a group of Touareg pulling water from a deep well in the desert. Built by a European donor, the well was over 100 meters deep. The Touareg pulled black leather bags of water from the well using a long rope harnessed to a camel saddle horn. The camel would stride off down a well-worn track down the incline from the well until the leather water bag finally appeared at the top. A waiting Touareg poured water into larger containers that would later be borne away by another camel.

We arrived in Gao in mid-afternoon. Gao lay on the north side of the Niger and we had to be rafted across the river in a rickety wooden ferry powered by a pained sounding outboard motor, onto which Ali drove the Land Cruiser without hesitation. This being the rainy season, the river was as swollen as I'd ever seen it.

It was possible to travel from Bamako to Gao by river boat during five months of the year when the river had sufficient water to be navigable. The river boats that made the trip up from Koulikoro near Bamako, stopping at Segou, Mopti, the port near Timbuktu, then arriving eventually in Gao, usually taking six days each way. There were two river boats which made the run, the *Tomboctou* and the *Generale Soumare,* if they weren't broken down. The boats had four classes ranging from deluxe to third class, second and third class being very difficult with swarms of people, screaming children, mounds of cargo, and only the most rudimentary of facilities. I had heard tales of unsuspecting foreigners booking passage on the river boats thinking they were in for an idyllic, romantic luxury cruise ride down the Niger, only to find to their horror they were in for days of near torture. At the raft we were told the *Generale Soumare* was expected to arrive in town soon.

Gao had a population of about 25,000, mostly Songhai and Touareg. Its population had grown after the droughts had killed much of the former cattle herds, forcing many former herders to move to the city and look for other work. Gao was even hotter than the rest of Mali, the temperature easily reaching 48 degrees Centigrade during the day.

I had flown into Gao twice before and knew the city fairly well. Gao had streets of sand, and several wide boulevards that were, despite the oppressive heat, tree lined with fast growing acacias that had been planted after a drought in the mid-seventies when donors had poured some money into the Gao area. Gao was pretty rudimentary after the bright lights and distractions of Bamako, but entering from the desert, particularly if you had just crossed the Sahara, it must have looked pretty fancy.

Had this been the 1930s, Gao would have been the perfect setting for a French Foreign Legion movie. Gao had an ancient gas station with pumps from the thirties or forties still functioning, a forlorn hotel — the improbably named Atlantique — still the best within hundreds of miles, three open air markets, one possibly functioning bank, and a large regional assembly government building. It didn't take too long for the streets and low banco dwellings of Gao to fade into the desert and end. On the outskirts of Gao to the east was the airport where I had had my earlier adventure with the smoldering Air Mali 737.

Ali Badara was now back on his own home turf and he was obviously happy to be home. He had a wife and new baby of his own he told us. Ali drove us to the small guest house we rented in Gao and we unloaded. The guest house was rudimentary and not often used, but it was clean and the generator worked well enough to run a refrigerator and the lights. Except for the considerable local color of the Hotel Atlantique, this was the place to be.

Gao's most impressive building was the large clay pyramid-shaped tomb of Askia Mohammed. Askia Mohammed ruled the Songhai Empire at the height of its glory, dying in 1491. The Songhai Empire grew in significance beginning in 1335 when the Songhai broke away from the Mali Empire and used a well-trained army with horsemen to conquer the surrounding area. The empire was lead in the fifteenth century by Sonni Ali, who was a great military commander, defeating competing armies of Touaregs from the north and Mossi from the south. Askia Mohammed stretched the borders of his empire to its greatest extent, to the Senegal River in the west, well into the Sahara to the north, and down into present day Nigeria to the south. The empire declined with the defeat of the Songhai by Berber invaders from Morocco at the battle of Tondibi not far from present day Gao.

Gao was a fascinating place but it was tempting to conclude that ever since the days of Askia Mohammed, most events of any wordly significance had been passing Gao by.

There was one worldly event that still touched Gao. The annual Paris-Dakar Rally, depending on the shifting route they chose to transit the Sahara, would sometimes pass through town. This year the Rally had come through several weeks previously, stranding a couple of drivers and leaving one or two vehicles broken down in the vicinity. Gao was the end of the road for these guys. Otherwise, the customized rally vehicles roared through town and were quickly gone, scattering terrified local children and animals in their wake as they careened their way through the Sahel towards far-off Dakar.

We always inspected the local markets. The handicraft market sold Touareg boxes, tea pots and swords and some of the local weavings which were simpler than those you could find in Mopti. I found the most interesting item to be the slabs of salt for sale that were still mined in the far reaches of Mali's northern desert and transported south by camel caravan. This system had been in place for centuries and still continued, though the camel was being hard pressed by the small truck as the preferred mode of desert transport.

We were met at the guest house by an agronomist who was under contract to provide technical assistance to the project. Dat Van Tran was a slight, soft-spoken Vietnamese scientist, who had left Vietnam in the mid-seventies and proceeded on to reestablish himself in the U.S. The Vietnamese knew rice and spoke French and Dat had been willing to live in Gao. Dat would be an essential part of our evaluation group, giving us his insights and advice.

As it was too hot to sleep in the guest house, Jerry and I hauled our mattresses up and slept on the roof under the stars. We awoke with the sun for three good reasons — when the sun came up it was soon too hot to sleep, the local mosque was broadcasting a recorded prayer call to the faithful amplified to volume ten, and sunrise signaled the start of the flies' strafing runs on our heads.

It was time to get up and work.

The project we were evaluating had been designed three years before as a follow on to a World Bank-financed drought relief effort. The Bank had begun work to increase agricultural production on 2,000 hectares of Niger River flood plain.

At the request of the Malian Government, our people had designed a project that was intended to increase local cereal production and introduce farmers to technological advances in growing rice. Increased local production would save the tremendous expense of paying for imported rice. The transport cost alone of importing rice to Gao could more than double the local price.

The original plan was to improve rice production on 5,000 hectares by constructing dikes that would be insubmersible to the Niger flood while also introducing improved rice varieties, improve rice production in an additional 5,000 hectares using traditional submersible dikes, improve sorghum production, and finally, construct a field research station.

The insubmersible dikes were the largest and most expensive item in the project and thought to be the key to protecting the increased rice plantings in the sheltered areas. The dikes would assure that water was neither too little or too much. Too much water in the fields at the wrong time of the growing cycle could drown the rice shoots, while too little water could stress them to death.

The new dikes were thought to be an improvement over the traditional ones as they were more permanent, being soundly engineered and compacted by machinery, therefore needing little or no repair and thus less likely to break during the rice growing season. The traditional hand-made submersible dikes also served the purpose of keeping the rising river water at bay while the rice matured, but as the plants matured, the dikes were eventually inundated by water. By this time the plants should have been tall enough to survive the rising water, but tremendous labor had to go into repairing the dikes in preparation for the next planting season.

The design team had estimated that the project would aid some 20,000 poor farm families in the region and some 140,000 grain consumers in the Gao area. Like in Dire with *Action Ble,* increased grain production would save a large sum of foreign exchange that went to pay for imported rice. Like Dire and wheat, there was a long history of cultivation of rice in the Gao area using traditional varieties.

Jerry, Dat and I began with a visit to the Malian Director of *Action Riz Sorgho,* Amadou Togola, an open and cooperative man who had been with the Ministry of Agriculture for years and was accustomed to working with Americans.

Togola received us in his office and warmly greeted us. He was dressed in his dark blue boubou and lit a Gaulloise as he motioned for us to sit. He seemed happy to see us and listened intently as we explained the purpose of the evaluation. He pledged his cooperation with our evaluation and offered to set up appointments for us to talk to his technical staff, credit people, extension agents, whomever we wished. Otherwise we were free to roam the project area and talk to farmers and anyone else as we wanted.

Togola explained the project's progress and problems. Construction of the insubmersible dikes had taken far longer than planned. Dikes had finally been mostly completed on the flood plains outside Gao but only 1,300 hectares had been protected, not the intended 5,000.

The repair of traditional dikes and flood gates was going on but these applied to only 1,000 hectares and not the planned 5,000. Fish screens were being applied to the flood gates to keep out rice-eating fish, but again in far fewer numbers than originally planned. Fish screens were vital because what was the purpose of increasing rice yields if it only benefitted the fish?

The better news, said Togola, was sorghum production was higher than planned and the construction of the long-delayed research station had finally begun and was expected to be operational in seven months. Rice production was up too, though the prior planting season had been a temporary setback.

Togola paused. "I know we've had a slow start, but we are starting to make progress."

Jerry and I asked Togola if he had any complaints about support from our office in Bamako.

"Eh oui, ca alors." Oh, yeah, well that.

"The main problem we have with your agriculture office in Bamako is the time it takes you to disburse the funds to us in Gao. After an initial advance, we have to provide all your documentation and then wait for it to be approved before you process our next advance. The advances are too small for our needs and take too long to get. The worst thing, though, is when your office buys project commodities without our knowledge.

This reduces our budget that we have planned to use on other items that we need desperately."

Togola went on.

"Part of the problem with the rice production last year was that we had to get our improved rice seed sent up from Mopti. This cost $35,000 a truck load, and though the Mopti station was too slow to ship, we didn't have the funds from you to make the payments."

This sounded like a legitimate complaint and we had heard some of it before from Malians working on other projects. The other bit of information was also startling. Why did rice seed cost $35,000 a truckload and why was it being brought in from Mopti? Surely this was not a sustainable expense, at the very least.

We were ready to start our visits and interviews with other project personnel and farmers. I had the same feeling though about Gao as I had had not too long ago in Dire. If it wasn't the end of the earth, you could certainly see it from here.

Gao was 700 miles from Bamako. The road past Mopti was in terrible shape, though we understood that plans were underway for the Mopti-Gao portion to be paved. The river was navigable only five months of the year to ship project commodities and materials. Some goods could be bought in Niamey in neighboring Niger, but these were expensive. Logistics problems may not have been completely insurmountable, but they looked to be a significant issue.

Jerry, Dat and I visited a couple of the local night spots of Gao that evening, the "Oasis" and the "Twist Bar." Sociological research. These bars were frequented by various grades of disreputable clientele, but we liked their profound level of local color and the giant beers they served were at least cool if not cold. A really cold beer was one of Africa's most rare commodities, but cool was fine especially for Gao. The "Oasis" even had a great collection of Fleetwood Mac records, though in terrible shape from the sand that permeated everything.

Jerry, Dat and I spent the next two days interviewing *Action Riz Sorgho* personnel before heading out to inspect the insubmersible dikes built near the villages of Tacharane and Gargouna. Seventeen kilometers of new dikes had been finished and to me it seemed somewhat impressive that something this new and modern could have been constructed at all in Gao. The new dikes covered far less area than planned because their construction cost was that much higher. Therefore it seemed that the construction had followed the contours of higher ground in the interior of the flood plain — leaving other good rice land outside the control area. We tried to understand the detailed working of the dikes, though our engineer from Abidjan would soon arrive for a thorough technical review.

The interview with the credit specialist back at headquarters in Gao had been the most disturbing. The credit fund had been designed to sell plows and improved seed to farmers, and mopeds to extension agents. We would talk to extension agents about the seed sales, but it was clear that the credit for plows and mopeds was being handled in a haphazard manner as the credit agent was unable to describe his procedures for granting credit and repayment.

The next meeting with a group of seven extension agents at headquarters was telling. Two were Bambara from near Bamako and couldn't speak the local language, Songhai, rendering them almost useless. Two complained of the inability of his village farmers to understand how to cultivate the new rice varieties the project had purchased. One of these even said that Action Riz Sorgho would have to "oblige" the farmers to get with the technical program. His meaning was clear enough. He thought it was up to him to force the farmers to do things his way. Others spoke of the difficulty of trying to sell rice seed on credit, and being unable to extend credit to provide for its proper storage. All the agents had purchased mopeds on credit from the fund.

On Saturday afternoon and all day Sunday we rested. We visited the Sakia Mohammed tomb in the morning and on Saturday evening after the heat of the day, met up with Dat and several Peace Corps Volunteers posted in Gao for a picnic near the river. Dat had brought a beat up guitar and we took turns playing. A tall, graceful barefooted Malian dribbled a soccer ball alone in the distance along the river bank. After the picnic, we paid a few hundred Malian Francs to a Songhai pirogue-man who gave us a ride on the river while we watched the hippos play from a safe distance. When hippos are near the surface, they stick their nose, eyes and ears out of the water while twitching their ears rapidly in a circular motion, constantly on the watch for intruders.

On Sunday I attended Protestant church service at a small wooden church on a little side street of Gao. Being from the southern U.S.A., I had spent my share of time in churches as a child, and though I wasn't from the buckle of the Bible Belt, I had certainly grown up within shouting distance. I wasn't a regular churchgoer these days and was certainly not doing penance for going to the "Twist Bar," but had noticed the little church on a previous visit and was intrigued by the idea of church service in Gao.

The minister was an American in his late forties, born, he said, right here in Gao. He had taken over the church from his father who had retired after thirty years of his own in Gao and returned to Georgia. The service, presented in Songhai and French, was simple and heartfelt. In all his years in Gao, the minister told me afterwards, he had converted only three people from Islam to Christianity. He didn't seem discouraged at all by this track record and told us stories about his church's activities and of the very different town Gao had been back in the colonial days under the French where food, farm equipment, and other goods were available directly from France.

The next day we visited villages north of Gao and talked to individual local farmers. Neither Jerry nor I spoke Songhai but in each village we found a good Bambara or French speaker to translate for us. Ali Badara stood by to help. Several older farmers were *"anciens combatants,"* former soldiers in the French colonial army. One bent old fellow who now walked slowly with the help of a carved wooded cane told us of fighting in the Battle of the Marne during World War I.

The farmers were very helpful, which was only natural since they were the ones the project was supposed to be benefitting in the first place. Those farmers in the zone of the new insubmersible dikes mostly liked them because they were not prone to breaching like the traditional dikes. This, they said, was despite the fact that they had never been consulted about the location of the dikes during the planning and construction stages. But since the new dikes didn't break, families slept better and much labor was saved, including women's labor. Also, the insubmersible dikes wouldn't need extensive repairs after the planting season like the traditional dikes that eventually disappeared under the rising flood waters each planting season.

The main problem was that while the dike controlled water entry, without level fields the water stood too shallow or too deep on the same fields, thereby affecting yields. Some also complained that project extension agents had no technical knowledge and nothing to offer. Several said that the new rice varieties were fine, but they were being distributed in insufficient quantities. Particularly if a first planting died from a lack of moisture, there was not enough seed available to replant.

The criticisms about seed and extension had the ring of truth. But the comments about lower yields in the newly diked fields due to unlevel fields shook us up. Had the original design team overlooked this factor? I had read the original project document and I could recall no mention of land leveling anywhere in the report. Leveling was very costly, and how would this additional expense impact on the economic feasibility of the project if it was undertaken now or at some point in the future? And if leveling wasn't planned, could yields really be sufficiently increased to the planned levels?

I had not been around development very long but I already knew the lore: it was obligatory and basic to consult with the ultimate beneficiaries — in this case the farmers — during the course of a project design. I was beginning to wonder how often though this was done in order to seek local experience, expertise, ideas and advice as opposed to simply satisfying the design guidelines. Or did someone here simply think that because we did it like this in Thailand or we knew it worked in Louisiana that it will work here?

To Jerry, long time resident of Mali and anthropologist, this seeming lack of consultation with the farmers at the planning stage was the most galling thing of all.

He shook his head. "Look's like it was another parachute drop design team," he said. "These guys fly in from the outside, they don't know the area except from reading a few reports, lots of times their French isn't very good, and they've only got a couple of weeks to gather data and come up with the outlines of a design."

"If they don't get sick from the local food and water, they leave and write up the project document back where they came from and you just have to hope they got it right. Look's like this time they didn't."

I asked a question.

"But the design was done for our office in Mali. Why didn't we provide or arrange the expertise locally, or better yet why didn't we do the design ourselves?" I was thinking to myself, after all, the in-country expertise argument is one major way we say we differentiate ourselves from other donors, for example the World Bank, which is more prone to design a project in great detail then turn over the money to the host government for implementation.

"Ha," answered Jerry. "Part of the answer is that we were just getting established in Mali back then and didn't have enough personnel with the answers either. We should have done better somehow, though. I think they were in such a hurry to try to help on the after effects of the drought, that they got sloppy. You can never predict that a project will be a smashing success in the Sahel even under the best of circumstances, but for sure you have to do your homework correctly."

On the way back to Gao, Jerry asked Ali Badara to stop the Land Cruiser. We got out and walked through a grassy plain flanked by low hills. Jerry explained that this was the ancient battlefield of Tondibi where invading Berbers from Morocco under Sheik Judar Pasha had defeated the Songhai empire once and for all in 1585. The Moroccans controlled the former empire for awhile, until their own efforts to manage such a large land area and number of people so far from home finally resulted in the growth of a smaller number of less powerful states, none of them strong enough to bring peace and prosperity to the region.

We made one other stop — to see a modern slaughterhouse that had been built outside Gao with the assistance of the Government of Yugoslavia. The slaughterhouse was clean and modern, gleaming modern metal machinery looking out of place in Gao. It was also shut down completely and had been ever since it had been constructed. The drought's decimation of the local cattle population had made the slaughter business so unprofitable that the plant had never opened its doors. Not one head of cattle had ever met its maker there. Where were the TV journalists from Yugoslavian "60 Minutes?"

We spent two weeks in Gao, finishing our interviews and coming to a few preliminary findings:

The project was really just getting underway. The planned time table for dike construction and construction of the research station had been far too optimistic. Construction costs were much higher than anticipated and their benefits would be far less than originally estimated because less rice growing area was under their control. Also, because fields within the dikes had not been leveled, water control was less significant a factor. Despite all that, the new dikes were useful and were having a positive impact on increased yields.

But the project planners had been essentially wrong. The insubmersible dikes could not be the key ingredient in increasing production as the planners had thought. That meant more energy should have been devoted to increasing yields in the traditional rice areas outside the new dikes. Why had project designers not thought of using water pumps in these areas, for example?

Also, delays in constructing and operating the research station had obliged the project to bring in rice seed from elsewhere. The seed coming from Mopti was too expensive, not available in sufficient quantities, and not that well adapted to local conditions. As Dat recommended, a research program was needed that looked at improving traditional cultivation patterns using the existing submersible dikes.

Finally, extension agents were poorly trained and were trying to extend farmers technologies that were inappropriate. Therefore, the project's credit program — which was poorly run — did not make sense either. Other alternatives to a project-led credit program for seed and other project inputs to farmers should have been explored.

We also were worried that the credit fund was not being well managed. That of course could mean funds would be used for other project purposes such as regular operating expenses or "diverted", a nice way of saying stolen.

Back in Bamako, Jerry and I spent the next three weeks writing up our report and waiting for our engineer to corroborate our own findings about the dikes. Our report would reflect those major negative findings we had seen firsthand in Gao but also emphasize the positive with recommendations to overcome many of the problems.

While it wasn't pleasant telling the Malians and our colleagues that all was not rosy, the news was certainly not all bad. Design mistakes notwithstanding, we felt there was enough right about the project to work. Rice and sorghum yields were increasing, the new dikes worked after a fashion, a traditional system could be improved, the new research station could have implications on new technologies that could eventually improve production, the top *Action Riz Sorgho* managers were well qualified, and most project personnel worked hard and were motivated. And despite the formidable logistic challenges of working in Gao, progress could still be made.

Hopefully in the time remaining in the project's funding life — and assuming the evaluation itself was correct — we could try to convince the *Action Riz Sorgho* folks and our own bosses to adopt our recommendations and maximize the project's potential.

Based on my experience with Action Ble and now with Action Riz Sorgho, I was starting to form an answer to my own earlier question about food self-sufficiency. Self-sufficiency seemed to make sense only if you could afford it and the resources were there to permit it. But in Mali, at least in the short-term, it seemed to me that a more sensible and achievable goal should be increasing food production and food security rather full self-sufficiency. Self-sufficiency — based on my admitted limited experience so far — seemed unaffordable and difficult to achieve.

There was also the policy factor to consider. Farmer incentives for food production should exist, like being able to sell freely on an open market, rather than having the present disencentives of setting consumer and producer prices artificially low. Even in poverty-stricken Mali, it seemed to me too that there was a role for higher value exports whose potential should be maximized. With the foreign exchange earned from higher value exports, the Malians would be in a better position to import food needed to cover shortfalls. I knew that cotton exports from southern Mali, for example, were Mali's largest foreign exchange earner. Exports too were dependent upon favorable economic policies inside and outside Mali and — one other important factor — someone to sell to.

I resolved to see how other projects underway in Mali would fit in with the lessons I was absorbing.

Joy had departed for the States soon after I returned from Gao, very pregnant but still able to fly in accordance with the airline's rules. I planned to leave three weeks before the baby's due date to insure I would be there with her in Texas in plenty of time.

I finished my sections of the report on Thursday morning. The Air Afrique flight left late that night direct for Paris and I planned to be on it and immediately proceed to New York and then on to Texas.

The phone rang in the office before noon with an international call. It was rare for overseas call to get through and to my surprise Joy was on the line from Texas. The transmission was very broken but I made out the words "water broke today" and soon after a few desperate yells to reestablish contact the line went totally dead.

There was absolutely nothing I could do. There was no flight out earlier than the one I was on that night, and a nurse friend confirmed my suspicion that once the water breaks, the birth is not far behind. Unable to call and knowing nothing more, I boarded the late-night Air Afrique DC-10 for Paris.

I immediately called Texas from Charles De Gaulle Airport at six in the morning Paris time and my father-in-law answered. "Congratulations!" he yelled. "You have a baby girl and everyone is fine."

Back in Austin, I spent some time dumbfounded by my new beautiful baldheaded daughter whom we had decided to name Allison. I was also thankful for the robust health of my wife, who had been forced to go through the whole birthing affair without me, and her supportive family.

I was also struck with a new appreciation of the incredible richness of my American surroundings — the perfect roads, the immaculate lawns, the greenery, the stores. The second night back, Joy and I left Allison with her grandmother and went to see Ry Cooder in concert downtown, and we reveled in the perfect sound and the healthy-looking young faces around us. The magic hand of America that made the traffic lights change in proper sequence and everything appear to be so well groomed and organized was truly impressive. I walked the aisles of Safeway in amazement, especially the produce section. I wondered if the management would mind if I came back later with my camera and took a few pictures to show to people back in Bamako and to remind myself later that it was all real.

We especially noticed the people. Robust, well-nourished and mostly prosperous, but so very many overweight people, the likes of which were unknown in Africa or our part of it anyway.

Joy felt the change in another way. She broke into tears seeing her visiting sister dump plates of hardly touched food from a Sunday feast down the garbage disposal.

We also wondered what it would be like exposing our newborn to life in the Sahel when we returned.

6
Jumping In with Both Feet

I had returned to Mali alone. Joy's doctor in Austin had recommended we wait until the baby was three months old before she was subjected to the health conditions of Mali, and we agreed that it would be better for her to be a little older. After several weeks in Texas, however, the vacation time I had accumulated was used up and I had no choice but to return.

When I changed planes in Dallas to fly to New York and then to Mali via Paris, I had been seated beside a friendly young woman who said she went to college in Dallas. She asked me where I was from. This question was getting more and more difficult to answer, but when I replied that I presently lived in Africa, she exclaimed, "Africa! That's amazing. What's the capital of Africa?"

I could already tell that the stories we'd heard about babies changing your lives were true, but Joy and I were happy about the change. I resolved to stay busy to make the time pass quickly until they returned. The transition from winter in the U.S. to Mali in the middle of the hot season was the ultimate shock to the system. Back again on Planet Mali.

Bamako was more or less the same. The hot season was going full blast but the Selingue Dam was operating and we had electricity now nearly full time. Work had recommenced still again on widening the Koulikoro Road. A new Vietnamese restaurant of all things had opened up where the old Bonbonniere had been and one could reportedly eat there and live to tell the story. Softball games were still held on Sundays and the Tuesday movies at the Marine house continued. Alex was thinking about putting on another play. Jerry and Barbara were delighted with their own new daughter. My Iranian friend Mickey had received a short-term visa for he and Ellie to travel to Italy where Ellie was due to give birth to their own first child, so they were off in Rome.

Pregnancy had been fashionable of late and of the eleven new babies already born or soon to be born among our colleagues and other friends, all eleven were girls. "It must be the water," Joy would explain, even boiled and filtered.

On the bad side, Kent's replacement in the administrative office had arrived, and one of his first acts was to fire our friend, the impressive Moktar Diakite, the head of procurement. Moktar had evidently been caught taking a kick-back from a local supplier and he was gone. Also, one of my favorite Malian colleagues, Dramane Coulibaly, who worked in the agriculture office, had been run over by a drunk driver while walking along the road in his Bamako neighborhood and killed. This was a terrible blow to the morale in the office as Dramane had been one of our most impressive and popular employees. My first act back in Bamako was to visit his grieving extended family in their compound and offer condolences.

Badji excitedly made arrangements to set up the new baby's room. She promised to babysit and keep Allison calm by carrying her Malian style on her back wrapped in her *pagne*. Yaya still slept on the job more deeply than ever since the electricity worked and therefore there was no loud generator to disturb his slumber. But Samba was missing. He was sick, Badji said, and had hardly come to work for the last two weeks.

This worried me. Samba had been very sick several months before, but eventually healed up and had come back to work. When I would ask about his health he assured me that now he was healthy and all was well.

I found Coulibaly, a friend of Samba's in my neighborhood who knew where Samba lived, and he went with me in my car to show me the way. To see Samba's home was to have still another reminder of the vast difference between the comfort of the expatriate and the real world. His hut was tiny and the floor dirt and in an obviously very poor group of dusty compounds beside the railroad tracks near the Koulikoro Road. He lived alone in his one little rented room as he had told me that he was from a village near the border with Burkina Faso and was single with no real family in Bamako.

Samba was conscious but feverish and obviously very ill. He mumbled a greeting while I looked around and tried to decide what I should do.

"Samba, tell me what's wrong. Where does it hurt?"

I knew the problem was serious because the always friendly and effervescent Samba could only moan softly in reply, eyes half closed.

"Samba, have you tried to see a doctor? Have you taken any medicine?"

He managed to reply that he had been given some medicine that a woman in the compound had made for him.

I looked around the walls of Samba's little mud room and my heart broke. Stuck on the walls were pages of the fashion newspaper "W", a publication interested in high fashion world and habits of the international jet set, a subscription to which Joy's mother had for some reason given her perhaps to make up for the cultural depravity of our current setting. Samba had removed some old copies from the garbage at our house and was using the pages as his one and only home adornment.

I went outside to gather my thoughts and control the sinking feeling in the pit of my stomach.

"Coulibaly, let's talk to some of the people in the compound and see if they can give us any information."

No one spoke French in the compound, but we found the woman who normally made the meals for the compound that Samba shared and who had tried to treat him. What had she given him, Coulibaly asked in Bambara?

The woman pointed to a nearby mango tree, with a hand-sized section of bark missing from the trunk.

She had boiled water with the bark in it and had made Samba drink it, she told us. He was no better. Coulibaly said she thought Samba was getting worse.

We couldn't give up like that. I gave Coulibaly money to get himself a *bachee* back home and went back inside.

"Samba, I'm going to take you to a doctor. Please don't worry but I'm going to carry you to the car, so just hang on."

I opened the passenger door in my little Peugeot and inclined the seat as far back as it would go. Then I next picked Samba up and carried him across both arms and tried to lay him gently into the seat of the car. He was emaciated from his illness and not at all heavy.

I was turning the possibilities in my mind of what to do next. It was Saturday and now getting dark. The Embassy doctor was not supposed to deal with locals and was not at the Embassy on a Saturday. The nurse was on vacation. I didn't know a single local doctor nor where to find one. The Bamako hospitals were only to die in. My French doctor friend had gone back to France.

I had heard of one private local clinic in town so I headed there.

After winding around the back streets of Bamako for a while, I finally found the clinic. It was not a real clinic at all, it turned out, but some homeopathic laboratory. Worst of all it was dark and shut tight.

Samba was more alert and looked more alive now.

"*Patron*," he said, "I'm feeling better, thank you for helping me, but I want to go home."

"Samba, you are too sick, you need some help. Look, Samba, this place is closed. Do you know another clinic or where to find a real doctor?"

He didn't.

"Samba, will you let me take you to the Gabriel Toure Hospital?"

Samba shook his head no emphatically. He had told me during his first illness that he distrusted hospitals totally.

"No. No, *patron*, no hospital. I want to go home, please."

I was in a quandary. Samba was serious and determined about not going to a hospital, a common enough sentiment among the common folk of Mali, and convincing him to see any doctor even if I could find one was going to be difficult. Did I have the right to insist on it anyway? Finally, I caved in.

"Samba, OK, I'll take you home now, but if you feel worse, you get word to me through Coulibaly, and I'll come get you. First thing Monday when the Embassy doctor is there and things are open, I'll find out how to get you some treatment and we'll go from there."

Samba opened his eyes halfway and nodded his agreement.

I took him home and carried him back to his bed. I gave the cooking woman some money for food and care and got her to understand that she should contact Coulibaly if Samba got worse and that she should do her best to look after him in the meantime.

On the way back home in the dark, I wondered if I had done the right thing. Samba was not an old man and he had been sick before and had bounced back. He could do it again. Surely he'd be all right. On Sunday, I'd talk to friends who would know how to best handle this and I'd see the American doctor first thing Monday morning.

On Sunday at dusk, the bell rang. I was on the front porch of my house and Yaya opened the gate. It was Coulibaly. My first thought was that he had come to tell me how Samba was doing, but I knew better when I saw a group of somber older men dressed in their boubous following closely behind Coulibaly.

I knew that Samba was dead.

"*Patron*, Samba has gone."

I had been in Mali long enough to know that people died suddenly and with great frequency, but this was no longer an abstract concept, this was Samba.

Coulibaly went on. "His friends here don't speak French but have come to thank you for being kind to Samba, for being a good '*patron*'. He always spoke very good of you and said you treated him with respect and kindness. They would like to thank you for that."

They silently crowded around me and shook my hand, while I tried to maintain control and while thinking of all the things I should have done differently the day before.

Coulibaly went on. "Samba Traore was not a religious person but we have found an imam who will wash the body and will do the burial service. He will take care of everything for 17,000 francs."

I gave Coulibaly the money and after we sat on the porch and talked for a few minutes more, they made their good-byes and departed.

What would have happened if I had insisted that Samba go to the hospital? Should I have forced him against his wishes? What if I had taken him to the American doctor? I certainly would have if I'd realized his condition, but could this one doctor be expected to attend to the legions of sick Malians that worked for Americans?

And I thought about the strangeness of fate. Why had Samba been born into grinding poverty ending up with literally no more possessions than the ragged clothes on his back while I had been born into privilege in America? What kind of chance had Samba really had? He had been born poor in a poor country where health conditions were abysmal. He had virtually no access to health care of any kind and could not have paid for it had it been available. He lived simply, he worked, he got sick, and in the normal Malian pattern, he died.

And I could not get the images of the pages from "W" on his wall out of my mind.

Out of my sadness over Samba, there was an underlying happiness at anticipating Joy's and Allison's return. I had found a good crib for sale and installed it in the spare bedroom. Before too long, the airfreight that Joy and I had sent from Texas containing baby clothes for the next six months, cloth diapers and toys arrived and I set to work with Badji fixing up Allison's room.

Finally they arrived. Joy was as glad as I to get back to our own home in Korofina and establish a new baby-oriented routine. Allison thrived even in the heat and thankfully seemed to be completely healthy. When she did cry, Badji would scoop her up and tie her on her back as promised. All babies seemed to like this kind of close contact and Allison's crying would immediately stop, little bald white head sticking out incongruously from the Malian *pagne*. The cloth diapers were washed either at midnight when occasionally the water pressure was enough to fill the machine, or during the day when the machine had to be filled with the garden hose.

When Allison got older and it was time to sleep all night, Joy decided to stop the middle of the night feeding and for a couple of nights purposefully let Allison cry herself to sleep. This didn't go over well with Yaya who pounded on our window saying, *"Madame, Madame, le bebe, le bebe."* Obviously the technique we were using was not popular among Malians and Yaya surely thought us heartless and strange.

At work, I had been asked by my colleague John Ford, who had earlier invited us to his house to meet Miriam Makeba, to do him a favor. Our office had undertaken a small low-cost project to deliver modest quantities of agricultural equipment and other inputs to a number of villages in the western-most region of Kayes. All the equipment had been procured and delivered to the villages and someone was needed to verify that it had in fact been installed properly and was being used. I decided to help John out and volunteered to be that person.

The real project manager of the activity was another colleague named Joe who worked directly for John. Joe was a bit on the odd side and never seemed to be too busy, but more to the point, was totally incapable of communicating in French. I didn't know much about Joe's background, but he was full of grandiose stories about the Korean War and other heroic-sounding exploits that he had had in Asia. He would later be fired and put on the next plane out of Mali for the less than intelligent transgression of writing a performance award for himself and forging his boss's — John's — signature on the document.

Joe's stories of Asia were at least partly corroborated by the presence of his young Philippine wife, Maria. She had confided to Barbara that she had met Joe under less than ideal circumstances. He had advertised for a wife in the classified section of a Manila newspaper and friends of Maria had turned in her name as a joke. Some friends. It was not a joke to Maria's parents, however, who saw money and security coming their way, and so, unbelievably, she had been married off to Joe and transported to Mali — totally disoriented and unhappy.

Since Joe couldn't adequately communicate in French and didn't seem to be learning it particularly rapidly, I went in his place. The equipment had been donated to a Malian women's group, the National Union of Malian Women, headquartered in Bamako but with representatives throughout the country. Using this organization made sense because much of the donated equipment in question were items like millet grinding mills, small water pumps, and gardening equipment that directly impacted on the duties and lives of rural women.

We rarely did projects like this. Normally we tried to operate at a higher level of investment and production, in line with development strategy of increasing food self-sufficiency, and backed up a supporting policy dialogue with the government. This little project was no attempt at sustainable development however. It was a good thing to do that would perhaps help a worthwhile national women's organization and would make the work of a few rural women a bit easier, at least for a while.

The plan was for me to take the train to Kayes and meet the Union women there. We would proceed south into the First Region by vehicle. That was fine with me as I had yet to experience train travel in Mali and I wanted no repeat of my earlier nearly disastrous Mali Air Service trip to Kayes.

The train wasn't as bad as the stories I'd heard. I had a reserved seat in First Class on the newer Senegalese train, and though this was no luxury, it was a seat and insulated from the free-for-all of second class, which was accompanied by crowds of people pushing and shoving for space, with piles of goods everywhere amidst the occasional squawking chicken and baaing sheep. Also, the train didn't break down, the view of the little villages and rudimentary towns along the way was interesting, and it didn't start to get unbearably hot until later in the day.

When the train finally arrived in Kayes, three women from the Union were there to meet me. There were Aminata and Binta from the national office in Bamako and Fanta from Kayes. They greeted me cordially and properly. Aminata who looked to be in her late thirties was obviously a strong women and very much in charge. All three women were dressed in printed African *pagnes* wrapped around their waists with the same pattern used for the blouse. Their long hair was neatly braided into long rows which I knew had taken hours of work to achieve.

Aminata took one look at my baggage and smiled, undoubtedly thinking how strange toubobs were to carry so many unnecessary provisions. I had only brought a small pack, a gas lantern in a cardboard box, a light-weight sleeping bag, and a Thermos of filtered water. The women carried only small hand bags. For them, this was plenty.

We piled in the project Land Rover and off we went, south from Kayes roughly paralleling the border with Senegal toward the villages of San-diola, Dialafara, and Narena. The Union had installed mills and pumps in these and other villages along the way and back to the northeast. The idea was to inspect the most of the villages to the south and go in a big loop winding back to the railhead at Bafoulabe east of Kayes.

I liked all three women immediately, but Aminata was the most impressive and outgoing and the easiest to talk to. All three couldn't have cared less about impressing me, the representative of the donor agency that had financed the whole project. Many times the donor-recipient relationship could be strained — the recipient wanting to be grateful while maintaining pride at the same time, but realizing that words and performance could always be judged negatively by the donor. The money could be cut off.

Sometimes this kind of dependency bred resentment toward the donor — 'why don't they just give us the money and leave?' — while the donor had the responsibility to try to assure that projects succeeded and that funds were well used and accounted for. It could make for strained relationships.

There was certainly no such weirdness between Aminata, Binta, Fanta and myself. Pandering and impressing me were not at all on their minds. With Aminata setting the tone, they were off on a working field trip to see how their people were using the equipment that my organization had happened to donate to a project that they considered to be totally theirs. It was fine for me to accompany them, but the trip was not being undertaken for my benefit. It was mostly for them and this was quickly clear.

I'm sure they thought my employer's generosity to be fine, but they weren't going to waste their time or mine thanking me for it, and deferent and shy — thank heavens — they were not. The fact that the relationships spawned by a week together at close range would be straightforward and uncomplicated was a relief. It looked like a fun trip. And my first impression of Aminata was that if she lived in the U.S. or Europe instead of Mali, she'd be CEO of a successful up-and-coming company and have several hundred employees.

The first day we stopped and spent the night at Sadiola. We were all tired from the heat and bouncing on the dirt road and slept soundly in the local encampment. We briefly greeted and visited the local dignitaries and saw a couple of millet mills in action, and then pressed on for Dialafara.

Dialafara was a large village that looked more modern than some and well run, and though obviously poor, the locals seemed to be trying to do the best with what they had. I had now been in enough Malian villages to recognize the ones that had good local leadership. The goods ones had a school, a neat gendarmerie, a well or wells that were cared for and maintained, and roads in and out that were passable.

Our reception was warm in Dialafara. We were met by the village chief, the prefect and the local representatives of the Union and shown the millet mills donated to the village, all properly installed in their own sheds and working away. In response to a question from Aminata, they explained the system for running the machines and financing the milling operation. Each user paid a small fee for each grinding which in turn financed fuel and maintenance. All fees received and paid were duly recorded in a ledger kept by the Union representative. A mechanic in town had carefully installed the machines with their long moving belts and was available to fix the machines when they had problems. I hoped that the fees earned could finance replacement mills when the present ones wore out.

The Union women and the other local women we talked to loved the mills, as they saved hours of hard labor that otherwise would have been spent pounding the millet into flour the old fashioned way, using the extended mortar and pestle method that was the ball and chain of so many West African women.

There were a couple of families of American missionaries living outside Dialafara near the main road. They were from a southern U.S. denomination that emphasized development work and education as well as soul-saving, they said, and even had their own small plane that brought in supplies. These missionaries said they were long-termers, and determined to stay in Mali for the duration of their professional lives.

The road south to Narena was long and dusty and in worse shape than the previous portions. While we tried to chat in the Land Rover between jolts in the road we also swatted at tsetse flies that flew in through the open windows. Tsetse flies were the source of sleeping sickness that effected mainly cattle but humans were not immune from the disease. Occasionally a fly would succeed in getting in a painful bite. I reminded myself to ask the doctor when I returned if one could get sleeping sickness from only several tsetse bites. These flies were aggressive and would sit on the outside of our now closed windows and on the hood of the car despite the movement of the vehicle, waiting a chance to infect us all, I imagined.

Our stay in Narena gave me the chance to see Aminata in action. After the opening formalities and introductions with the local officials, we went off to see women's gardens being irrigated with a few small pumps provided by the project, and several of the now familiar millet mills. The Union women in Narena had not yet set up a system for charging milling fees and there were no ledgers as in Dialafara. Aminata politely but very firmly took the hapless local Union woman aside, and with Fanta providing moral support, let the local woman know that she would be expected to have these problems solved in short order. At least that's what she told me she said, because the language had switched to rapid fire Bambara.

"Ehh. What's the use of giving them mills if the local women don't make sure that they run them like a business and take care of them so they last a full life?" Aminata said to me when we returned to the Land Rover.

We spent the night in a large rounded house with the traditional thatched roof that was split up into separate rooms. The house was clean with a concrete floor and the beds had whole mosquito nets for protection. We took bucket showers in slow succession, me going last, that felt wonderful after the dust and the heat.

I loved this area of Mali, where Mali, Senegal, and Guinea came together. The people, almost all of the Malinke ethnic group, seemed peaceful and the villages mostly old and well established. There was a lot of vegetation due to higher rainfall and the fields and gardens looked healthy. Far from paved roads and without any of the modern conveniences of electricity, telephones, or television, this was probably someone's idea of a pastoral Eden. On an earlier trip almost down to the Guinea border at Faraba, I listened fascinated as men in the village discussed in great detail the agricultural policies and internal politics from across the border in Guinea, and the latest actions of the Malinke despot that ran it, Sekou Toure.

After the shower and dressing, I moved out of the room to get some air outside. My three companions sat on benches on the concrete floor beside the house, dressed in fresh *pagnes,* Fanta washing her sandals and Binta fixing Aminata's long braids.

"Hey, Luke, come over and sit here with us," said Aminata careful not to turn her head too much.

Luke was the pronunciation of my last name in French and since this was a perfectly good French name, this was how I usually introduced myself. I found this was easier than using the English pronunciation of either my first or last names which were totally incomprehensible by most native French speakers.

"So, Luke, how do you find the trip so far?" asked Aminata. She was barefooted and still a little damp from the bucket shower.

I told her that everything had been much better than expected. I was happy to see that the equipment had been delivered and that most of it was working as planned. I also told her that I liked this area of Mali and had wanted to return here.

"Do you think the Americans you work for like this project?"

I replied that my colleagues who were implementing it with the Union had seemed pleased, but that was really what I was here to find out. I said from what I had seen so far, I thought the investment was worthwhile. This was especially so, I thought to myself, since the investment was so comparatively small to what we spent on most other projects.

I told Aminata that when I first arrived in Mali, I had had no appreciation for how hard people had to work to survive, and just how much of that work was done by women. I told her about my trips to around Mopti and the northern areas where just the search for and hauling of firewood and water could take hours of the day, not to mention all the other duties expected of women such as tending rice fields, cultivating vegetable gardens, child care and many more.

"*Eh, oui,* you've got that right," said Aminata. "Women in the countryside may carry heavy firewood for ten kilometers or even more every day. And water too. Life is sweeter in the city, but it's still not easy for most people. If you have the means, you can live well, but since the droughts so many new people have come into Bamako from the countryside and there is not enough work or money for everyone."

I told Aminata that the other realization I had was that good health care was so inaccessible to most people and disease so widespread.

"That's true too," said Aminata. "We just die like cattle it seems. You go to the pharmacy when you are sick, and do you know what they give you?" I shook my head.

"Vitamin shots. Vitamins! Can you imagine? They cost a lot and do nothing. People spend several days' money or more to buy medicine they need desperately, and they are given vitamin shots."

She went on. "I have lost a child to malaria and so has Binta here."

Binta nodded and kept braiding.

I told them how sorry I was about that and that my wife had recently returned from the States with our firstborn.

"That's good, congratulations, but don't worry. You don't get sick like the Malians, and if you do you have good doctors and treatment and you will go to America to recover."

To a large degree she was right on target, and despite the fact that many expatriates' children seemed to thrive in Mali, I still worried a little for Allison.

I asked Aminata why she had become involved with the women's union and what she hoped to accomplish.

"Well, the Union is connected with national politics you know and that's part of it. But the real reason I got involved is that we are one of the few organizations here that tries to organize both urban and rural woman in this country, and we need more of this. Women do so much of the work here but we're at the bottom when it comes to passing out the benefits. If we have some other skills to offer, like what this project lets us do, we can help women use their time for something more than the routine work. And if we can get some technical training to learn more skills, we can be even more productive inside and outside the home. We will be better off and our families will be better off. Too often we are wasted potential."

It may have sounded like the start of social revolution to some conservative Malians, but seemed like basic good sense and development to me.

Aminata wasn't quite finished and she smiled in my general direction as Binta pulled on her braids. "I also like it so I can get away from my family for a little while and travel with nice foreigners."

"*Merci,*" I said, "but I promise you I'm getting at least as much benefit out of this trip as you."

The next part of the trip was back to the north the way we had come, until near the village of Yatera where we branched off to the northeast. The road became more of a track than before and even Fanta who was from the region said she did not know this zone very well. The further northeast we went, the villages became smaller and further apart and more settlements of one or two poor looking compounds rather than real villages. Fanta said we needed to visit two villages in this area where project equipment had been installed.

The first we reached by a wooden ferry over a small river, really nothing more than a floating raft powered by one ski-cap wearing lanky

Malian teenager and one wooded pole that he used to propel us, Land Rover and all, to the opposite bank. This ferry had definitely never passed a safety inspection from anyone and I knew that if we went into the river, it would be a long wet hike through the wilderness back to civilization.

Women's gardens watered with our project pumps grew on the other side of the river bank. The one millet mill that had been delivered to the village was not yet installed and functioning, however, prompting another aside talk with the local woman official.

In the next little village, I had the surprise of my Mali stay so far. Someone had told the village elders that a toubab would be inspecting the local donated equipment, and they had obviously been led to believe that it was a big shot "eminence gris" dignitary kind of toubab rather than a thirty-year-old semi-neophyte.

The entire village of what must have been over a thousand people were assembled, and after the *dougou-tigi,* the village chief, had pronounced his official welcome to our party, and it seemed particularly to me, we made our way to inspect the one millet mill that had been donated.

This was obviously a poor village way off the beaten path and the gift of a simple millet mill was the local equivalent of winning the New York State Lottery. Led by the village chief with the other village notables and our group lagging behind, we were taken to see the millet mill in action. It ran and the village had a supply of diesel fuel in a barrel in the corner of the shed. The long drive belts running to the mill, however, seemed to me to be attached at such an angle that they would soon fly off. Aminata made another quiet speech to the Union representative about this and we moved on to ask about their plans for organizing the user fees and so forth.

Now it was time for the speeches and the dances. The entire village was still assembled and waiting for our return from seeing the mill. The village chief made the first speech — totally in Malinke — which was understandable to my Bambara-speaking companions but not to me. Fanta whispered the translation in my ear.

The chief, thin, in his sixties I guessed, and dressed in his finest boubou, seemed to be extolling the virtues of my employer which had financed their millet mill, the Union women for selecting their village as a recipient, and me for having honored them with my presence. We consider this a great, great honor he said, and a major event in the history of the community. This is good for the women and good for us all. This is real development, not just the words that we hear all the time. This will help us make our lives easier and for that we are appreciative.

It was now time for someone in our group to make a speech in response. Aminata was looking at me from aside and she whispered, "Luke, you have to speak. Go ahead."

Ready or not, I made my way to the front of the dignitaries and faced the hundreds of upturned faces. I was the only white face in sight and I had the feeling that, trivial matters like skin color aside, since I represented the donor agency and had been so highly praised by the chief, some bit of wisdom was required to be imparted.

I hadn't made an impromptu speech in French to such a big crowd before, particularly one that was to be totally off the cuff. I thought about the previous American Ambassador's failed speech in front of high Malian officials over a year ago.

Formal speeches in French were always a bit on the flowery side, and an acquired art form for foreigners to learn. At least I knew how to start:

"Monsieur le chef du village, messieurs les representants du Prefet de la Premiere Region du Mali, madames les repesentants de la Union National des Femmes du Mali, madames et messieurs."

So much for the introductions. I decided to relax and wing the speech as best I could. Nothing bad would happen if I made a mistake or two, and though the big build-up made it desirable that I do my best to shine, it was best to smile and do what I could. I figured only a few of the crowd understood French anyway, but to handle the language problem a young educated French-speaking man from the village stood by to translate every sentence into Malinke.

I expressed my sincere appreciation for their reception and for the kind words of the chief. I was honored to be here and to represent my employer and very pleased that the equipment donated here was so appreciated and would be so useful. It was important to operate it in such a way that it was self-financing and that it would last and be maintained. It was good to provide donations like the mill, and if the entire village thought of it as their own property and responsibility, it could be a productive resource for a long time to come. As a foreigner in Mali, I was very impressed with the people and the hard work that everyone, including women, had to perform every day. Used correctly, this machine could make less the daily work of many women, and for this we should all be grateful.

I continued a bit more, thanked them again for their hospitality and stopped. The translation of every sentence into Malinke had seemed to give an aura of significance to my simple words though none of it was in reality very profound. To my surprise there had been complete silence while I had been speaking and the crowd had seemed to hang on every word. True, this village probably didn't get too many outside visitors and cable TV was a half a millennium off in the future. But Aminata looked pleased so I knew that it had gone well.

It was time for the dances. I and my companions from the Union were seated in a place of honor in the dusty village square beside the chief.

The chief held a large black umbrella in his hand to shield himself from the blazing sun. Drums began beating.

First, a large group of little girls came in, wearing green kerchiefs, smiling shyly and dancing barefoot in the dust while they swung calabashes — hollowed out gourds cut in half — side to side in time to the beating drums. Cowrie shells, currency in the pre-European days, were attached to the calabashes and they clicked as the girls twirled them around.

Next came a group of young men, all wearing leather gris-gris — charms tied in leather strips around their arms to keep evil spirits away — dancing acrobatically to the beat of the drums, turning cartwheels one minute and pairing off for mock wrestling the next.

Finally a young male acrobat appeared, turning backward flips from a standing position and then walking on his hands in front of our group of dignitaries. Coins spilled from his up-turned pants pocket but he kept up his performance, sweating profusely in the heat.

We applauded each performance enthusiastically and after a decent interval expressed our thanks and made our way to the waiting Land Rover. We were supposed to drive the rest of the way to Mahina-Bafoulabe back on the railway line by dusk, and therefore had to refuse their invitation to stay for dinner in the village. As we turned to drive away, the acrobat from earlier ran up to the car with three live chickens dangling upside down from a line in his hand. A gift from the chief, he said, and thank you again.

We arrived as the sun set in Bafoulabe, an occasional cluck still rising from the chickens in the back. A generator in town lit a few store lights and street lights and it seemed that we were back in civilization. Bafoulabe was by far the liveliest place we had seen since leaving Kayes at the start of the trip.

My plan was to get the local Malian train coming from Kayes and go on to Bamako that night. I would leave Aminata, Binta and Fanta to inspect equipment donated in Bafoulabe and several other nearby villages. They would then return to Kayes to finish other Union business and drop off Fanta, then Aminata and Binta would return to Bamako by a later train.

I made my goodbyes to Aminata and the others, and reiterated my appreciation for having been able to accompany them. I admired the work they were doing and hoped to see them again. I had accomplished what I needed to do to assure the project equipment had been properly dispersed and that most of it was working properly, but I was more convinced than ever of my earlier observation — I had received a lot more than I had given on this trip, and for that I was grateful.

The train was late arriving in Bafoulabe and in much worse shape than the Senegalese train I had taken coming out. The seating system, if there ever had been one, had broken down and I grabbed any seat I could. It was hot and the train seemed to crawl through the dark wilderness of Mali in the direction of Bamako. Occasionally we would come to a complete stop in the middle of nowhere for no apparent reason and the one light bulb in the car would frequently go out. *"Energie du Mal"* muttered the Malian man in front of me, all but the sound of his voice lost in the total darkness.

I was glad to be met at the Bamako train station by our driver Maiga, who had driven my little Peugeot up from Abidjan some months after our arrival in Mali. Maiga grabbed my possessions from my hand and drove me home, negotiating the craziness of the Koulikoro road by himself while I re-absorbed the night-time bustle of Bamako and shook my head to remove that other-planet feeling that I always felt when I emerged from the bush.

7
Talking 'bout Timbuktu

I was happy to be home and Allison was in great shape, still as bald as a cue ball. The air freight from Texas with the diapers and baby clothes and other equipment had arrived and Badji and Joy had the baby care routine down by now. All thankfully was well.

It was also our month for the VCR. Though we were incredibly rich by Malian standards, we were too poor by our own standards to afford our own VCR so we split one with three other couples, rotating it every month and keeping a liberal visitation policy for our even more deprived friends. Joy had set up the VCR in the spare bedroom. A few tapes of long-ago-played college basketball games had arrived from my sister in North Carolina and I knew I would soon have every minute of every game committed to memory.

Joy was full of other news. Mike, the World Bank resident representative who was a friend with a tendency toward spaciness, had been hit by a train while crossing the tracks in his Peugeot on the Koulikoro Road on his way to work. Fortunately, by some miracle he had not been seriously injured. Also, Mickey and Ellie had returned to Mali from Rome where their daughter had been born. Mickey had been feeling a bit overwhelmed at the responsibility of having a child before he left for Italy, especially given that he was still a man without a country, so I wanted to talk with him soon.

Joy reported one item of interest from work. Our office building had been broken into over the weekend and most of our calculators, a few typewriters, and some of our electrical transformers had been stolen. Everyone knew immediately where they could be found — for sale in town at the *marché des voleurs,* the so-called thieves market. The administrative office had given Vieux Diallo, the head janitor, use of a vehicle and some money, and he had gone and negotiated the repurchase of all of our things and reinstalled them as before. Joy said there was a special line item in our budget that covered the repurchase of our own, stolen equipment.

The next day we drove out to the airport to say farewell to our friend who had been the Commercial Officer at the Embassy. There was not much commerce between the U.S. and Mali — used clothes was one of the principal U.S. export items at the time — and I wondered if this didn't account for the fact that this guy had the time to become such a good tennis player. Dan had always given me the impression that he liked Mali, but his wife Megan evidently had had no such feeling. We had gone and would continue to go to the airport many times to send off friends as they departed the country but Megan was the only person I ever remember sprinting across the tarmac to the waiting Air Afrique plane, not looking back.

At work I settled back into a bit of a routine, staying busy with a project redesign as well as a couple of evaluations. My immediate boss was consumed by a design of the next phase of a livestock project we had financed since the end of the drought, and was working incredibly long hours on that, letting me and Jerry work away on our own.

The news we occasionally heard about *Action Ble-Dire* continued to be bad. Charlotte and Dave's contracts had ended and they had returned to New York where Dave planned to finish his Masters Degree in history at Columbia University. The revolving fund for the pumps had still not been set up and other management problems persisted with the new Director of *Action Ble*. David, the Bamako project manager, had been transferred down to Conakry, Guinea and had been replaced by someone very junior who had recently arrived from Washington. Dire had not become any more accessible than before and I wondered how much longer we would or should keep the project going.

With *Action Riz Sorgho* in Gao, our bosses and the Malians in Gao were still trying to decide what to do about our recent project evaluation report. Indications were that our recommendations would be included in a new project phase that would be designed and presented to our Washington office for approval.

When Jerry and I heard that the charter Twin Otter plane was flying to Gao to pick up a passenger and could take us, we decided on the spur of the moment to go up and discuss the completed evaluation results with Togola of ARS and see what if any changes in the project had already been undertaken.

I was happy to take a chance on still another Mali plane trip because the plane was to stop for a day in Timbuktu en route to drop supplies for a German aid project. I had yet to make it Timbuktu and this was a golden opportunity.

I asked Joy if she had any desire to go too, even though with the baby and her job I doubted she could get away. "No thanks," she said, "I've had about as much bush travel in Mali as I want."

"But this may be the only chance you'll have to visit Timbuktu in our entire stay in Mali," I said.

Joy replied, "That's OK. I really don't feel the need, but in the future if I do, I'll just lie and say I went there."

It was hard to argue with this so Jerry and I left alone. We flew directly from Bamako to Timbuktu, overflying the Niger floodplain. The town of Niafounke south of Goundam stood out from the air as a town surrounded by water with an impressive Soudanese-style mosque in the middle. We next flew near Dire and then crossed the Niger on our approach to the little Timbuktu airport.

There was an air of mystery about Timbuktu, even to those of us who lived relatively close by in another part of Mali. Part of the charm was the stories of the city's past glories and its inaccessibility. Some people I had talked to in the States had thought Timbuktu wasn't even real but rather made up and in story books only.

On the other hand, there was a differing point of view about Timbuktu and its perception by the westerner as being located at the nether reaches of the planet. One of Mali's most famous musicians, Ali Farka Toure, a Songhai who came from a village outside Timbuktu and now was making well-selling CD's and performing to appreciative audiences in Europe and the U.S., wrote the following about Timbuktu:

"For some people when you say 'Timbuktu' it is like the end of the world, but that is not true. I am from Timbuktu, and I can tell you that we are at the heart of the world."

My father-in-law, a graduate of Texas A&M University, even knew a totally politically incorrect Aggie joke about Timbuktu. He had told it to me like this:

"An Aggie and a Tea-Sip (the Texas A&M term for an alumnus of the University of Texas) show up at the Pearly Gates together and are met by St. Peter. In a frivolous mood, St. Peter says they can enter only if they can use the word 'Timbuktu' in a poem. The Tea-Sip thinks for a moment and says:

On masted schooner we set sail
Storm swept passage through wind and hail
Plying deep the ocean blue
Destination, Timbuktu

Then it was the Aggie's turn:

Me and Tim 'a hikin' went
We spied three maidens in a tent
As they were three and we but two
I bucked one and Tim bucked two."

Timbuktu was a real place all right. I could see it from my low-flying plane. But to my surprise it was not on the Niger River at all but rather some six kilometers to the north, the river having sensibly shifted its bank southward over the centuries. The little port of Timbuktu was Kabara where the pinasses and the river boats plying downstream from Kolikoro and upstream from Gao would stop to load and unload freight and passengers.

From the air, Timbuktu looked smaller and more forlorn than I had imagined it, its red mud buildings darker than the desert that completely surrounded it. We circled the city, buzzed the little airport to make sure the runway was free of animals, then landed.

The pilot told us to meet him back at the airport for the continuation to Gao tomorrow morning and Jerry and I were off to town in a beat-up old Land Rover driven by a silent, turbaned Touareg at the wheel.

My first impression of Timbuktu, despite Ali Farka Toure's beautiful description, was that we had arrived five or six centuries too late.

I had heard and read stories of the fabulous wealth of the old Timbuktu. At the height of the glory of the Songhai Empire in the fifteenth century, Timbuktu, buoyed by trans-Saharan trade and taxes from subjugated peoples, had a population of over 100,000, two universities, and several world class mosques. The government of the day subsidized scholars, doctors and judges, and there was a professional army and civil service. When Leo Africanus, a Spanish Moor, visited Timbukti in 1494, he wrote that Timbuktu "had a great store of doctors, judges, priests and other learned men, that are bountifully maintained at the king's expense."

Several nineteenth century European explorers risked their lives to visit Timbuktu, even then much in decline: Frenchman Rene Caille, German Heinrich Barth, and Scotsman Gordon Laing. Laing was the first to reach Timbuktu but he was killed by one of his Arab escorts after leaving Timbuktu while on his way down to Segou. Caille came a bit later in 1828 disguised as an Arab and speaking Arabic. He lived to tell his tale back in Europe. Barth arrived in Timbuktu in 1853 during a five year trek through Africa from modern-day Libya to Morocco, down all the way to Nigeria and then back north to Timbuktu. He too barely escaped with his life and wrote a five volume account of his travels. Plaques marked the houses where each of these explorers stayed in Timbuktu, though now they were largely in ruins.

The modern Timbuktu seemed far different from the older more glorious descriptions and I knew that the present population was only around 15,000. Still, I was interested in the different culture of the Touaregs that lived in and around Timbuktu, the remains of the old mosques in the city, and the desert.

As tourist destinations in Mali went, Timbuktu would have had more tourists if it had been easier to get to. Some people wanted to come just to say they'd made it there, or better yet send a postcard with a postmark from Timbuktu, one of the real-life Ends of the Earth.

But you had to really try hard to get to Timbuktu.

There was a terrible road north from past Hombori — itself the middle of nowhere — off the Gao road, but that was supposedly a very difficult stretch with almost no traffic. The other route was north from Mopti but that road disappeared during the rainy season.

Air Mali flew in two times a week on the milk run, but a discerning traveller would avoid these dangerous, beat-up old Soviet planes at all costs.

I had a colleague working in our office in Dakar who had decided to add Timbuktu to her elderly New York Italian mother's Sahelian itinerary when she came over to visit her daughter. They reserved on Air Mali, but then the plane broke down after dropping them in Timbuktu and they were stranded. My colleague's mother ended up renting a private plane to come fetch them from Bamako, which cost a couple of thousand dollars and came only after the poor woman had spent several uncomfortable days not knowing if or how she was going to escape Timbuktu, and wondering why in the world she had ever left New York.

The river boats were also a possibility but they only ran half the year and these were only for the very adventurous. The best way I knew of getting to Timbuktu was to do like Jerry and I had done — find a reliable plane going there and ask for a ride. Our friend and colleague Alex had also used this technique successfully — waiting at the private plane section of the Bamako airport and hitching a ride with two Western journalists who had rented a plane and had an extra seat.

Before exploring the town, Jerry and I decided to try to check into the local *campement*, the hotel, as we knew there were very few places to spend the night. There were probably a few other very rudimentary places to stay in Timbuktu, but we had heard that the *campement* was the best. The best of Timbuktu was still pretty basic.

Our Land Rover dropped us at a low concrete building built on a concrete slab at the edge of town and the start of the serious desert — sand dunes and Touaregs on camels several hundred meters away. We'd check in soon, but Jerry and I were hot and very thirsty. A little bar stood off to one side and we both went over.

"*Bonjour*," I said. "Could we please get some bottled water? Cold if you have it."

The man behind the bar shook his head. "Sorry, chef, but the water is finished."

"That's OK. Do you have any juice or a soft drink?"

"No, *patron*, it is finished too."

This didn't look good. "How about a beer?", I said. A beer is what we really wanted anyway.

The beer was finished also.

"Well, what do you have?" I remembered the story about the African restaurant with an elaborate menu with page after page of items that the waiter patiently explained they were out of. After being asked in frustration by the customer what he did have, he was told, "The only thing we have is '*steak-frites*'," steak and french fries.

"*Patron*, I'm sorry but we don't have anything here now. It is all finished."

Jerry and I looked at each other and I turned back to ask the barman a question that only a toubab would ask, and that I was too slowly beginning to understand had no place in West Africa.

"Well, if you don't have anything to sell, then why are you here standing here behind the bar?"

The man looked at me like I was strange. "I am here because I am the barman and this is the bar where I work."

Jerry and I gave up and headed to the primitive outdoor reception desk. After the bar episode, I was afraid that we'd be told there were no rooms either but the reception man gave us a little form to fill out so it looked promising. There was sand everywhere, including the corners of our eyes and nostrils.

The guy behind the counter turned to me first. "Monsieur, would you like a room with an air conditioner?"

This was the last thing I expected to be asked. Jerry and I had prepared ourselves to grin and bear the heat and the absolute most we had hoped for in the way of cooling had been a electric fan.

"Air conditioner?," I said. "That sounds great. You bet I'd like an air conditioned room. Thanks a lot."

The problem was, the man explained, that there was only one room with an air conditioner available.

Jerry solved the problem. "Look, I'm fine in a regular room. I've been in Mali for years and we never had even a fan in my old village. Take it, man, I don't need it."

Great, we were all set. We'd throw our bags in the room, explore Timbuktu, find a place for dinner, watch the sun go down over the desert, wander around some more, and then sleep and leave for Gao in the morning.

I unlocked the louvered metal door to my room and went inside. The door and the two windows were the same — metal and louvered without glass or screen and totally open to the elements. This meant the air conditioner wasn't going to do much good. Then I saw the air conditioner itself. It sat on the floor in the corner of the room, disassembled and in several large pieces. It was obvious that it had not worked for years, maybe even twenty.

I next made a final discovery: there was not a drop of electricity in Timbuktu nor had there been for two months. The German aid program had donated a new large generator to the town of Timbuktu that would have been a considerable improvement over their older, smaller generator. The Malians had poured a new concrete pad for the new generator and then installed it.

Alas, though, there was WAWA to consider.

The Malians failed to let the concrete dry and cure sufficiently and started the generator prematurely. It worked only long enough to shake its pad to pieces, finally falling on its side damaged beyond repair. Timbuktu was now totally without power with no prospect in sight for it being restored. My air conditioner wouldn't have worked even if it had been new and whole.

The story about the air conditioner had one final footnote. The next morning when I paid my bill, I looked carefully at the charges: they had charged me twenty-five per cent extra for a room with an air conditioner.

I thought about asking another toubab-like question about why had I been charged extra for an air conditioner that was in pieces in a town with no current, but stopped myself in time. I decided that it was worth the extra money to have received another insightful lesson about the ways of Africa and the complete and total irrelevance of Western logic. And maybe, I thought, someday it just may make a good story if anyone actually believed me.

Timbuktu, as much because of the air conditioner story as anything, had been as interesting as I had hoped. We found a restaurant called The Golden Chicken that had no chicken but some roasted lamb and, wonder of wonders, a bottle of Schaefer beer that somehow had travelled the distance from the U.S. to Timbuktu. The locally baked wheat pita-like bread they served and that could be found all over Timbuktu would have been excellent except for the sand that permeated it. We noted that there was not much food for sale in the local open market but I learned later than many items are sold in bulk out of merchants' homes.

We wandered the streets of the old section of town and saw what was left of the house where Rene Caille had lived, marked by a metal plaque. We also passed by the interesting but rather unimpressive remains of the three old mosques, one of which had served as both a mosque and a university that by the sixteenth century was one of the largest schools in the Muslim world with more than 2,500 students.

Sunset over the desert was spectacular and the Touaregs looked as they were intended, emerging from the desert on camels, all but their eyes covered by their indigo burnooses. I reminded myself that the nomadic Touareg way of life had been terribly affected by the droughts of the seventies and camps of Touareg refugees had been established for these proud people outside of Timbuktu.

Touareg camel caravans still did ply the desert between Timbuktu and the salt mines of Taoudeni far to the north. The first stop of the caravans to Taoudeni was a spot in the middle of the desert called Araoune some 257 kilometers north of Timbuktu and only a third of the way to Taoudeni. Timbuktu, like Gao, looked pretty good after crossing that desert, I imagined.

Jerry and I made it to the plane on time the next morning. Leaving Timbuktu, we overflew the *Ile de Paix* (Peace Island) development scheme run by a Belgian group that used large pumps to cultivate several hundred hectares of irrigated rice. Jerry said they were successful in growing rice and thus were alleviating the food shortage problem, but the technology of using large pumps made the project too complex for successful long-term Malian management in this remote setting. Therefore the project was not a good development model, but growing domestic rice at below the price of imported rice still seemed a worthy accomplishment.

We overflew the town of Bourem thirty minutes later, a barren-looking spot where the Niger River finally stopped its eastern flow through the desert and turned south for the rest of its journey, eventually passing through Niger and into Nigeria, finally emptying into the far off Gulf of Guinea and the Atlantic Ocean.

We landed at the now familiar Gao airport and immediately went to the *Action Riz Sorgho* office where we hoped to find Ali Badara. He wasn't there but one of the chauffeurs there knew where to find him and went to fetch him. Ali Badara was glad to see us and vice versa, and we piled ourselves and our little packs into his Land Rover to be dropped at our guest house. I noticed a new movie poster at the Gao theater near the market. Bruce Lee, well known and loved in the Third World, had even made it to Gao.

Jerry and I carried out our latest mission to Gao in just several days. We looked deeper into alternative ways of providing farmer credit and distributing rice seed through existing cooperatives rather than through project extension agents. We met with Director Togola who had read our report by this time and who wanted to comment. He agreed with much of what we said but believed in continuing to use project extension agents, but wanted them better trained. He said he was working to clear up the credit fund that we had found to be in poor shape. Then he said he would soon be leaving the project to return to the Ministry of Agriculture in Bamako and he hoped his deputy in Gao would move up to succeed him.

Remember that this project is just getting underway, he said. Keep supporting us here and we can eventually show increases in production and food security.

Jerry wanted to visit and study a couple more of the European-financed cooperatives we had visited during our previous trip to the south of Gao, towards Ansongo. We took off, stopping en route to again see our insubmersible dikes. At one stop along the way, villagers told us that they had just seen a group of giraffes nearby, supposedly one of the few collections of giraffes remaining in West Africa. The few large wild animals left in West Africa were depleted almost to the point of extinction and the tiny number of remaining elephants and giraffes were under the constant threat of poachers. We resisted the urge to go searching for the giraffes, hoping we would get lucky and see them from the road.

With the work accomplished, Ali Badara drove us the bone-jarring two day trip back to Bamako. True to the rumors we had heard, road construction was underway north of Mopti — they were actually starting to pave the Mopti-Gao road which represented a potential quantum leap in improving logistics of the Gao project and our ability to monitor and track its implementation.

All was well on the home front though the sight of all our carpets outside draped over the bushes in the front garden had given me pause as I walked in the door. Not to worry, Joy said. While the water had been cut, she had tried the tap and since there was no water had left it on by mistake. When the water came on while she was out, the sink had overflowed and we ended up with a major indoor flood. The rugs would dry eventually.

8
The Manantali Dam:
Not Treading Water

Work had for once settled into more of a routine and I took fewer trips far from Bamako. Staying closer to home gave me the chance to concentrate on the implementation of a few projects I had only been slightly involved in previously. The design of a credit program in the High Valleys was being reevaluated and the redesign of our livestock project continued.

My immediate boss Bob was still possessed by the livestock design, often working late on it night after night, sometimes sleeping only a few hours in the office and continuing to work. His dedication was admirable but it seemed to me he was becoming completely exhausted by his schedule and I worried about his health. He could not keep going at the present rate, that much was clear.

On the home front, Joy and I were spending more and more time with our Iranian friends, Mickey and Ellie. Our daughter Allison and their daughter Roya were now almost two years old and fellow toddlers and playmates.

Mickey was absorbed with trying to reform the credit program of the AID project where he was an advisor and was having big trouble with the head of the Malian *'Operation'* that ran the program, much like Charlotte and Dave had problems with *'Action Ble-Dire'* earlier. Mickey was trying to set up a credit program that actually worked and was sustainable, with less subsidized interest rates and policies that required farmers to pay back loans — not the way that many Malian credit programs were traditionally run. The default rate of most credit programs oriented towards small farmers in Mali was enormous, the normal pattern being that farmers would refuse to pay and the lending institution would not bother to try to collect. Mickey was giving it his best to run a serious program that would be sustainable and continue to provide rudimentary financial services to farmers seeking to expand agricultural production.

In the meantime, he was tormented by resistance to change from the Malian Director of the *'Operation'* and had begun to suspect him of shady dealings.

Mickey was the most Americanized of any Iranian I had ever known, speaking imperfect Farsi, yet impeccable English and French. In addition to loving baseball, Mickey was likely one of the few Iranians around with an extensive collection of American country and bluegrass music. Therefore, Mickey's angst over his inability to return to the United States where he wasn't allowed to go, nor to Iran where he dare not go, and the responsibility of having his new family stuck in Mali, lay very heavy on his mind.

Western authorities were cracking down even further on Iranian passport holders. The U.S. was still totally out of the question and was granting no visas to Iranians, but now even the previously more tolerant Swiss, Italians, and French were granting fewer and fewer visas to Iranians. Cut off from the U.S. and now from Switzerland where his parents resided, Mickey seemed to sink a little deeper into reflection and depression, though he was able to still snap back to being his old self, full of vinegar and wit, when he was with friends.

Back at the office, we were approaching a watershed in our whole approach to development in Mali. Despite our efforts to keep our far-flung food production projects in Mali afloat, it seemed that some disagreeable handwriting was clearly on the wall.

There was no point in denying that the *Action-Ble* project in Dire, for reasons of logistics, management and pure economics, was a failure. *Action Riz-Sorgho* in Gao, though more successful than the Dire project and with more long-term potential, Jerry and I thought, had the same kind of logistics problems as Dire and had suffered from its own design flaws and problems of mismanagement. Though Jerry and I had worked hard to identify the issues and come up with a strategy to help the project succeed, we understood that our Washington office was not now enthusiastic about accepting our recommendation to add modest new funding and carry out the revised next phase of the project.

On top of that, an audit report of our large millet production project in the Mopti region had just come out. I had had virtually no involvement in this project and had assumed that it was proceeding on course. I had accompanied my former boss Ron Levin and ex-Ambassador Byrne to a dedication ceremony of the project's Mopti headquarters almost three years previously during my first visit to the Fifth Region, and everyone then was full of promise and hope about the project.

The auditors' findings, however, were devastating. They concluded that the project had been poorly designed and was overly ambitious, that our agriculture office had done a poor job of project management, and that the responsible Malian counterpart organization had little institutional capability. Further, the project's purpose of increasing millet production was seriously undercut by the Government of Mali's policy of setting grain prices artificially low. Project procurement had been a disaster, credit funds had disappeared, and the project's financial records were found to be in such poor condition that the auditors considered them to be unauditable.

I was very shaken by the report. We had many experiences where Malian project management had proven deficient so this was not new. What was bad about the millet project was that it was us more than the Malians who seemed to have failed so miserably. If we had done a better job of managing the project, surely we could have helped our Malian colleagues avoid trouble too. Project management — the process by which we designed, approved, funded, implemented, and evaluated a project, and normally one of our attributes that defined how we ran development projects and that we used to justify our large overseas field staff — was found to be virtually non-existent. The auditors had a final jarring recommendation: the project should be immediately terminated.

The millet evaluation report hit at about the same time we ran out of patience with *Action Ble-Dire* and *Action Riz Sorgho-Gao*. The conclusion was finally inescapable: in orchestrating a rapid response to drought and human suffering, we had put together a generation of projects that was too broad and tried to tackle too many problems at once. Our staff energies and our financial resources were dispersed across too many miles and too many activities for us to manage them effectively. Finally, in our determination to reestablish food production, we had not yet focussed enough on restructuring Mali's cereals policy that undercut our efforts in agriculture.

I had seen the good effects of our projects and our hard work in a hundred ways scattered across Mali, but the systematic impact of all our assistance was much harder to gauge. I sadly had to admit that I agreed with the consensus we were coming to: in a world of very limited resources that could be devoted to economic development — and especially in harsh environment like Mali's — we had to better focus our assistance on fewer well-defined problems and focus it better geographically, where returns on our investments could be more feasible and much more cost-effective.

We decided to phase out of *Action Ble* and *Riz Sorgho* and, as recommended, the Mopti millet project was terminated. Plans for a new project in Kayes in the First Region were dropped. Though the process didn't happen overnight, we began to redefine our priorities toward the fields of agriculture, child survival and family planning, management and planning improvement, and economic policy reform. Consensus was also building that we would begin to concentrate our activities in Mali's Second Region — the area south of Bamako — where higher-than-average population densities and rainfall as well as better infrastructure would make impact and success more likely. This process too would take several years to fully achieve, but it was important to begin.

It was the middle of March and my big boss David Wilson wanted to see Jerry and me in his office. A cable had come in from headquarters in Washington informing us of the results of an international donor's meeting that had just been held in Paris. The meeting had been to discuss something called the Senegal River Basin Development Authority, which was evidently known by its French acronym of OMVS. The OMVS was a regional development organization founded in 1972 composed of the countries along the Senegal River: Senegal, Mali and Mauritania. The official function of the OMVS was to promote and coordinate research, planning, and fund-raising to further the development of the river basin.

The Senegal River originated, like the Niger, in the highlands of Guinea as a smaller tributary known as the Bafing, first flowing northward into the Mali's First Region, and finally turning west to become the Senegal River near Kayes and flowing on toward the Atlantic. Exiting Mali, the Senegal River formed the border dividing the countries of Senegal and Mauritania before emptying into the Atlantic near the old French colonial city of St. Louis.

The OMVS states, with considerable help from donors such as the UN and France, were devising a plan to develop large scale irrigated agriculture along the river, developing the appropriate agricultural dikes, polders and other schemes that, once completed, would provide a more secure, i.e. drought-proof, source of food production.

The waters would be controlled by the construction of two dams. The first, a so-called salt-intrusion dam, was to be completed near the mouth of the Senegal at a place called Diama. The Diama dam would keep salty ocean water from intruding upstream during the dry season, therefore providing protection for the fresh-water dependent agriculture that was to be developed along the river basin. The second dam was to be a large impoundment dam that would block a tributary of the Senegal far upstream, forming a large man-made lake whose waters could then be released as needed, creating in essence a constant all-season flow of water that could promote all year agriculture production to an estimated potential of 375,000 hectares in the Senegal River Basin, independent of seasonal floods and unreliable rainfall.

Not only would agriculture benefit from the dam, it would also in principle provide for year-round navigation of the Senegal River between Saint Louis and Kayes, opening up land-locked Mali to increased trade with Senegal and Mauritania. This seemed like a good idea because I knew that transport costs for traded goods in Mali came to almost a third of their value, making imports expensive and most exports non-competitive.

A final stated purpose of the impoundment dam — to produce one billion kilowatt hours per year in electrical generation for industrialization — seemed to me a little more dubious. I knew western Mali somewhat already, and there was nothing much there but wilderness with hardly even any roads or tracks, much less any budding industry. Electrical power could be produced, I supposed, but it would be very costly to distribute. And to where and for what purpose?

The impoundment dam was to be constructed at the estimated cost of some $584 million in western Mali at a place called Manantali, a village some 90 kilometers southeast of Bafoulabe in Mali's First Region. Bafoulabe was the place where not long ago I had left my Malian Women's Union companions to return to Bamako by train. Neither Jerry nor I had ever heard of Manantali.

There were a few technical problems with the OMVS scheme that I would hear about for the next few years, but one of the most inconvenient details was that the lake formed by the dam at Manantali was to be located over the villages and farms of what seemed to be some 12,000 rural Malian peasants.

The head of my organization's Washington-based Africa section had attended the donors' pledging session in Paris and had declined our participation in the construction of either of the two dams. As a development agency, we normally didn't do this type of large infrastructure work anymore, preferring to concentrate on "the poorest of the poor."

Other donors however, particularly the Saudis, the Kuwaitis, Germans, Abu Dhabi, the European Economic Community, and the African Development Bank, had already pledged some $800 million for the two OMVS dams and other related infrastructure. However, our boss for Africa had said that we would be glad to support the OMVS's downstream development program once the dams had been built. We would, she also said, be happy to design and finance the resettlement of the 12,000 rural Malian villagers away from the Manantali impoundment zone.

We were being presented a *fait accompli* on the issue of Manantali resettlement. Not only was this type of activity not fully consistent with the new strategic focus for Mali we were now grappling with, it was completely inconsistent with our plans to focus projects on more accessible geographical areas. Besides, I had read a couple of case studies about other resettlement programs in Africa and had yet to read one where the effort could have been considered even a partial, qualified success. In fact most or all resettlement programs, particularly forced ones as opposed to voluntary, seemed to be unqualified disasters. This kind of project could likely land us someday on "60 Minutes" or the like as journalistic cannon-fodder, but since our Washington boss had made a commitment for us to do the project, there was to be no further discussion.

In addition to the announcement that we would be designing and implementing the Manantali resettlement, David Wilson had two more things to say. The first was that Jerry and I would be leading the design process. Second, I was appointed to be our representative for all matters related to the OMVS.

Living in Mali and being preoccupied with its development problems alone, I had not been aware of what was going on with the OMVS, based as it was in Dakar. Given my new charge as our OMVS person in Mali, I tried to find out what else was going on I didn't know about.

I found out that in the 1970s, our Dakar office had provided some $17 million in funding to analyze the hydro-agricultural potential of the Senegal River Basin and to identify the environmental effects of dam construction. We had mapped the entire basin through aerial surveys and had compiled a mass of socioeconomic data on the basin and its people. These activities had proven influential in the decisions of the international donors to contribute to the OMVS development program.

The director of our Dakar office was organizing a strategy session in Dakar to discuss the design of our OMVS support program. I had briefly worked with the Dakar director, David Shear, on the Sahel drought relief program back in Washington before coming to Mali. I found Shear to be smooth, bright and totally dedicated to development and considered him to be a development visionary. Shear had been instrumental in putting together the first U.S. response to the Sahel drought back in the 1970s.

The idea now was to develop a strategy and program for supporting the OMVS that would proceed apace with the construction of the OMVS dams, and that would be ready and in place once the dams were finished. Jerry, David Wilson and I made plans to attend the meeting where we would participate and listen, and learn more about Manantali.

The Government of Mali's local counterpart to the OMVS was the Hydrological Service of the Ministry of Industrial Development and Tourism. Since *Hydraulique* would be the Government's representative on any resettlement project, we had to establish a close working relationship with them from the start and get as much help from them as soon as possible. Jerry had met one young Malian engineer who worked for *Hydraulique* named Robert Dembele. Robert was unexperienced but eager, and upon meeting, we thought one who could be our resettlement liaison with the Malian Government. Knowing we would have to worry about a Malian counterpart in due course, Jerry and I made an appointment to see the *Hydraulique* Director whose office was a short walk from ours.

Malian government offices were rarely a beehive of motion and activity, but the Hydrological Service headquarters seemed particularly devoid of life and movement. We let ourselves in from a dusty courtyard into a waiting area that was hot from the afternoon heat, completely silent and almost totally dark.

We could make out the outlines of a secretary at a desk in the waiting area. I had seen more than a few Malian government employees asleep at empty desks before but this one was unique. She was asleep face down and nose-first on the keys of her old manual typewriter. When I gently leaned over and told her we had a meeting with the Director and asked directions to his office, she raised her head only slightly from the keyboard and pointed silently down the hall. I noticed that the typewriter keys remained pressed down in the shape of her face.

Mamadou Sacko was in his office and very much awake. He was a powerful looking man in his mid-forties, trained as a hydrological engineer in the Soviet Union he said and, I found out later, married to a Russian woman.

Sacko shifted the folds of his dark blue boubou higher on his shoulders and lit a Gaulloise. Yes, he knew about the plans for the Manantali Dam and he was aware of the need to resettle the villagers from the reservoir area. He knew too of our pledge to finance resettlement, but nothing more. His communications with the OMVS were evidently haphazard at best, and it was clear that this operation would be managed from Bamako anyway, certainly not Dakar.

"We want to work with you and we need your help," we told Sacko.

We explained how we planned to begin. First, we would attend the OMVS planning meeting in Dakar where we would, among other things, try to find a copy of a 1977 report that represented the sole feasibility study done to date on Manantali resettlement. Then we would return to Bamako and survey the Manantali area ourselves for the first time to begin to understand the zone, its inhabitants and the challenge we would be facing as we proceeded with a detailed resettlement plan over the coming months. We would much appreciate it if he, Sacko, could name a representative from his office to work with us on a daily basis and be our primary working level liaison with the Hydrological Service.

"Fine," said Sacko. "I will also set up a resettlement coordination committee. I will get representatives of all the interested agencies of the government to be members. It can serve a role in assigning tasks in the design and implementation process and can also serve to disseminate information about Manantali."

He went on. "There is another option for this project that you haven't discussed." Sacko was no pushover and it was clear he was a natural leader.

"What's that?" I asked.

We were truly not experts in resettlement and we were just beginning what would surely prove to be an enormously complex undertaking.

"You could just give me the money and we'll implement the resettlement project ourselves."

This comment was one we were used to and would not be at all far-fetched in some settings, with some donors, and with some projects.

"Well, I think the point for us is to work effectively with you as a team," I said. "We have our rules about how we operate, and while these rules require us to control and account for the money, we consider this to be much more your project than ours. We'll do our best to operate it like that. We'll work with the *Hydraulique* counterpart that you name and coordinate with you and him during the whole process."

Jerry then mentioned that we knew and liked Robert Dembele and that we would appreciate Sacko considering him for the job as our government counterpart.

Sacko nodded resignedly. "I'll have your counterpart named by the time you return from Dakar," he said, rising to shake our hands as we made ready to depart.

Jerry and I passed the secretary still asleep facedown on the typewriter and proceeded back to our office, wondering how two people so thoroughly ignorant of a subject so potentially explosive as forced resettlement could end up being in charge of it.

David Wilson, Jerry and I flew to Dakar, this time with mostly work on our minds. Our hotel bordered on Dakar's *"Petite Corniche"* by the sea, and each room had a private veranda that overlooked the ocean. Dakar seemed as beautiful as ever to the landlocked veterans of the Sahel and I reminded myself again that there was serious work to do.

The meetings organized by our Dakar office were well run and informative. The meetings were held in the former office of the firm that had completed aerial photography of the river basin and had recently pulled up stakes and departed. The villa's parking lot was littered with the remains of numerous U.S. manufactured pick-up trucks and other vehicles that had been used for the project, and that had inevitably suffered a premature demise due to the bad roads and harsh conditions of Africa.

Though like our small Bamako contingent there was another little group from our office up in Nouakchott, Mauritania, most of the attendees were based in Dakar, including newly arrived members of a design team that were to work throughout the river basis designing a detailed $60 million project that would be the centerpiece of our support to the OMVS. I had never heard of my employer financing such a high-priced project in Africa, and had certainly never heard of hiring a large, special design team that would work for months and months just on the design and spend perhaps well over a million dollars on that exercise alone. I wasn't as inexperienced at this business as I once was, but all the normal rules seemed to have been thrown out the window.

We learned a lot about the planned OMVS program during the meeting, but far less about Manantali. The discussion about Manantali was pretty simple — we were going to finance, design and execute the project, and that was about it. The people worried about the main OMVS support project were only too happy to leave Manantali to those of us from Bamako. Their plates were already full.

We did learn a few salient facts. Manantali dam construction activities were due to begin in a matter of months, starting with the access road from the railhead to the dam site. The road would be completed within a period of about ten months. Concurrently, rail facilities at Mahina-Bafoulabe would be upgraded to accommodate the influx and equipment and supplies and then actual construction on the dam would commence. The reservoir would begin to fill about five years from the date the access road was completed and the dam itself would be completed less than a year later.

The bad news was that resettlement was a complex and difficult undertaking with great potential for disaster — that and the fact we didn't yet know much at all about the subject matter. The good news was that, despite the complexity, we seemed to have enough time to learn what we needed to do in order to be successful, and then do resettlement right. If we organized ourselves and the Malians, and started the design and planning process soon, maybe we would avoid our nightmare scenario of dropping life jackets to scores of poor villagers huddled together as the waters rose around them, followed by a press conference broadcast on the American evening network news to explain what we had done wrong.

Despite the high potential for failure, I looked forward to the professional challenge. We would be starting a project totally from scratch and clearly have the leadership role for the entire process. We would be working in a remote and new (to me) area of the country which I looked forward to seeing firsthand. Also, since the 12,000 or so villagers had no choice but to move, if we studied the lessons of the past, planned thoroughly, and worked closely with villagers constantly throughout the process, we could possibly carry out the project in as least a disruptive manner as possible and perhaps even reinstall these people in somewhat better developmental conditions than before, such as through improved water supply, agricultural conditions, access to improved health facilities and education. The idea of actually improving conditions, we realized, may have been too optimistic given the time and money available, but this would be the subject of a future debate. Regardless, the main point was to reestablish 12,000 poor villagers with homes and livelihoods intact. Without doubt, the resettlement program would be a first class challenge.

There was a reception that night at the home of the Dakar-based American colleague heading our entire OMVS support operation. I would get to know Vito much better in the coming years and he would go to be in charge of U.S. energy policy as Deputy Assistant Secretary of Energy in the early 1990s, but for the moment Vito's responsibility was to pull a coherent OMVS project design out of a huge team of development specialists.

David Wilson and I left the reception and forgot about Manantali for awhile. The NCAA basketball championship game was being played that night in far-away New Orleans, and my old university was playing. I knew that Armed Forces Radio would broadcast the game on short-wave. Ben, a Dakar resident friend from Indiana — as similar a group of college basketball fanatics to those of us from North Carolina as could be found — had offered his house and big short-wave radio for the game. This involved staying up practically all night given the time difference to the U.S., but David and I gladly sacrificed. We panicked when, with the lead changing with every possession and less than two minutes remaining in the game, the broadcast disappeared from the short-wave frequency we were using. Scrambling, I found the game on another frequency and we listened intently as my team pulled out the game by one point, hitting the winning shot with 19 seconds to go.

David and I headed for the airport the next day to return to Bamako, exhausted but happy. Jerry, who had perhaps sensibly wanted no part of staying up all night listening to a basketball game from the far-off U.S., felt fine.

With us we took a copy of the one earlier feasibility study on Manantali settlement that had been carried out to date. The study had been made years previously and, to our knowledge, no one had returned to the area to further plan the effort or consult with the villagers to be affected. If villagers had heard about or believed that they would have to move from their villages five years ago, they most likely would not believe it now.

Back in Bamako, Jerry and I checked back in with Sacko and made plans to visit the Manantali zone for the first time. True to his word, Sacko had named our counterpart and had taken us up on our suggestion of Robert Dembele. We found out that Robert — a rare Malian Christian — was off on vacation in his home village near the border with Burkina Faso, and therefore we would have to take our first trip to Manantali without him.

Jerry and I pulled out our maps of Mali to figure the best way to get to Manantali. Once the access road from the railhead at Mahina was constructed, we could drive due west from Bamako the 150 or so kilometers to Bafoulabe-Mahina over a passable road of rock and dirt, and then head due south to Manantali. But the access road wasn't constructed yet and we had to find another way. After consulting what few maps of the region that existed, we chose to go west along the western Kayes road before turning southwest in the direction of Manantali through a region that neither Jerry nor I had ever previously visited. This area would prove to be an increasingly isolated and primitive part of the country the further away from the main road and into the bush we went.

For the occasion, we brought our Gao-based driver Ali Badara down to Bamako. Ali was given charge of one of our still-new red and white Toyota Land Cruisers that seemed to stand up to the Africa roads better than anything else we had seen and that had earlier impressed us by crossing deep water without conking out. Those of us who traveled a lot in the bush had become convinced that the Land Cruiser was the most dependable and indestructible vehicle that could be had. This was the era when American vehicles were still in decline and until they crawled their way back toward the top of the automotive heap and became more durable and reliable, I and my colleagues who traveled into the nether reaches of the Sahel by vehicle only wanted to do it by Land Cruiser.

We packed the Land Cruiser with almost everything that either we or the car would consume for the next two weeks. Manantali was in the far reaches of the First Region where there would be no gas, no paved roads, no amenities at all, and possibly no easily accessible food. We would be disappearing from the trappings of civilization for the duration of the trip.

Jerry had taken care to design roof racks for the vehicle where we could stack our numerous gasoline jerry cans and that would keep us from having to inhale gas fumes on the trip had we been forced to keep them inside. With the inside free, we stacked boxes of food, cooler, cots, a tent, and other camping equipment. We had one more technological innovation installed for the trip — a two-way radio that we hoped would connect us back to the office in case of an emergency.

Ali Badara headed us east from Bamako, passing the dreaded hospital on the heights of Point G, past the little town of Kati still near Bamako, and west through the towns of Negala and Sebekoro toward the larger Malian town of Kita. The dirt road was torn up and still muddy from the rainy season and, even with the skilled Ali at the wheel, we were beaten and bruised by the time we made it to Kita. We spent the night at the former guest house of a United Nations electrical transmission project that had been run by a group of French-Canadians we had known, and who had now finished the project and departed the country. An

144 WAITING FOR RAIN

impressive peanut oil processing plant had also been built in Kita and was still run by Germans, though we understood at only a fraction of its potential capacity.

We turned southwest off the main road as planned and headed into the deep bush, villages becoming more isolated and the road more a track the further we went. Bridges across streams were crude log affairs when they existed at all, but more often we would forge streams by try-ing to pick the most shallow spot we could, and then holding our breath as Ali put the Land Cruiser into four-wheel drive and pulled us up on the opposite bank. Cultivated fields too gave way to forest and wilder-ness, and we passed and saw fewer and fewer people.

The track we were following became rougher and muddier and Ali could go no faster than a crawl in many places. To my amazement, even the venerable Ali Badara — magician driver and negotiator of the desert sands — got the Land Cruiser stuck in the mud. Even though we had no choice but to take it all in stride, I could tell that Ali Badara was terribly ashamed and upset about for once being at least temporarily defeated by the elements.

After about fourteen hours of this kind of driving, no more than a few stops to negotiate river crossings and our eventual liberation from being stuck in deep mud, we were approaching the future dam area from its southern end. We had not passed nor seen another single vehicle since leaving Kita. A few villages appeared and true to the information we had been given, they were, Jerry pointed out, inhabited by the Malinke ethnic group.

It was dark by this time and after passing through an area of particu-larly thick woods, we emerged into what seemed to be a good-sized vil-lage. Our map indicated this was Keniekenieko — a fact confirmed by a teenager we passed beside the muddy track. We were welcome to put up our tent and sleep the night at the edge of the village, he said, and we complied, unloading tent and provisions as quickly as our tired bodies could manage.

Bright morning sunshine revealed Keniekenieko to be one of the more major villages of the dam impoundment site, and our first encounter with a village that would be forced to relocate. It was still a few kilome-ters south of Manantali village itself — for now a much more insignifi-cant Malinke village than Kenienkenieko — but soon to be the site of the main dam construction effort. Kenienkenieko was also nested on the banks of the Bafing river that, still in its undammed state, flowed serene-ly northwards from its source in Guinea.

The camp site we had chosen in the dark turned out to be very near the banks of the Bafing, and we soon discovered we could hear hippos splashing around in the nearby water below. We had pitched our tent near a very grand communal rounded house with thatched roof of the type I had seen on earlier trips to the First Region.

The recent rains had brought out tall, lush green grass around wooded Kenienkenieko, and the sight of the Malinke village laid out beside the river with smoke from its cooking fires rising to the clear blue sky, gave the impression of isolated pastoral serenity that I knew, unfortunately, would not last for much longer, at least not here. These people would soon, like it or not, have their lives turned completely upside down.

Jerry and I, aided by Ali Badara, worked on our campsite a bit that morning, putting up a tarpaulin outside the tent and setting up the card table we had brought. Jerry pulled out a red checked table cloth for the table and set up our little camp stove while Ali Badara unloaded most of our water cans from the Land Cruiser. On subsequent trips to the Manantali area, we would continue to use Keniekenieko as our base camp, fanning out in all directions to cover the zone, improving the campsite more each time.

We were soon to discover that Keniekenieko had an American Protestant missionary living nearby. It was still a surprise to us, despite our contacts with other missionaries scattered throughout Mali in the most unlikely of settings, that a missionary would be living here in the supreme isolation of Keniekenieko. Gene had quickly discovered through the village grapevine that we were camped on the outskirts of town and drove over in his old model beat-up Land Rover to greet us. His Land Rover had an exhaust pipe that curved all the way up the back of the vehicle ending at roof-top level, a necessary innovation for crossing rivers, streams and roads inundated by water.

Gene gave religious classes to the villagers, he said, preached in the big round house near our tent, and tried to do a little amateur medical work when he had to. I was of the opinion that the best missionaries were those that did more work on health, agriculture or other development areas and less on saving souls, especially in areas such as this that had no access to health or education infrastructure, but Gene had been in Kenienkienko for twelve years, he told us, and seemed nice and dedicated enough. I suspect too that he enjoyed seeing some fellow countrymen and being able to speak English again.

Yes, he knew about the coming dam and the citizens of Keniekenieko knew about it too, but the villagers believed the news far less than Gene. Our presence alone, he said, would serve to help convince the skeptics that the dam and resettlement were really coming.

Sitting around the card table with maps spread out on the red checked table cloth, Jerry and I reviewed the purpose of our trip. The first idea was to generally familiarize ourselves with the entire impoundment area — the roads, the topography, the population density, agriculture, vegetation, etc. This knowledge was of course a prerequisite to designing a resettlement project and carrying out all the more detailed tasks that would come later. Second, we would attempt to survey the various villages and hamlets in the impoundment zone and begin to gather general information about their actual location, ethnicity, agricultural patterns, water availability, health situation, etc. Third, since resettlement sites for new villages would have to be soon selected, we needed to gain a preliminary understanding of where present villages could envision themselves resettling. And if the villagers knew where they wanted to go, what were our impressions of the new selected sites — from the perspective of soils and agricultural potential, water, vegetation, health conditions, environmental issues, land tenure and so forth? Though these subjects would have to be studied in far more detail later, a general survey now was necessary. Fourth, and though the decision would be a bit later on, we needed to decide how to actually carry out the resettlement — whether to pay villagers to move themselves, provide most or all of the assistance to carry out resettlement for them, or devise some sort of combination.

In preparation for our trip to Manantali, Jerry and I had begun to study other recent cases of forced resettlement in Africa. The case that we decided most relevant to our own case had been the resettlement carried out in conjunction with the construction of the Selingue dam — also in Mali 130 kilometers south of Bamako — the construction of which had helped Energie du Mali make Bamako's electricity supply actually reliable.

As with Manantali, the effected population of Selingue had numbered about 12,500 people inhabiting about 30 villages and hamlets. A number of detailed studies leading up to actual resettlement had been undertaken that covered many of the technical questions, but, at the end of the day, there were two principal problems in execution of the program: one, there had been inadequate time available for actual transfer of the people to new sites, land preparation and village construction because the planners had underestimated the time required; and, two, there was inadequate funding available to carry out the transfer, land preparation and village construction. The United Nations, the project financier, had spent 70% of their funds just on studies, so that when the reservoir was filling up, only about two-thirds of the required new buildings had been constructed.

In some of the Selingue cases, insufficient building materials were provided, and then only for sleeping quarters and kitchens, leaving nothing for granaries, chicken houses and so forth that would have helped villagers reestablish agricultural production. Fields were insufficiently cleared, lost fruit trees were not compensated in cash or kind, and newly dug wells provided insufficient water due to non-existent or poorly functioning pumps. Also, food that was supposed to be distributed to

newly established villages was done so insufficiently due to poorly executed village censuses.

Selingue-area villagers complained that, in general, their new land
was of inferior quality to the land they had left behind and that cleared
fields were not chosen for their optimal agricultural potential. Women
complained about inadequate space to reestablish gardens as well.
Finally, in what must have been the crowning blow, inadequate archaeological work was done on the impoundment area, and when rising
waters flooded an important archaeological and cultural site across the
southern border in Guinea, Guinea sued Mali for damages in international courts.

Jerry and I resolved that we would apply as many of the positive and
negative lessons of Selingue to Manantali as possible. We had begun to
boil down the Selingue and other resettlement case studies into a few
salient lessons: the need for careful and detailed resettlement planning
and sufficient time to carry these out; the need for multidisciplinary
research on potential sites, the resettling people, people already there,
and the variety of alternatives for carrying out the actual transfer; understanding the physical and social stress of those resettled; the need to
avoid economic innovations until villagers are firmly reestablished in
new villages; the need to take women's potential economic losses into
account; maintenance of existing ethnic boundaries; the need for constant monitoring of resettlement; respecting cultural and religious beliefs
of settlers; and the need to involve settlers in the process of planning and
actual resettlement to the extent feasible. To Jerry and me, the last point
— participation by the villagers to be affected by the move — seemed the
most important and one that we would try hard to not forget.

Using our maps and the original 1977 OMVS feasibility study, Jerry
and I divided the Manantali impoundment zone into four general areas
that included, as nearly as we could determine, all the estimated 39 villages and hamlets that would be flooded out by the Manantali Dam. We
would do our best to cover parts of all four of these sections — northeastern, northwestern, eastern, and southeastern — during this, our first
survey trip, depending on several factors: if our maps and other information proved correct enough to allow us to even find the villages, if there
were roads or tracks that would get us there, and, in the case of the
northwestern section villages, if we could figure a way to cross the
Bafing River to start to look for them.

As for crossing the Bafing, there certainly was no bridge of any kind
anywhere nearby, and the Bafing River was far too broad and deep to
ford in the Land Cruiser, at least judging it from its appearance at Keniekenieko. From the map, it seemed that the most feasible option of
crossing the river was to bang our way north up the small, rough track

past Manantali village itself all the way to the railroad bridge at Bafoul-abe — some 75 kilometers away — drive carefully across the railroad bridge to the other side of the river, and come back down the other bank, assuming there was even a track there, all the way back to a site more or less directly across the Bafing from Keniekenieko. If we could make it at all, it looked like more than a full day's drive just to end up on the other side of the river within a good rock throw from where we started, and with another full day's return trip in front of us.

We decided to figure all this out later and start with some of the nearer villages on the east side of the river. As we set off to the northeast in the Land Cruiser, we passed first through the rest of Keniekenieko toward Manantali and the future dam sight. The village of Manantali was small and unimpressive but the rock walls and formations there on either side of the river that sloped toward the river demonstrated why this site had been selected for the dam. A villager pointed out to us the exact spot where the dam would be built, but the future upheaval was hard to visualize. The site was still completely in its natural pristine state except for a painted mark on the rock walls that marked the future dam — no construction, no equipment, no improved roads, and no foreigners with the exception of ourselves. No nothing except for the large bird that sailed serenely over the site hovering on the wind currents; and with our engine stopped as we stared up at the rock walls, total silence.

As we made our way east of Manantali toward the first village we planned to visit, I was struck how different this area was to others in Mali I had seen. First, the vegetation was different — thicker with more trees than you normally saw, almost forest-like in places. Second, there were very few people. Most other non-desert regions I had seen in Mali had a more dense population of villages, with the accompanying infrastructure of rough roads and markets, but there was little of this sort of thing here. Only a very few people were visible in fields, and only an occasional passer-by was seen on the rough tracks of the zone.

In a word, the Manantali zone was as close to a vegetated wilderness area I had seen anywhere in Mali, excluding Mali's vast tracks of open desert or savannah. It was, to use the French word, *sauvage*. In conversations with a village hunter the day before in Keniekenieko, he had described the zone's agriculture, mostly subsistence with only some small amounts of peanuts leaving the immediate area. He had also said that the zone was very *enclavé*, or extremely isolated, with few manufactured goods entering the zone. Accordingly, he said, even such basic items as canned instant coffee and milk, flashlights and batteries, and cigarettes — fundamental village items in every other part of Mali I had seen — were rare indeed here.

The hunter, who hunted at night with the help of a light mounted on the top of a home-made helmet that he eagerly demonstrated to us, told us another item of interest: except for the occasional presence or visit by a Western missionary, there had been practically no European or Western penetration into this zone.

I was soon to experience personally one manifestation of this fact — some of the little village children ran in terror when they first spotted Jerry and me — until their laughing parents calmed them down and assured them that we were harmless. The parents explained: the kids had never before seen white people and had assumed we were ghosts.

From the dam site, we doubled back further east toward the small village of Nigui which we had chosen to conduct our first interview with the people soon to be affected by the dam construction. As we bumped and banged our way at a snail's pace toward Nigui, Jerry and I reviewed the purpose of village visits. Though all of the 39 villages and numerous hamlets to be affected by dam construction would have to be visited and studied multiple times prior to relocation, this trip was the first contact and our questions should set the stage for future work and stick to basics.

Our questions would start at the beginning: Do you know about the planned construction of the Manantali Dam and do you know that you will have to relocate? Where would the village like to relocate? With which other villages would you prefer to be amalgamated? The latter question was based on the practical reality of our need to save money and achieve economies of scale by grouping as many small hamlets and villagers as possible and practical into larger and fewer new village units.

Also, what form of assistance would be necessary in order to construct new villages? We were beginning to grapple with three forms of village reconstruction — provide funds to the villagers to reconstruct new villages on their own, reconstruct the entire new village for them ourselves, or a possible sharing of these alternatives with villagers taking charge of some tasks while the project did others. Finally, we planned to ask questions about well construction and, based on how the meeting was going, explore whatever topics the villagers wanted to bring up.

We were not expected in Nigui and as we got out of our red and white Land Cruiser which Ali had stopped near the village center, it took a while for a crowd to gather to see what the strange foreigners wanted. Finally, the village chief emerged from a nearby hut and greeted us warmly, and surprising to me, without any visible hint of suspicion.

Jerry explained who we were and why we had come. With that, the village chief escorted us directly to the village center and motioned us to sit on a log while he sent word for the heads of family and village elders to assemble. Nigui was a small village and it seemed we had picked a day when there were few people away working in the fields. Once a good-sized crowd had gathered including a number of grizzled older men who represented the main families of Nigui, Jerry — consummate Mali anthropologist that he was — turned to the chief and began to address him in ceremonial Bambara, which was close enough to Malinke to be understood by everyone.

It was important to know the proper way to address the villagers. This was done by talking directly to the village chief who would turn and transmit the same information to the elders, family heads and others and solicit their views on the topic at hand. Their opinions would then be retransmitted verbally back to the interviewer which would then constitute the official opinion of the village. It sounded stilted as an approach, but we were to find that using the necessary cultural parameters of respect for the villagers' modus operandi, lively debate and discussion would invariably result.

Yes, they said, we have heard about the dam but we have not seen anyone around here talking about it to us since 1977. Jerry and I knew this referred to the original site visit by the OMVS feasibility study team. We thought they must have decided not to build it, they told us, but now since you are here, we know they still intend to.

Jerry and I had our notebooks out and were scribbling furiously. Jerry asked the village chief the main family names of Nigui and asked if they had relatives living in other villages nearby. Yes, they replied, and when asked if they would be willing to amalgamate into a larger village unit with their relatives, they replied that this would be their preference.

Villagers had sharply differing views on how to reestablish their new village — some said the new village, wells, and its agricultural fields should be constructed and established completely from the outside, while others argued that they should take charge of some of the work themselves.

I was surprised as to how flexible and understanding the villagers had been during the entire conversation — to reconfirmation that their homes and ancestral lands would be lost forever one minute, to discussing the best means for reestablishing their new village the next. Such an undertaking in the U.S. or Europe, I knew, would now likely be met by hostility, protest, lawsuits and countersuits, the raising of environmental issues and the like, and the whole process — if it were allowed to proceed at all — could take years and years.

The citizens of Nigui, however, seemed not eager but willing to accept their fate and were even ready to propose a site for the new village — between the villages of Bankasi and Keniekeniedala they said — which Jerry and I would later try to locate on our map and then in person in the field.

We ended our discussion after about an hour by thanking the village chief and the villagers for their help and cooperation and explaining what we thought would be the next steps in the process: we would visit all the other effected villages and ask them the same questions we asked in Nigui. Nigui would then later be visited again by ourselves or others in the project and more progress would be made — in determining the new village site, in deciding finally who and how the reconstruction would be carried out, in surveying the new site in terms of agriculture, water potential, land clearing needs, health and sanitation issues, land tenure, and so forth.

As we proceeded out of Nigui and back toward the main track which would lead us to our next village, Jerry and I compared impressions. This process was obviously going to take time and a lot of work. Given the number of villages to cover and the studies to be undertaken in the old and proposed new sites, we — Jerry and I — would be relying a lot on our Malian colleagues and eventually on an expatriate technical team to carry the work to the next stage. Our role now was clearer than before — we were really capable of only beginning the exploratory process and preparing the ground for the detailed work that would come later. We also seemed even more determined in our view that if this was going to work, villager participation and agreement was necessary throughout.

We reached the main track again and headed south toward the larger village of Kenieba which according to our map was located near the eastern shore of the Bafing. We found Kenieba with no difficulty despite the rough road and terrain, and the interview process began again. This time however the sun had broken through the clouds and the day had become beautiful. The villagers of Kenieba ushered us to a place of honor in the village square which was framed by several huge cottonwood trees not far from the banks of the blue Bafing. While the villagers assembled I mused what a shame it was that such a beautiful physical setting would soon be inundated.

The questions and many of the answers of Nigui would be repeated in Kenieba, except the beginning was rough. In answer to Jerry's question of whether they knew that the construction of a dam was going to require them to move, the village chief hesitated.

"Yes," he replied. "We were visited some years ago by people who said that a dam was coming and we would have to move."

"But," he continued, "the problem is that we don't know what a dam is."

"Oh, God," I thought to myself, "this could be hard."

Bill Cosby's old comedy routine about Noah and the Ark with God asking, "How long can you tread water?" came to my mind and stuck there.

The chief's reply had shaken me up a bit but Jerry, unflappable, began to explain.

"A dam," he began — rather majestically I thought — "is a large wall of stone that will be built across the river at Manantali. It will block the entire river and cause the water to rise upstream and form a huge lake."

Jerry pointed to the mid-way point of the village's highest cottonwood tree while the assembled villagers stared upwards together.

"The waters will rise to about that point on the tree and will flood your homes and fields. That's why you have to move. We're here now to help you plan to move to a new site that will be as good or better than your village now."

After that, the interview went well and the villagers gave many similar responses as the people of Nigui. They identified their own kinsmen in the area and spoke of where they would like to be relocated — near Djinfiti which they described to us, but that Jerry and I could not later locate on the map and that we finally concluded was not a village at all but rather a geographical place name whose location for now we could only guess.

We covered two more villages that same day, making careful notes and finally arriving back in Keniekenieko as the sun set. As Ali Badara went with a little money to a nearby compound to purchase rice and sauce for dinner which would be supplemented with some of our Bamako canned goods, Jerry and I took wonderful feeling bucket showers with water we hauled out of the river, followed by a warm Masters liter-sized beer that we had carefully packed in Bamako to avoid breaking on the rough roads. Next trip, we decided over dinner, we would come better equipped and do it right: we would bring someone with us to cook and clean up, we would set up a better campsite with a protected tarp area where we could write, and maybe even we could figure out how to have the beer cooled. In Africa, after a long, hot day in the bush, the little things like a cool beer went a long way in restoring one's civility and initiative.

For the next five days we repeated the pattern of the first days explorations — hitting on the average another four villages a day, making extensive notes on the villagers' reactions and replies, and contemplating what we were beginning to understand as major issues we would have to plan for in the coming months. Once we understood who should be amalgamated with whom in new villages and a methodology for reestablishing new villages, we had to plan for new site surveys. Would land in the new sites be as agriculturally productive as in the old villages? Would there be sufficient water? What should we try to do, if anything, about sacred objects in the old villages — the village fetish or the sacred rock for example? Who owned or occupied, if anyone, the land in the proposed new sites? How would villagers live from the time they moved to the new sites and until agricultural production was established there and food was available? Who would clear fields at the new sites?

One thing was clear to us: with only about $13 million available from us for the entire undertaking, we needed help in the form of in-kind and monetary contributions from the Malian Government as well as other donors in order to avoid a disaster — the image of helicopters dropping life jackets to villagers amid rising waters still a worry at such times.

In one far-removed area we had a flat tire, which Ali Badara began to change, followed by his patching of the old tire. With some time to kill, I went on by foot alone, glad to be out of the vehicle and enjoying the absolute stillness and isolation of my wooded surroundings. Crossing through an area of thick brush down the track in the direction of the next village, I had a strange sense of being followed — by what I had no idea — but it was a strange sensation quite unlike anything I had experienced before.

Ali finished his work on the tires and eventually caught up with me in the Land Cruiser. When we arrived at the next village, we were warned in passing — a head of cattle had been lost the previous night to a lion. There are lions in the area, we were told, be careful. I gave a shudder at the thought of having been possibly stalked by a lion, but realized once again, this area of Mali was more wild than any I had ever seen and the idea of there being lions seemed unsurprising and perfectly natural.

By the time we were ready to return to Bamako — dictated by dwindling supplies and especially gasoline — we had surveyed about half of the main Manantali-zone villages and several of the smaller hamlets. Villagers had continued to completely cooperate with a surprising degree of openness and friendliness. They seemed completely understanding of the need to amalgamate with other villages to form larger units, and mostly knew with whom they would be willing to live.

There was however one small village — Goumbalan — with whom no other group would be willing to associate. We had visited Goumbalan and had found the people there indeed a bit strange and stand-offish, avoiding an answer to the question of whom they would like to move in with among the other villages. The Goumbalan villagers had identified themselves to us as a village of blacksmiths.

"What's the problem with Goumbalan?", we asked people in the other villages.

"They are sorcerers," we were told. "They do black magic there and we do not want to have anything to do with them."

"OK," we thought, "so we'll have several large new amalgamated villages and one very small one. We're flexible."

When we finally headed for home, reaching small and normally unimpressive Kita once again, we were again struck by the modernity of its peanut oil plant and even the occasional electric light as we emerged from another time and era on our way back home to Bamako — itself a space-age city compared to where we had just come.

I was always glad to get home after these trips, to catch up on family business and friends, play with Allison in the pool, go to the parties and private dinners that were still the main forms of expatriate entertainment in the Sahel, see if any new tennis players had arrived in town, and go over to the new "American Club" across the Niger River in the Manyambougou neighborhood where the English language movies were now shown and where the weekly softball games were now played.

Jerry and Barbara, now American community stalwarts in addition to their other attributes, had been instrumental in founding the American Club in Manyambougou and negotiating additions such as a tennis court, generator, bar and swimming pool. Given the dearth of entertainment in Bamako, the Club quickly became a magnet among Bamako's outlet-starved English-speaking expatriates.

I settled back into somewhat of a normal routine at work for a few days while Jerry and I took stock of what we had learned about Manantali resettlement and the immediately needed next steps. The first of these was to inform Robert Dembele from *Hydraulique* of what we'd been doing and get him and others from his office more involved.

We were interrupted however by another crisis at work. My boss Bob's eighteen hour work days on the livestock project design had finally caught up with him and his resulting run-down condition had turned into a far more serious case of stomach problems, whether ulcers or worse we didn't know. A medical evacuation to the U.S. was immediately ordered, and I suddenly found myself not knowing whether my boss was suffering from a life-threatening injury and was gone from Mali forever, or whether perhaps he might later return. In any event, I had inherited management responsibility for our office and a bigger workload.

In the meantime, Jerry and I were serious in recognizing the importance of the Malian government involvement in Manantali resettlement. This was philosophically correct — it was their country and involved their people — as well as operationally. We needed their close cooperation for the extra planning and implementation manpower they could provide as well as the coordination with other donors that we had quickly figured out was needed to help us with resettlement-related activities — such as land-clearing and food provision that we could not hope to fund out of our own limited project funds.

We immediately sought out our counterpart from *Hydralique*, Robert Dembele. Robert listened intently as we told him of what we'd accomplished during our first Mantantali trip. Robert was only in his mid-twenties and had never before been entrusted with such a big responsibility in his professional career. Though I wondered privately what level of engineering training Robert could have hoped to obtain in Malian schools, he was our first and so far only counterpart and we had to work with him.

Jerry and I were in fact very glad about Robert's appointment: he was bright, eager and seemed like he would be cooperative rather than act like a few of the more seasoned bureaucrats that we had seen or worked with in other projects. This breed could easily have resisted ever going to the wilds of Manantali in order to stay in the relative comfort of Bamako, or worse, could have looked upon such a job as an opportunity for personal gain from the donor's money. This was a mind set that I had now seen many times in Mali and though it certainly didn't apply to a majority, it did often enough. To be exposed to this mentality had disappointed me at first.

"Why should I," I asked myself, "care more about Mali's development than the Malian counterparts I work with?"

It took me a while to learn the answer to the question but I finally did: with the pervasive poverty, tiny government salaries and the pressures to support an extended family, it was no wonder that many Malians looked at the chance to deal with donor-financed projects and donor money with keen anticipation. They were poor, the thinking went, and the donors so obviously rich. One had to take advantage of such situations when they presented themselves and very quickly, because the chance surely wouldn't be available for long and may not ever present itself again.

We didn't need these complications with Manantali and with Robert it was clear that we all had the same interests and agenda. Jerry and I hoped that Robert would be the first of many dedicated Malians covering a range of professional disciplines that would be assigned to the Manantali project. For the moment though, Sacko of *Hydraulique* seemed uninterested in assigning anyone else to help us, so Robert would have to do for the time being.

Almost immediately, we began making plans for a return to Manantali. We planned to take two vehicles this time and the office equipped them both with two-way radios that in principle would allow us to talk to our Bamako office from Manantali. Jerry and I also scrounged extra jerry cans, water containers, lanterns, chairs, and an extra tent and tarp so that we could be more comfortable in the field and stay out longer.

It was not just comfort we were worried about — our group was going to be much larger than before with two drivers, Robert Dembele, Jerry, myself, and an American anthropologist, David, from our regional office in Abidjan whom we had invited up to join us. Finally, we had located another key member of the team — Amadou — who had agreed to accompany us in function as our camp cook and cleaner. With the back of both Land Cruisers loaded to the brim with supplies and the roof racks topped-off with jerry cans full of gasoline, we set off for Manantali once again. We decided to try a different route this time, west through Kita and all the way to Bafoulabe, then south to Manantali by the track that the Germans were soon supposed to begin turning into the promised dam access road.

We made it to Keniekenieko in two days, this time arriving from the north. At the railhead of Bafoulabe we noticed a storage area full of newly-arrived road building equipment — the first sign of the coming construction of the dam access road, and the first concrete indication that Manantali resettlement was not an abstract concept. This was seeming more and more like serious business.

For now though, the track leading southeast to Keniekenieko from Bafoulabe was terrible and we could hardly make more than twenty kilometers an hour. Finally arriving at Manantali, nothing appeared changed at the future dam site as we continued on our way southeast.

We made camp at Keniekenieko at the same site as before, but this time with a difference. In addition to our two tents and tarp, we purchased two large straw mats in the village and used them to set up a shower area as well as latrine. Amadou got with the program and laid rocks in the shower to make a floor so we could clean up without getting our feet muddy. I had ordered a "sun shower" from a mail-order catalogue in the States, and if the thing actually worked, after leaving the water-filled bag in the afternoon sun, we could even have a warm shower at the end of a long day's work.

Gene, the missionary, soon showed up and seemed happy to see us again. He made admiring remarks about how improved our campsite was — by this time we had the red checked tablecloth out on the card table with folding chairs and lanterns were hung waiting for night fall.

Jerry, non-abstaining Irish-American liberal Democrat that he was, did not however look entirely happy.

"What's the matter?" asked Gene.

"Well, it's just that we haven't figured out how to get the beer cold," admitted Jerry even to a missionary.

Gene didn't hesitate for long. "Well, I suppose you could put them in my refrigerator."

Gene walked the twenty meters to the large round thatched hut that he used for his religious classes, and opened the door to reveal, of all unlikely things for Keniekenieko, a functioning kerosene refrigerator. Jerry's and my eyes bugged out. With as many liter-sized Masters Beer bottles stuffed into the little refrigerator as we could manage, life suddenly seemed devoid of major problems. Our opinion too of missionaries was much improved.

Logistically, we were set. The only problem was that our two-way radio refused to raise our Bamako office. Though we changed the position of the Land Cruiser and tried to transmit from hilltops, nothing worked. Once we thought we picked up someone trying to answer our call, but the signal was incomprehensible and we soon had to give up.

We now turned our attention to Amadou. Amadou proved to be a Bamako born-and-bred city person and none too comfortable about being in the deep bush of western Mali. But he dutifully unpacked our cooking gear and made arrangements to prepare meals, gathering wood and setting up a cooking area. I knew that many Malians were superstitious about spirits, especially at night, and would therefore feel very uneasy about sleeping in tents outside. Amadou confirmed this. No, sir, he absolutely did not want to sleep outside in any tent, he said, but since there really was no alternative, sleep in the tent he did.

Amadou seemed to be adjusting and feeling better about his new environment until I told him the story about our near encounter with lions in the area during our previous trip, which together with his worries about spirits, sent him into a near apoplectic fit. I imagine that Amadou hardly slept a wink the whole trip, but we couldn't do much about him except hope that his trauma subsided and didn't overly affect his cooking.

Jerry and I had briefed our Abidjan colleague, David, thoroughly on the road about the results of our last trip, so there remained only the task of planning the best means of covering the remaining villages. We would try to find and finish first the villages on our side of the river, and then figure how to get a vehicle across the Bafing west bank and cover the as yet unseen villages over there.

David, a PhD. anthropologist, was fascinated by the task at hand and eager to get to work. David and I shared one important trait: our lack of fluency in the local language rendered us dependent on Jerry as interviewer and translator, except for the few cases where we encountered village French speakers. Robert would be another help in the communication department too, though for now he seemed very much in awe of his new surroundings and the task at hand.

We got to work again surveying the remaining villages in the eastern, southeastern, and northeastern sectors, Robert and David quickly catching on to the routine. In turn we visited villages with names like Kollogo, Diba, Koba, Sitaninkoto, Sitafeto and so on. Most numbered several hundred inhabitants each and everyone was, as with the other villages visited, largely dependent on subsistence agriculture to live. The main crops grown were millet, sorghum, corn, beans, peanuts, and rice. As a sign of their isolation, not even Islam had penetrated these villages, most people continuing to be spirit-worshipping animists.

I had visited enough villagers by this time in my more than three years in Mali, to be able to discern the difference between a "good" or progressive village and the ones less progressive. Though this could be an entire anthropological study in itself, the progressive village — even in an isolated and poverty-stricken area — tended to look and feel differ-ent than its poorer-run counterpart.

The progressive village's chief tended to be more able and capable of mobilizing heads of family around certain important village issues, such as measures to improve water supply, health, rudimentary education and village sanitation, for examples, or mediate disputes, organize celebra-tions and festivals and so on. The village would normally be composed of compounds grouped in a circle around a common center, and overall seemed neater and more ordered.

The poorer-run village and its compounds would often appear to be arranged in no discernible order and poorly maintained. Far fewer deci-sions affecting village well-being were made by the chief, with a similar inattention to addressing such issues as clean water, sanitation, health, education and so forth.

I had the feeling that some of the poorer looking villagers were that way for reasons of health. A few villages seemed to have been decimated by onchocerciasis — river blindness — where a rite of passage into blind-ness at about the age of forty seemed the norm. Most of the older people in several villagers were blind after a lifetime of exposure to the disease, and sadly had to be guided by a young village boy.

The Manantali villages covered the normal gamut of excellent to poor-er villages with, in my view, most tending despite pervasive poverty and isolation toward the well-managed. While health problems struck me as the most severe in the zone, availability of water and sufficient and pro-ductive agricultural land were not serious problems among the Malinke to be relocated. I wondered if we would be able to assure equally pro-ductive land and sufficient water in the new villages.

Together, our little group was making progress surveying the villages to the east of the Bafing. We had effectively spread the news that relocation was necessary and had discovered — at least for the east-bank villagers — most knew where they preferred to move and with whom. Our preliminary work indicated that we could probably amalgamate thirty-five old smaller villages into eleven new larger villages, with the exception of the sorcerer village which was to be moved and left by itself. It was also emerging that villagers neither wanted to be moved into completely re-constructed villages financed by the project, nor paid to completely reconstruct villages all by themselves. A combination — some activities financed by the project and some carried out by villagers themselves (exactly what we'd define a bit later) — seemed to be the preferred modus operandi. This preference seemed reasonable to us, would probably prove cheaper than the project-financed alternative, and fit in with our view that resettlement had a better chance to succeed and be less disruptive over the long-term if villagers were intimately involved in decision-making as well as the physical process of the move.

We were all working with a purpose now and still fascinated with the challenge and uniqueness of the task at hand, as well as with the isolation and nether-worldness of the Manantali zone. Our two new Bamako-based drivers — Ali Badara had returned to Gao — had never been to the area before and seemed taken by its wildness. For several days as we swept through the east bank villages, we had fallen into a comfortable pattern: leave early from Kenkiekenieko, bounce and bang our ways to the day's villages, bang our way in the direction home, stopping alongside an empty millet field as the sun headed down.

Neither Jerry nor I were particularly dedicated hunters, but at this point we would pull our shotguns out from the rear of the Land Cruisers and go hunting for dinner — usually quail or wild guinea fowl. We were invariably successful, arriving back at camp to drop the birds off with Amadou to prepare while we headed for the river or the shower stall to swim or clean up slowly.

When choosing the river, care was to be used: hippos played and lurked nearby and it was important not to mistakenly invade the area of a baby hippo, as an enraged and protective mother could be extremely dangerous.

At Keniekenieko the river flowed at a slow, steady pace which we figured would minimize the chances of our contracting either schistosomiasis — which resulted in dangerous liver worms that entered the human body and bloodstream from still or stagnant water, or onchocerciasis — river blindness — which resulted from bites of a small black fly that bred in tree branches hanging over swift-running water. We were beginning to see more and more signs of river blindness in our villages, but we had been told this disease, however terrible, required longer-term exposure to contract.

We normally went ahead and plunged into the Bafing after the obligatory reconnaissance for hippos. From what basic medical knowledge we possessed about schistosomiasis and onchocerciasis, we felt that swimming in the river was a little risky but not so much as to not do it. Somehow our resolve to be careful about our own health and not swim in the Bafing faded away in direct proportion to the heat and the dust accumulated after a long day's work.

After the swim and changing clothes, Amadou would be just finishing preparing our dinner of pheasant over rice. With that and a cool beer from the missionary's refrigerator, we felt very pleased with ourselves and, for a little while at least, complete masters of our remote little corner of West Africa.

The day finally came to start work on the west bank of the Bafing. Jerry and David volunteered to make the trip in one Land Cruiser all the way back to Mahina-Bafoulabe, crossing the Bafing there using the railroad bridge, then snaking their way back down the west side track, ending up as close to Kenienkienko as they could manage. Leaving the camp at dawn, Jerry estimated that they would be back in camp perhaps by nightfall, assuming the unknown road was passable and the vehicle held together.

Around nine o'clock that night, I finally heard voices from the river below the camp. Jerry, David and the driver stumbled up the bank from the little pirogue that had ferried them back across the river. The Land Cruiser was somewhere off on the other side of the river where we would keep it as long as we worked the western zone. Jerry and David were exhausted and glad to be back, but the trip, while long and difficult, had gone well.

After our normal breakfast of strong instant Nescafe coffee from the Ivory Coast, supplemented with pre-sweetened canned milk and sections of the French-style baguette we had preserved as best we could wrapped in plastic, we made ready to depart. We set off by pirogue back across the river, taking a couple of trips to carry our group and some more of our gear. The vehicle was a ways back from the river, so we did like the folks in the old Tarzan movies: we hired a few bearers who carried our few boxes of equipment in authentic fashion — on their heads.

The western zone seemed just as remote as where we had come from, if not more so. Villagers in Bamafle, Samantoutou, Tima and Badioke listened intently as we explained the effects the filling of the reservoir would have on their lives and opined in much the same fashion as their Malinke brethren on the other side of the Bafing.

We continued to press the subject of how villagers wished to be reestablished in the new amalgamated village sites, though we knew that simply providing cash compensation to villagers to move and rebuild new villages in a new site by a certain date would be the simplest and cheapest alternative. But this method had been used in some Selingue villages a couple of years previously — due to lack of time to use an alternative means — and it had failed. The money provided was general-ly spent on things other than reestablishing households and fields.

So far, only one Manantali village had expressed its desire for the whole compensation option. The village chief in Bamafle was representa-tive of all the other villages: he said, "If you just give us the money, we'll spend it and there will soon be nothing left to use to rebuild." And then we appear on *"60 Minutes"* to explain a disaster, I thought.

Wisely, I thought, the villagers almost universally saw the need to be involved in the construction of their new villages, being provided some building materials where that was appropriate for villagers to do part of the labor themselves, and being assisted in moving cattle and belong-ings, digging new wells, clearing new fields and so forth where it was not reasonable to expect the villagers to do it themselves. This option seemed best to preserve our strategy for maximizing villager participa-tion in resettlement while assuring that a not unreasonable amount of physical labor on their part would be required.

We also continued to seek ideas about the composition of the new amalgamated villages, but a couple of village chiefs had started to voice objections to such a plan: there would be increased distances from home to their new fields and there would be a loss of the old village's historical identity. We began to suspect too that the chiefs had realized that bigger village units meant that they would not be exercising the same kind of political influence when previously autonomous communities were joined. We hadn't thought about this before and didn't know how it would play out. After all, funds were limited and it would cost far more to resettle all the existing individual villages and hamlets separately. We would have to worry about this one later.

Also, though the selected resettlement zones did not seem to be dense-ly populated, it was unlikely that they were totally devoid of people which meant that there had to be future consultations and planning with the people already living in the new sites.

Thoughts were beginning to coalesce in our heads about how to implement resettlement, though we were still a ways from deciding for sure. It seemed that the project should contract for clearing new village sites and fields; improving access tracks to the new sites; digging wells; providing warehouses for project materials; and transporting people and their possessions to the new villages. Also, food would have to be pro-vided from somewhere while agriculture production was reestablished in the new sites, and homes and offices would have to be provided for project staff, both Malian and expatriates. It seemed sensible that villagers in turn would be provided materials to build granaries, com-pound walls, garden fences, corrals, chicken coops, latrines and the like, but the villagers would do the actual building. Also, while fields would be cleared of brush and non-productive trees, the farmers would be expected to plant their new fields themselves in traditional ways.

Coming back to camp at Keniekienko was the Tarzan movie in reverse — bearers carrying our gear atop their heads from the Land Cruiser, through head-high dry brush, and down to the waiting pirogues for the trip across the river. Jerry and I stood behind the rest of the group with shotguns again unsheathed, looking for quail which we were generally lucky enough to find. Little village boys competed to extract the birds from the heavy brush, for which we gladly paid them.

Our Malian colleague, Robert, who had been an enthusiastic participant in the field work so far, still seemed a bit awed by the whole scene. I assumed this was partly because of the complexity of the task at hand, the new and strange part of the country he was seeing for the first time, and the odd ways of his American colleagues whose fate now seemed interlocked with his.

We had been in the Manantali zone for another two weeks now, and had succeeded in surveying all the major villages of the zones and a few of the smaller hamlets. We had filled a couple of large notebooks with information that we would take back to Bamako and try to make sense of and come with at least a preliminary planning document.

We had been completely out of touch with Bamako or otherwise outside civilization, with the exception of the BBC news that I tried to pick up on my little short-wave radio early every morning. The two-way radio in one of the Land Cruisers still refused to raise the home office. We were also again low on food and supplies and had just enough gasoline in our spare jerry cans to get us home. Jerry and I both had toddler daughters that we hadn't seen in far too long. It was time to leave.

Jerry and I stayed back in camp for a few hours to begin to write up our notes while one of the drivers plus Robert and the hardy David drove back north along the west bank track to Mahina-Bafoulbe and once again across the railroad bridge. We then broke camp, said farewell to Gene and the folks at Keniekenieko, and headed back up the other slightly better and faster track, meeting up with the other vehicle in late afternoon in Bafoulable.

Back in Bamako, we reported straight back to David Wilson and then, accompanied by Robert, to Sacko at the Hydrological Service. Jerry and I explained to him the results of our now completed first stage survey of the zone and presented our preliminary thoughts on how we and the Malian Government should organize and ultimately implement resettlement. Robert kept quiet during the meeting with Sacko and it struck me that he seemed quite intimidated by him.

On the home front, Joy and Allison were thriving as we entered our fourth Malian hot season. Joy had stopped her executive office work before returning home for the baby's birth, but now that Allison was no longer breast-feeding and we had help from Badji, Joy went back to work part-time for a U.S. consulting firm that was implementing our on-going livestock project. She had survived her seventh bout with intestinal amoeba — even with all my bush travel I had yet to have a single amoeba problem — and was in overall good health and good spirits.

By this time, our friends Chris and Elizabeth had departed Mali to work in Uganda still with CARE, but Pat, Africa's best softball fast pitcher, was still around and had married his Arizona girlfriend Roberta to boot. Roberta moved to Mali bearing a good attitude, a sense of humor, and more than a few recipes for Tex-Mex cuisine — the latter ensuring her popularity among Sahel-bound expatriates. Of course Jerry and Barbara were still around, as were Mickey and Ellie. Joy and I were very happy to note that Mickey seemed much more at ease and content in his role as husband and father. Their daughter Roya was a dark haired little beauty and Allison's favorite playmate.

The credit program Mickey was managing for *Operation Haute Vallee* still was problematic, he describing in greater detail than ever the resistance he was encountering from the *Operation's* Malian director. Mickey's U.S. visa problem had not improved, however, and while certainly not forgotten, he seemed more relaxed about it at least for the moment. The change in Mickey's personal life however was palatable, and a relief to his friends who had worried about him.

Mickey's older brother, Firouz, a former Iranian high government official under the Shah and presently working for an American consulting firm, came to visit Mickey and Ellie. Firouz was followed by Mickey's parents who had arrived from their exile residence in Geneva. Mickey's father, the former Ambassador, looked miserable in his proper dress in Bamako's heat, but seemed content enough to be reunited with the family. All this seemed to combine to infinitely lift Mickey's spirits.

I was in for a small surprise at work: Jerry was named to finish the redesign of the livestock project since Bob was still on medical evacuation in the U.S. With Jerry suddenly immersed on livestock, Manantali resettlement fell completely on me. My immediate task was to write a preliminary resettlement design document which would be submitted to our Washington office for review and approval. Washington didn't always require this kind of scrutiny, but given the sensitive nature of the project, they had opted to review even the preliminary document there.

I summarized as best in the document our ideas for proceeding to the next stage in designing the project, and described our findings to date: the lessons learned from earlier resettlement projects; what preliminary studies would be required to install new villages; how the Malian Government would participate in the process; how we viewed the role of villager participation in resettlement; possible implementation modes, and so forth.

I wrote the paper, submitted the document through David Wilson to Washington, and then jumped on a plane to return to Washington myself to defend the document in the sometimes collegial, sometimes inquisitorial process by which we approved major new projects.

This was my first time to defend any project back at the home office and I was determined to be thoroughly studied and prepared. Later I would figure out that it was usually difficult for a Washington-based panel to seriously second guess a well-prepared, field-based development person on a subject that few had had any direct exposure to, but I worked extra hard to be ready for any eventuality.

I was not prepared for the opening statement of the senior professional colleague who chaired the review meeting. "Now tell us," he addressed me, "why shouldn't we just give these people bus tickets to Dakar?"

The fact that our financing of the project was assured due to our previous international commitment lay heavy in the air.

Irrespective of the surprise beginning, the meeting went well and the document received the review panel's seal of approval, allowing us to proceed past the conceptual stage and on to the real design work where we would have to come up with detailed implementation plans and responses to our hundred unanswered questions.

Back in Bamako, Jerry was finally finishing the redesign of our livestock project, one that seemed complex to me, but one that Jerry and people in our agriculture office believed had good prospects for success. I hoped so for Bob's sake if nothing else. Bob's health had been temporarily broken by his obsession with the livestock project, I felt, though I was no doctor. What we heard from Bob, still in the U.S., was not good. He had serious stomach trouble it was reported, but all we knew for sure was that he would not be returning to Mali anytime soon.

It had become clear to us that while our own Manantali project would be able to finance the actual move and reinstallation of villagers in new sites and some related works such as improving tracks to the new village sites, field clearing, well digging and the like, we did not have sufficient funds to carry out a range of other related and essential support activities. These included detailed socioeconomic studies of the Manantali area, compiling inventories of physical structures to be rebuilt, updating census data, clearing new agricultural fields, providing food while agriculture was reestablished, and detailing the layouts of new villages. It had also become clear that the Government of Mali needed a far more formal involvement in the project than Robert Dembele's participation and reports back to his boss Sacko at *Hydraulique*.

While I had been in Washington, Jerry had been coordinating with a couple of other important donor organizations on these questions. Help and salvation came first in the form of the United Nations Development Program, the UNDP. The UNDP first thankfully agreed to finance a Resettlement Project Unit which would be attached to the Hydrological Service and would be the Government's main resettlement coordination and implementation arm. Robert Dembele would become the head of this unit.

The UNDP also came through with funds to finance soils and hydrological studies at the new potential village sites. The results of these studies would be crucial in determining the sites' suitability for occupation and agriculture. Finally, UNDP agreed to finance not only aerial photography of all existing villages so that spatial arrangements could be replicated if desired in the new locations, but also village level censuses of people and physical structures.

With this crucial support promised from the UNDP, Jerry and I proceeded to visit the Bamako offices of the World Food Program and the German aid program. The WFP was interested in providing food support until agricultural production could be reestablished at the new sites, which we estimated would be a contribution of over $5 million. The Germans were already planning to finance the deforestation or clearing of the new Manantali reservoir and responded positively to aiding resettlement by offering to finance some more Manantali area road improvement at the same time.

Though a good deal of the Manantali resettlement design was taking shape in our heads, it was clear that a number of technicians would be needed in a number of specialized fields: engineering, agronomy, forestry, anthropology, health, and economics. In line with the existence of the new Malian Resettlement Project Unit, we determined to have as many Malian experts participate in the design as possible, including our friend Robert Dembele as well as two of his new colleagues, Yacouba Konate, a rural sociologist, and Djibril Diallo, like Robert, a civil engineer. The rest would come from a variety of sources — some our U.S. colleagues in Mali and some from the U.S. and Europe. The rest of the design process, we estimated, would take another six months or so to complete.

The detailed work to come would be based upon the preliminary outline that we — primarily Jerry and myself — had already produced. The project would involve three stages: resettlement site selection; resettlement planning and coordination; and site survey, preparation, village reconstruction and population transfer.

New village site selections would be made based on various studies at the potential sites: soils, water, health, transport, land tenure, socioeconomic and so forth, some of which the UNDP was already getting underway in coordination with the Malian Resettlement Project Unit. Once the studies were done and the results in, consultations would be held with the resettling villagers to confirm or select alternative sites as appropriate, with special attention paid to people already living in the new resettlement zones.

The second stage would involve institutional planning and coordination between ourselves as primary resettlement financiers, the Government of Mali, and other international donors. There were several points here: to assure that the negative and positive lessons of Selingue resettlement were well-known and not forgotten during implementation, that proper planning was carried out, that the Malian Government's Resettlement Project Unit was well integrated with ourselves as well as other appropriate parts of the Government (the Ministries of Public Works and Public Health for example), and that mutually reinforcing coordination with donors of the type that was already paying off with the UNDP continued throughout the project. Also important was to maintain coordination with the OMVS in Dakar as Manantali resettlement was part of their overall Senegal River Basin Development scheme.

The final stage was to be the actual process of resettlement: censuses carried out of families, fields, buildings; surveys to lay out new villages and access roads; land clearing, road construction, well drilling, nursery establishment, training of villagers (for example in pump repair), construction of public infrastructure, construction of granaries and homes, field clearing; and finally population transfer to the new village sites along with all of their belongings and animals, provision of food, and provision of technical assistance in the reestablishment of agriculture, fruit trees and gardens in the new villages.

The more we studied and thought about resettlement, the more we realized how complicated it was. It was hard enough in other less complex projects to coordinate effectively with the host government and other donors. Could we maintain this coordination for the life of the project?

What would be the influences of actual dam construction on the affected villagers? Would more people move in and settle in the area attracted by construction jobs, further complicating resettlement? What would we do if there were serious water and land tenure problems in the new sites? Would resettlement or filling of the reservoir complicate the already serious health situation in the area? Would villagers really be willing to amalgamate into larger villager units and reconstruct some of their own homes and villages when the time came?

The list of questions and worries went on and on with Bill Cosby's faint voice in the background, "How long can you tread water?"

My next trip to Manantali came several months later, the interim time being filled with more work on the design as well as a number of other work obligations. The three OMVS Heads of State were to dedicate a plaque at the future site of the Manantali Dam, and as the "OMVS Coordinator" and to date co-designer of the resettlement project, it fell to me to represent my office at the ceremony. The Malian Government was arranging air transportation and I was told to be at the Bamako airport at 8:00 A.M.

To my shock and consternation, the transportation arranged was on a Mali Air Force paratrooper plane, one of the very few in their fleet, and like all but one of the Air Mali planes, an old Soviet-built relic.

With all of my near misses in the Mali airplane travel department, I wanted no part of flying on that plane. To do so violated what had become my Mali bush travel creed and modus operandi: if you can possibly drive there, do so. Even if it takes several days more to drive than to fly, drive. Don't fly. Life is already too short without the complications of air travel in the uncertain conditions of West Africa.

I admit that as a result of my various near aerial mishaps in Mali, I had developed a bit of a fear of flying unless the plane was a 747 or equivalent. I would not term this an irrational fear either — it was based on real, palpable experiences of Sahelian flying. But I was in a quandary — it was too late to drive again to Manantali and arrive within two days of the ceremony, and in my heart of hearts I really wanted to be there.

I had been breathing and living resettlement for the past six months and this ceremony meant that dam construction work was actually beginning, meaning our own efforts on resettlement were timely and more important than ever. So, together with various other donor representatives, press people, and Malian Government officials, I took courage, piled into the paratrooper plane, and belted myself onto the side bench where the paratroopers were supposed to go.

The flight to Manantali only lasted a bit more than fifty minutes but to me it seemed like hours. I wonder when this plane was last maintained, I asked myself, trying to appear nonchalant. The Malian Government minister sitting beside me must of thought me odd to be staring at my watch every other minute, but soon we were descending into the Manantali area and fortunately landed smoothly with no problem whatsoever.

We had landed north of Manantali village on a dirt strip that had not existed several months previously. Numerous four wheel drive vehicles — another novelty for Manantali — lined the airstrip to ferry passengers to the ceremony site, using to my amazement the newly constructed

Manantali access road. I had known the access road was being built now by the Germans, but I was not prepared for the abrupt change. Where very recently we had crawled and banged our way for hours on the merest of tracks toward Bafoulabe, there now stood a wide, smooth road that was the Malian equivalent of a high-speed interstate highway. Not satisfied to have just built one of the finest roads in the country, albeit still dirt, the Germans had added honest-to-God authentic autobahn road signs along the way, indicating not the exits for Munchen or Mannheim, but rather for Manantali and Bakouroufata. Mein Gott, I thought.

More planes were landing behind us, perhaps Moussa Traore himself, I thought. As we were ushered to the ceremony area, draped in the yellow, red and green Malian national colors and with the three countries' flags on prominent display, it was clear from the bustle of advance people that the arrival of important personages was imminent.

I looked at the large cloth covering the plaque that had been installed on the rock walls of the future dam site. This was the exact spot where Jerry, I and Ali Badara had stood months earlier in silence watching a lone bird float on the wind currents of the deserted site. It was deserted no more, and beyond the banners, Malian flags, and assembling people, stood vast bare tracts of freshly bulldozed reddish earth — part of the construction site as well as the new workers village.

Moussa Traore, President of Mali, arrived first in his makeshift motorcade, dressed in his flowing light blue 'grand boubou', decorated with elaborate gold and darker blue braid. A formal white fez was perched on his head and white pointed sandals were on his feet.

Next followed President Abdou Diouf of Senegal who looked distinguished and subdued. Diouf was an impressive six feet seven inches tall and dressed à la Nixon in dark suit and striped tie more suitable for Europe or Wall Street than the heat of Mali's First Region. Diouf's bodyguard intently surveyed the crowd behind dark glasses for signs of suspicious behavior.

The Mauritanian President came last, his lighter Moorish features and little beard standing out in the crowd of mostly black faces. I couldn't remember the Mauritanian President's name, but Mauritania had had several recent coup d'etats and it was a little hard to keep track.

The three presidents in turn made short speeches lauding this as a great and auspicious day in the lives of the three countries and the downstream agricultural development that the dam would permit. Traore mentioned in his speech that while 12,000 Malian villagers would be displaced from their homes, this sacrifice would be in the overall national interest and more than compensated by the economic benefits that the dam would bring. I guess I wasn't so sure about that yet, and such a statement would have rung truer to me if it had been made by one of the folks to be affected and not by a politician.

But move they would, and at least the villagers were not forgotten in the speeches. One large banner read "Manantali: Here begins the future." Another said "36 villages and 24 hamlets will sacrifice their ancestral lands for the common good."

Speeches were followed by the plaque's unveiling and organized presentations of dancing villagers. Soon, the three delegations roared toward the Manantali airstrip and took off once again for their respective capitals. My fellow comrades from the paratrooper plane and I were last to go, but go we did, and safely. I looked a little less at my watch on the return flight, with memories of a transformed and transforming Manantali running through my mind.

Arriving back home in Korofino at sunset, I noticed a new face where Yaya, the ever sleepy night guard, had been for so long.

Joy explained, "The office fired Yaya. One of the neighbors told me that he had been selling our diesel fuel right in front of the house. He was pumping it out of the barrel in the generator house into the containers that people would bring to him. Some nerve. Anyway, he's gone."

Well, that explains why we were going through the diesel so fast, despite having a relatively steady supply of electricity these days thanks to the Selingue Dam and therefore not having to use the generator all that much. I was disappointed with this turn of events since I had financed Yaya's latest marriage, a divorce, a new roof, cement for the walls of his house, a bicycle and money for all the major Moslem holidays, but such was life.

I saw him later at the office when he came to pick up his last bit of back pay.

"*Bonjour, patron, ca va?*" Hi, boss, how's everything?

Yaya smiled widely, waved enthusiastically and continued away for good on his still new bicycle.

9
The Bamako-Dakar Express

I needed to get out of Mali for a vacation. After three and a half years in Mali, our fourth hot season, and admittedly, the occasional frustration of trying to move development projects forward under the work conditions of the Sahel, Joy and I were feeling a bit beaten down and in need of relief. Though we had never made so many good expatriate and local friends in our lives and our daughter was healthy — and for that we were grateful — sometimes a radical change from the Sahelian scene was absolutely necessary to maintain sanity and motivation. This was one of those times.

My employer required us to spend several weeks in the U.S. every second year on "Home Leave" in order to become reacquainted with our own culture, undergo physical examinations, and — my personal theory — to spend all of your accumulated savings in one fell swoop, thus boosting your hometown's economy and obliging you to return overseas once more to work. Joy and I and Allison had completed our Home Leave in Texas the previous year, having a wonderful time and spending almost every cent of money we had been able to save.

On the odd year between "Home Leaves," we were permitted a Rest and Recuperation trip, which in the case of Mali provided us with round trip airfare to Paris. We could use or change the tickets for another destination if we preferred and if we were willing to pay any extra travel expense ourselves. We had been thrilled when we learned about R&R — what an advantage to be able to get out of the Sahel and have free transportation to visit another totally different country.

France sounded like a pretty acceptable destination to us. We made plans to begin our trip in Paris, go down by train to Lyon where I had gone to school ten years previously, and then travel through Provence to Nice, finally returning to Mali via Marseilles. We knew that traveling with a two year old wouldn't be easy, but we figured we would manage somehow.

In the meantime, Jerry and family had just returned from their own R&R in the U.S. While in Indiana, however, Jerry had been given some disturbing news by his university: there were to be no further extensions on his doctoral dissertation. He had ten months to finish writing it or there was to be no PhD. Jerry and Barbara had spent years working off and on on their research in and out of remote Malian villages, and it seemed inconceivable that the ultimate goal could now be at risk. Jerry had simply been sucked into working full time on development at the expenses of his original purpose, fortunately for me and my colleagues. Now Jerry saw no choice: he decided to concentrate on the dissertation full time for a month, then return to work while continuing to work on the dissertation at night and on weekends until it was finished and submitted.

I knew all this meant work would grind to a halt on our Manantali design for a while, but the UNDP was working away on the preliminary studies and the Malians were beginning to get organized in the Resettlement Planning Unit. We knew that for the moment anyway we still had time to plan properly, assemble a technical design team, produce the final design and begin implementation in time to avoid disaster — if nothing major went wrong. Joy and I therefore determined to have a good trip to France.

Our three weeks passed too quickly. The Latin Quarter of Paris and Lyon were as beautiful as I remembered. Our French doctor friend we had known in Bamako and his Norwegian wife now lived in Nice on the Riviera where he was a cardiologist. We explored the towns above Monte Carlo and near Nice with them and exalted in the beauty and quaintness of the little Cote d'Azur towns far off the tourist circuit. Our ex-neighbors from Korofina, Dan and Anne, now lived outside of a small, idyllic medieval Provence village north of Marseilles, where Dan worked for the U.S. Consulate. Surrounded by beauty of Provence and bathed in the light of Monet, Dan and I contemplated the deeper truth and sublime subtleties of the local wines and cheeses and caught up on old times.

Loaded down with camberbert, saucisson, and pâté, Joy, Allison and I caught the UTA flight in Marseille direct to Bamako. Allison had been a great traveler — hardly ever crying and fussing and taking plane and train travel completely in stride. She had been flying and otherwise traveling internationally since she had been born, was growing up in Mali and had been exposed to more experiences and places than most kids received in half a lifetime.

"Poor thing," said Joy, "she probably thinks this is a normal life." I was glad however that the firstborn seemed to be so much with the program.

As daylight faded and the plane approached the savannah part of Mali south of the desert and began its descent for landing, the outside air filled with angry black smoke. As was their custom, the farmers far below were burning the grasslands to clear fields for the coming planting season.

Back in the office, turmoil seemed to be the order of the day. Gail, my agriculture economist colleague from New York City, had become disillusioned with her work and her career choice and had resigned. She and her husband were gone for good and had returned home to New York.

Then my colleague Jon, who was still doing his best to manage a solar energy project, came to me with some even more disturbing news. Our slightly warped but lovable head engineer, George Thompson, had also decided to quit.

This was especially hard to fathom. While George never looked or dressed the part of your normal organizational man or typical engineer, he was a conscientious worker and by all accounts a very competent engineer. I also knew that he, more than any of our colleagues, loved Mali with all his heart. I suspected that part of the answer had to do with George's tendency toward alcohol, which unfortunately seemed to be getting worse. Beer was the drink of choice in Mali and I knew that George consumed far more than his share. I recalled leaving many a late-night party over the past three years with George totally plastered after downing far too many liter-sized Masters or Somalibo's. His drunken behavior in diving on top of the airplane in Alex's pool was not the only example of his problem.

I ran into Jon, one of George's closest friends, in the office courtyard and he explained to me as best he could. Jon and I had become friends slowly over the past couple of years and his girl friend Oumou was about the most impressive Malian woman I had met and certainly one of my favorites.

"It was the alcohol," Jon explained. "George got really out of control and it was like there was another person talking. He actually did submit his resignation. I couldn't believe it when he told me."

I asked Jon what he planned to do.

"I already did it while you were on R&R", replied Jon. "I went straight to David Wilson and he was great. He said there was no way we were going to let George down when he needed us the most, and that he didn't believe for one second either that George really wanted to quit his job."

Jon went on. "The home office in Washington has some arrangement with an institution evidently called 'The Farm' in West Virginia, I think, to treat people who can't deal with alcohol. They work with acute alcoholics and try to rehabilitate them so they can return to work and function."

"David already sent an immediate cable to Washington about George and they said they could get him admitted to the treatment facility. Wilson is a real hero."

"But," I asked Jon, "how can they admit an employee who just quit? George wrote a resignation letter."

"Dave Wilson dealt with that too," said Jon. "He told Washington the truth. He said that George was so whacked out on alcohol when he wrote it that his resignation should be disregarded. George is on board with the whole plan and will write another letter explaining that he was sick when he wrote the first one and didn't mean to resign."

This news had been a shock and I looked forward to talking first-hand to George. Jerry was in the office working on his dissertation, writing in his flowing longhand on page after page of yellow legal pad paper. We were glad to see each other but since I couldn't remember ever seeing him looking so harassed, I soon left and let him get back to work.

But then I discovered the worst news of all from my friend, Tom, still the head of our health programs: the wife of a colleague had actually committed suicide while we were gone. Peter was an Austrian-born physician who worked as a regional health advisor, and while he was not a close personal friend, I knew his professional reputation to be impeccable. His wife, whom I had met at several parties but did not know well, had evidently been in a deep depression and, unbelievably to me, had killed herself at home one afternoon while Peter and their son were out.

It was hard to blame such problems as alcohol abuse and depression on life in Mali, but the difficulties of living and working there could wear one down. Everyone handled it differently though, and I suppose no one should have been surprised that for a few people there was evidently an unshakable dark undercurrent to their lives. Kent's replacement, for example, had lasted just a few months in Mali, himself succumbing to severe alcohol abuse and soon being permanently evacuated back to the U.S. never to return.

Joy and I were perhaps too young and inexperienced to judge the depth or even the source of discontent among the expatriates in Mali, but felt glad that we had fallen in with a pretty happy and positive crowd that, all in all, still liked being where we were and appreciated the good side of life in Mali while not naively refusing to acknowledge the bad.

I went to see David Wilson in his big upstairs corner office and thanked him for what he had done for George. Welcoming me back and as humble as always, David simply replied that George would be departing soon for "The Farm" in the U.S. on a medical evacuation but that we expected him back eventually. While in work matters, David, despite his intelligence and interest in development, was not a desk banger or my vision of the world's most passionate development visionary. In his response and help for George, though, he had shown the stuff he was really made of.

"I'm glad you're back," said David. "The OMVS people in Dakar have suddenly become more interested in the Manantali resettlement project and want to hear from you how we plan to proceed with the detailed design. There will be a lot of talk about the big OMVS integrated development project the Dakar office is still working on and about other river basin development issues in general."

"We need to leave next Monday," he concluded. "I'm going too, so remember to bring along your racket."

Once more I packed for Dakar, a city that after all my travel there and my good memories of WAIST, was becoming like my second Sahelian home. David had already had reservations made for us both on the next day's Air Afrique flight, so after working a half day we picked up our tickets and headed out from the office through Badalabougou and out once again to the airport.

There was a large crowd of Europeans and Africans pushing and shoving in front of the Air Afrique counter, which wasn't unusual in itself, but this crowd looked a little more exercised than usual. After about thirty minutes or so of waiting, David and I finally made it to the counter, even though people behind us continued to push and put their own tickets down on the counter in front of us. The Malian Air Afrique agent calmly gave us our boarding passes and we headed from the departure area.

In the meantime our flight had arrived from Ouagadougou — a very promising event and one never taken for granted in West Africa — and I knew it shouldn't be too long before we boarded. I had noticed that once again there was no assigned seating on the flight — which meant that it would be a mad rush from the departure lounge out to the plane, the early arrivals on the plane much more assured of a seat than the stragglers. The reason for this state of affairs was that the normal practice of the airline was not to provide assigned seating on most flights, except those going to France. And for the inter-African flights, since the practice was to sell more tickets than there were available seats on the plane, it was every man and woman for themselves in a mad scramble across the tarmac to assure oneself a place onboard. The slow and the indifferent were often left behind.

This was about my least favorite thing about African travel: I just couldn't easily overcome my childhood training that one waited in lines in a civilized fashion and that it was tacky to push and shove anyone aside for a seat on an airplane. For that reason, while I often found myself near the front of the crowd waiting to leave the departure lounge, somehow by the time I reached the stairs leading up into the plane I was either the last or nearly the last to actually board, having been elbowed aside by everyone from government ministers to little old African grandmothers.

But this flight proved different. A group of about thirty Malians, mostly men, dressed in very traditional boubous and other garb, were escorted right by our group in the departure lounge and right onto the plane. Now this was out of the ordinary. What was going on?

Someone from Air Afrique stood off to one side of the lounge and he was immediately surrounded by a group of excited people — all waving their tickets and boarding passes in front of the poor guy. I wasn't close enough to the airline agent to hear what he told the group, but it obviously wasn't good news because there were now angry shouts rising from the group.

"This is unbelievable," shouted one man in French.

"It is totally *'insupportable'*," unacceptable, screamed one Frenchwoman.

This woman, obviously not a resident of West Africa, was clearly more outraged than anyone and seemed determined to lead a passenger rebellion against the Malian airport authorities.

David and I were as usual in the back of the crowd but as the vocal Frenchwoman swept my way, I asked her what was going on.

"It is *insupportable*," she said again. "Air Afrique has moved thirty religious pilgrims on their way to Mecca on the plane in our place. They don't have boarding passes! They don't even have tickets! Somebody just decided to put them on the plane in our place. There's no more room for us."

The Frenchwoman continued, "We must all go out on the tarmac and link arms in front of the plane. We have to demand that our seats be returned. We cannot accept this!"

I looked at David and David back at me. We'd both been in West Africa long enough to know about WAWA and that this sort of thing, however frustrating, happened with great regularity. If you got too upset when it did, you would only be making the problem worse not better. There was no way we were going to participate in any passenger rebellion like the one proposed. Good Lord, that woman could disappear in an African jail if she tried that, further complicating her leaving. Her's was a very bad idea.

No sir, there was a better way to handle this. We proceeded out the departure lounge to the now empty ticket counter where we eventually found someone from Air Afrique to talk to. She matter of factly and with no apology confirmed the facts in the case — and the fact that someone among the pilgrims had connections with the Minister of Transport. The pilgrims were going instead of us and that was all there was to it. The agent also said that he would switch our reservations to another Dakar flight the next day, so David and I found one of the beat-up taxis that hung out in front of the airport and we went home to await the next flight. This was the sensible African way of handling such matters and was much easier on the nervous system.

The next morning we were back at the airport and departed without further incident. The Frenchwoman from the day before was nowhere in sight and I wondered what had happened to her and the others. In an hour or so we were descending to land in Dakar, the DC-9 turning out over the Atlantic before turning for its final approach and landing at Yoff airport.

The meetings on the OMVS-related projects were intended to update everyone on what had been accomplished in terms of implementation and project design since the meeting the previous March. Whereas no one had much talked about or even enquired about Manantali resettlement during the prior meeting, we were now much more integrated into the program. The social scientists participating in the design of the huge OMVS Senegal River integrated development project seemed particularly curious as to how the design was proceeding and how we would structure implementation and monitor results. I made a presentation to the group about Jerry's and my work to date and described how I thought the Manantali project design would eventually turn out.

On the integrated development project itself, the huge number of people working on the design seemed to be all over the map, literally and conceptually. There seemed to have been little consensus achieved since the last review meeting, and though the team seemed dedicated and well-qualified, I wondered how long the process could go on like this. These experts cost a lot of money to employ, and with a back-of-the-envelope calculation I estimated that well over a half of a million dollars had already been spent just on the design — all for an uncertain result and a product that was not nearly achieved.

Vito, the coordinator for all the Dakar-based OMVS activities, seemed frustrated by the process. Vito was smart enough to understand that sufficient research and design time could pay benefits in the long run, but practical enough to realize that a implementable design had to be produced before too much longer.

Part of the pressure on Vito came from his boss, David Shear, the architect of the first Sahelian drought relief program I had worked on back in Washington and still the head of our Dakar office. Shear was determined that our integrated development project be the centerpiece of a large, multi-donor effort that would support the dam-based OMVS development scheme, the first part of which was already being implemented through the construction of the Manantali and Diama dams. Shear anticipated that a billion dollars or more could be invested in irrigation and other development infrastructure in the river basin based on the model of our project — there was a lot of Saudi, Kuwaiti, and Gulf

Arab donor money then — so he was determined that our project be designed correctly. In any event, I empathized with Vito and thought he had his head screwed on straight. We had several good conversations.

Three days into our stay in Dakar, Vito asked me to come to his office above Dakar's centrally located Independence Square. He wanted to talk to me about something important, he said.

Vito got right to the point. How would I like to move to Dakar to work for him and manage a large river basin project? The project he had in mind had nothing to do with the OMVS, he said, but rather another large river basin to the south of us — the Gambia River Basin, which Vito explained included eastern Senegal, part of Guinea, and the entire country of the Gambia. Another team, much smaller than the OMVS one, had earlier worked on the design down in the Gambia and was now getting final approval of the project back in Washington. It would be ready to start implementation in another month or so. Think about it, talk to David Wilson and let me know soon, said Vito.

I headed out of Vito's office and headed up Avenue Ponty in a daze. I would love to move to Dakar and head up a big river basin project of my own. Workwise, it would complement and broaden the experience I had received in Mali and make me a better development professional. Life in Dakar for the family would be far less harsh than Mali, and we would have the ocean — something I loved and missed very much about land-locked Mali. Also, I knew a number of American colleagues who felt as warmly about Senegal and the Senegalese as we now felt about Mali.

On the other hand, I still had a lot of work to do in Mali and felt committed to finish the work on Manantali resettlement. Also, our best friends in Mali — Mickey and Ellie, Barbara and Jerry, Pat and Roberta — were still there, and though it was difficult to explain, I knew there would be a special bond with these people for the rest of our lives.

I pondered my options. I knew that David Wilson would not want me to leave Mali even though I suspected he would eventually go along with whatever I really wanted to do. I also knew that moving on was an unavoidable part of living and working on development in a foreign country — and as much as we liked and loved Mali, we could move on either now or be required to move not long from now. Except for people like George Thompson who could somehow pull every conceivable trick to stay in Mali forever, four years was the normal limit of one's assignment, and four years for Joy and me was only about six months away.

If I had to leave Mali anyway, it probably made sense to go to a guaranteed good situation, and this seemed like a good situation. The work on Manantali had made me really feel, more than before, that I had something meaningful to contribute to development, and this new job offer would let me continue to be around similar work with some of the same issues as Manantali.

Though I wouldn't be around to finish work on Manantali, Jerry would still be there and he certainly would assure better than anyone that Manantali turned our right. Besides, as part of an office that worked exclusively on river basin development one country over from Mali, perhaps I could return to help Jerry finish the Manantali design.

I finally decided that the pluses far outweighed the minuses. I knew that Joy would go along with the move as she and I had already discussed Dakar as a possible next assignment, though Dakar then was such an attractive destination for development professionals in West Africa, we had hardly dared to hope that a job there would ever come through.

David Wilson and I were supposed to meet for lunch that day and I decided to ask his blessing for the move. Over Lebanese food, I told David about the job offer and told him that, considering everything, I thought I wanted to accept. After a few more sentences, I decided to say no more and wait for David's reaction.

David didn't look at all pleased and I could tell that he was taken aback by my question. He finally responded.

"Well, it's probably the best thing for your career," he said. "I'll never stop anyone from making a move that they really think is in their best interest, even though I think that Mali is a much better place to work."

I knew that David was probably wondering how he would replace me. Though certainly no one was irreplaceable, it was still very hard to find qualified French-speakers to live and work in Mali.

It wasn't exactly a ringing endorsement, but at least David really wanted me to stay in Mali — and that was better I supposed than enthusiastically welcoming my departure.

We played tennis that night at our hotel's lit court and David and his wicked spin serve polished me off good — not an entirely new experience by this time in our sporting relationship. At the hotel bar afterwards over a couple of beers — I had learned to never try to keep up with David Wilson in the alcohol consumption department — we talked more about the move.

"It's OK. You should take the job here," he conceded as he poured the remainder of his Flag beer into his glass.

"I meant what I said about Mali being a better place to work, but your assignment will be up and you'll have to leave soon anyway. Better to have a good position like the one they offered you to move into."

I gave Vito the news the next day and he seemed pleased. Though he was non-committal about my expressed desire to return to Mali to work on Manantali resettlement, I think he was pleased that I cared enough to want to continue to work on it despite what would be new, demanding responsibilities.

Meetings and discussions over, David and I returned to Bamako. The rainy season should have been well underway by this time and though I understood that the Dogons had already planted their millet up in the Mopti Region, not much rain had fallen. I fervently hoped that still another drought year would not be visited on the poor Malian farmers.

Joy took the news as I knew she would — happy about a good new city and country and more enthusiastic about her own professional prospects in Senegal — but very sad and pensive about leaving our present life and friends behind and bothered by all the uncertainties associated with a move and a new country. But she was clear headed enough to know that our time in any one place was always fleeting — and one could not sacrifice the inevitable future for a present that would soon end anyway.

David, Vito and I had agreed that I should arrive in the new job in two weeks time. This was very little time to prepare to move and then actually leave, but to me it seemed the best thing. The thought of having, say, several months to prepare to move and go through that long a period of saying farewell to friends and colleagues held no attraction to me. I would rather pack and make our good-byes rapidly and be gone rather than agonize over it for months. The latter was the pattern we had already seen so many other expatriates go through in Mali.

I planned to return to Mali someday, was determined to be involved in the Manantali project, and after all was only moving to next door Senegal. So despite the coming move I refused to disassociate myself mentally from Mali. This attitude was belied by the fact that we were now planning for packers to come, deciding how to ship Jenny the dog to Dakar, deciding how and when to break the news to Badji, and starting to say farewell to long time friends.

The Malians had seen expatriates come and go so many times before, but Joy and I were touched by the warmth and sincerity of our Malian friends and colleagues at the farewell party my office had arranged. Many of them had touched our lives over the past three and a half years, and saying good-bye was hard. Boubacar N'Dao made a speech on behalf of the Malian colleagues, followed by Jerry who said good-bye on behalf on the Americans. The office drivers all came up to shake my hand and wish me good luck. I had earlier made my sad farewells to Robert Dembele and several other Malian government employees with whom I had worked, some also for over three years.

It was going to be tough to say good-bye to Badji and I was glad that Joy would stay in Bamako a few days longer than I and would make the penultimate break with Badji herself. Joy and I had decided however to give her enough money upon our departure to permit Badji to make a major payment on the plot of land she was still trying to purchase outside of Bamako, enough that would finally permit construction of her new modest compound to begin. Badji was totally overwhelmed by the gift.

At another huge farewell party at Jerry's house, we said goodbye to all our expatriate friends. This was harder on Joy than me, because I had become convinced that in the relatively small fraternity of aid workers, paths tended to recross with great frequency. I knew I would probably work with at least Pat and Jerry again, and probably many others, it was just a question of timing and location.

With Mickey and Ellie it was a bit different and their visa problem had still not been solved. Mickey's father, the ex-Ambassador, had recently died in Switzerland and I had personally gone to the Swiss Embassy in Dakar during my last trip to persuade the Swiss diplomats to grant Mickey a visa to attend his father's funeral. I had succeeded with the Swiss that time, but now Mickey was trying to obtain still another Swiss visa to permit him a short visit to comfort his mother, now living alone in Geneva.

Though all was still not well with his credit program and his family's exile in Mali continued to weigh heavily on him, he forgot his troubles at least for the evening and we bid each other farewell. Mickey and Ellie had become very special friends with whom we would somehow maintain contact.

In order to depart Mali, Joy and Allison made the traditional plans to fly out on Air Afrique directly to Dakar with our dog in a portable cage, checked with our suitcases in the baggage compartment.

I however chose another route. I had heard about a few people who had made the trip to Dakar on a freight train while seated in their car. The car would be cabled fast onto a railroad flatcar and it was not unknown for an occasional adventurous owner to decide to go along.

This was how I decided to depart Mali. It was different and it would surely be a memorable trip. I could avoid having to sell my Peugeot 504 that I had purchased from a departing French policeman about a year before, and that I wanted to keep.

I would stock the car with enough provisions, especially water, and sit in the car for the estimated day and a half that would take the freight train to make its way through Mali and into Senegal. I was told that the paved road in Senegal began in the eastern Senegalese town of Tambacounda where I could be cut off the flatcar and continue by highway the rest of the way into Dakar. No sweat.

I looked forward to the adventure, but a few skeptics raised their voices in warning. "Don't do it," one said. "Freight train cars are sometimes unhitched for no apparent reason and pushed off to a siding for days or weeks at a time. If this happens, you could be in real trouble."

Part of the justification for riding in the car was to protect it. Lone cars shipped on flatbeds often arrived at their destinations without the benefit of tires, spares, major engine parts, fan belts, windshield wipers and the like. Physical presence in the car through the wilds of Africa, I was told, deterred such theft. Mostly it sounded like a great adventure and a chance not to be missed.

Joy was happy we would have a car immediately in Senegal but was worried too that I could be pushed off to some siding and never be seen again, or something else even worse could go wrong as was known to happen in West Africa.

"You better get down to the station and supervise the loading of the car on the flatcar," she said, "otherwise you could end up riding backwards all the way to Tambacounda."

Facing backwards towards Mali for the entire trip, however poetically fitting, would probably make me crazy but I decided to tempt fate and let the authorities deal with the positioning of the car without me.

But first I packed the car. Ice cooler with a bunch of juice, water and surely more than enough beers to last the entire trip was placed on the floor of the back seat within easy reach of the driver. Stereo and speakers, a few clothes, baby accoutrements, and a couple of other boxes of items Joy decided we would need in Dakar immediately upon arrival went into the trunk. A few favorite cassette tapes went in the front seat for playing during the trip, along beside my portable short-wave radio so I could listen to the BBC news and maybe Armed Forces Radio. A few more boxes went onto the back seat. Finally, I filled the Peugeot with gas and as a last touch recommended by more than a few friends, put my unloaded shotgun under the front seat. I was ready to go.

My office had made travel arrangements for my family and took care of the required paperwork that would permit the car to be placed on the freight train and shipped into Senegal. They paid the transport price for shipping the car and even paid a small additional fee that permitted me to sit in the car. I delivered the packed car to the office and it soon disappeared to be loaded onto the waiting flatcar.

I was to leave Bamako for good on Thursday afternoon. After riding the freight train all night, I should arrive the next afternoon or early evening at the border, and then arrive early Saturday morning in Tambacounda. If nothing went wrong, I would leave the train in Tambacounda and proceed for another six hours by modern paved road to Dakar. My new Dakar office had cabled that keys for my new house could be picked up from my Indiana friend Ben, at whose house I had spent much time and who would be our new neighbor. Joy, Allison and Jenny the dog would arrive on Monday from Bamako on the Air Afrique flight. I would pick them up in our own car and drive to our new home. It sounded organized and pretty straightforward.

After a temporary farewell to Joy and Allison, Pat and Roberta drove me to the quiet and deserted Bamako train station. I said my last good-bye to them and walked through the little station to the tracks. On a flatbed car near the end of the waiting freight train sat my white Peugeot — pointed due west toward Senegal and not east as Joy had feared. I would not be facing backwards the whole trip after all.

Climbing into the car alone in the silent station, the finality of departing Mali finally hit me. I was really leaving, and if not for good, nearly for good.

For the last three and half years in Mali, I had had the most continually profound experience of my life. I had arrived with a new wife and little else. I hadn't even had any expectations because I had known so little about what lay ahead. I had arrived knowing next to nothing about development, and now departed far more experienced — not wise but wiser — and more convinced that I may have had something to contribute to this business after all.

On a personal level, I was also departing with a new daughter, the same wife I had arrived with, and a group of profound friends with whom we had deeply experienced the frustrations, the happiness, the humanity, and all the accompanying lessons of the real West Africa.

It was a little past the train's planned departure time and soon there was a bustle of activity from the railroad workers and my departure looked imminent. To my surprise, two European men emerged from somewhere and got into the small burgundy Suzuki four wheel drive vehicle that was strapped in front of my Peugeot on my same flatbed. I would have company after all.

The train pulled out slowly from the station, gaining speed as it passed near the French Tennis Club, some old Malian Soudanese-style government buildings with their big mango trees, out past the neighborhood near Mickey and Ellie's house, and out of town past the Lido and its nice swimming pool. We were moving faster than I had thought and the dusty compounds of western Bamako soon faded to bush, occasionally interspersed by an isolated hamlet or little group of compounds off in the distance.

We kept moving at a good clip, and despite the stories about being stranded on a side track for days at a time, the train fortunately seemed inclined to keep moving. I opened a Masters beer from the cooler, and relaxed, helpless in the face of African fate, but trusting that somehow I would eventually make it to far-off Dakar and that my family would soon be there too.

The sun went down in my face and the breeze kept me cool. I tried to find the BBC on the radio but I was surrounded by too much metal for the reception to be any good, and figured I'd try again when and if the train stopped. As it got dark, my original plans to stay awake a little longer faded away. I declined the seat of the 504 to an almost prone position and slept soundly. I awoke once in the middle of the night to the sound of voices to realize that we had stopped — in Bafoulabe, I guessed, because it seemed to be a good-sized town — but before an hour or so had passed we were underway again.

So far, better than expected. I had even slept pretty well and the nighttime temperature had been pleasant. I awoke at dawn due to excitement as much as due to the increasing sunlight and poured myself some coffee from a thermos that Joy had provided me for the trip. I had the Bamako equivalent of a croissant to eat — decent but nothing like we had recently consumed with great frequency in France. The two human figures in the burgundy Suzuki in front of me stirred and stretched.

The temperature was rising and I hoped the train wouldn't be stopping long, as I knew I would roast in the heat. About ten thirty in the morning we pulled into Kayes and shuddered to a halt. I quickly realized that the heat was not to be avoided. We were in Kayes, supposedly the hottest continually inhabited city on earth, in the latter part of the hottest part of the year. The temperature in the car grew hotter and hotter.

There was a fair amount of activity in the Kayes railroad yard as cars were shifted and unhitched, then hitched. A group of little boys came by, staring at me, then moving on. When a railroad worked came by, I asked him, "Hey, do you know how much longer we'll be here or what time we'll be departing?"

I didn't want to abandon the car with all my possessions in it but if I knew I had a couple of hours to go, I'd lock the car, stretch my legs and get out of the sun. I knew that there was a "Hotel du Rail" in Kayes where I could perhaps even clean up a bit and wait it out in relative comfort.

But no, the railroad guy replied, "We're leaving *'toute de suite'*." Right away! *"Toute de suite!"*, he reiterated for emphasis.

I had been around Africa long enough to know that local measures of time and distance didn't necessarily conform to the toubob model. I had once been hiking in the bush with a Malian guide trying to find a village in the Dogon region.

"How far is it?" I had asked him.

"Not far, just over there," he had replied. Two hours and about ten similar questions later we had still not arrived in the village and the answer from the guide was still the same: "Not far, just over there." I recall we arrived after still a couple more hours hiking — definitely not my interpretation of "Not far, just over there."

I figured that there could be a similar phenomena at work here with *toute de suite,* but one could never be sure and I figured it wasn't worth the risk of watching one's car disappear over the horizon toward Senegal with no way to catch up. No, better to sit tight and hope that *toute de suite* meant *toute de suite.*

It didn't. By noon, I estimated the outside temperature in the Kayes railroad yard to be at least 115 degrees and probably hotter. I was dressed appropriately in T-shirt and shorts, but I was beginning to feel very dehydrated and a bit debilitated by the heat. I began to down my water in big gulps and was glad I had brought a sufficient supply. I even started the engine and flipped on the air conditioner for a minute, but the Peugeot 504's air conditioner only pumped out cool air when the car was moving, so I quickly dropped that idea and turned off the motor. Besides, I felt a bit ridiculous sitting in my car strapped to a flatcar with my engine running.

The group of little boys passed by the car again and this time asked if they could bring me anything. I was still set with food and water but the ice in my cooler had long since melted away. In two minutes two of the boys were back with several small blocks of ice in plastic bags for which I paid ten Malian Francs per bag. I held one to my brow for a few minutes and threw the rest in the cooler.

I also finally met my traveling companions in the Suzuki — two older Frenchmen who were obviously no strangers to Africa, traveling from Niamey, the capital of Niger, to Dakar. They too had finally climbed out of their car and we stood talking on the flatcar. They also were afraid to leave the area because of the admonition about our *toute de suite* departure.

These fellows, Marcel and Yves, had originally meant to drive the entire distance from Niamey until having been informed in Bamako that past Kayes the road into Senegal was often impassable. They had finally decided that going by freight train from Bamako was their best option.

These guys, in their late fifties or early sixties, told me they had spent most of their lives in Africa and were not at all bothered by the wait in Kayes. Marcel, the more grizzled of the two, said that he had not even returned to France since the 1950s and furthermore, had no real desire to go. I assured him that I personally thought he was making a big mistake since I had just come from there myself barely a month ago and it had been pretty fantastic.

Marcel and Yves took turns recounting to me war stories of the Africa of the 1930s or 1940s — settling in Madagascar, living on the Ile de Maurice, traveling through the Congo. It was clear that they had basically seen it all in Africa over the years and were not about to be seriously bothered by the mere heat or inconvenience of a wait in Kayes.

Finally about three-thirty in the afternoon, the railroad workers began to shout and run about, followed soon after by the first lurch of the train as we finally moved forward once again. We gathered some speed and began to cross into the western reaches of Mali, at this point further west than I had previously traveled by in Mali by land. It also seemed to me, unfortunately, that the train was moving far slower than it had in leaving Bamako the previous afternoon.

The wait in Kayes had really drained my energy and I was feeling dizzy from the heat and not nearly as fresh as the day before. Also, adding a bit to my worries, the train stopped several times in the middle of nowhere for no discernible reason, and though it was never longer than fifteen minutes or so, I recalled the stories about being abandoned for days off on a siding.

By the time the afternoon heat had finally subsided and the sun gone almost completely down, the train had once again come to a full stop. I got out of the car and peered ahead from the side of the flatcar. A small group of buildings stood on either side of the tracks — the border I wondered? I also noticed that the entire train had pulled off on a siding from the main track.

What was going on now? It was almost dark when a Malian official wearing military-looking trousers but an Africa shirt open on the sides approached our flatcar.

I greeted him and then asked "What's going on?" Marcel and Yves were standing on the side of the railroad car listening intently for the answer.

"We're at the border with Senegal," he replied, "and we're waiting for another freight train to pass us before we can get underway again. It is a special freight train hauling materials for the Manantali Dam."

"Oh."

I knew that Manantali construction was going full bore now and that almost all of the construction materials were to be brought in by rail from Senegal.

The official didn't volunteer how long he thought we would have to wait and I didn't expect any more information from him at all. But the man, in his forties and obviously as weary and baked by the sun as the rest of us, seemed to take an interest in the three strangers perched in their cars at the end of his freight train.

"Are you tourists?" he asked.

Marcel relied that he and Yves were travelers to Dakar, and I suspected that anyone with as much African experience as they would certainly not want to be classified as mere tourists.

I also wanted to reply in kind to a friendly question and said, "No, I'm not a tourist. I'm leaving Mali after working there for over three and a half years. I'm on my way to my new job in Dakar."

The Malian official nodded. "I see. Well, in any event I'll need to see your passports and customs documents before you enter Senegal."

We hadn't realized that the man doubled as a Malian customs agent, but we dutifully pulled out all our documents for his inspection.

Marcel and Yves were first and the Malian railroad-customs man seemed satisfied with them after a close examination. I was last and handed over my passport which contained my Senegalese visa, as well as a pink sheet of paper with some official looking Malian stamps and signatures that the office had given after making all of my car's shipping arrangements with the Bamako railroad people.

The man looked at my documents carefully then back up at me.

"These are fine," he said, "but where is your *fiche de douane*?" Your customs certificate?

I felt a lump in my throat.

"It's this pink form with the stamps, isn't it? This is the only document I was given after my office made all the car arrangements."

"See," I said pointing to the paper, "the document says we paid 54,000 CFA for the cost of the transport all the way to Tambacounda."

I was pointing to the stamps and signatures on the pink form. I was also hoping that this would take care of it, but it didn't look good.

"No," he replied. "The pink form only indicates you've paid for shipping yourself and your car, but there's a separate customs form that gives you the right to exit Mali. This is missing."

"Oh, God," I thought to myself, "the office blew it this time. They didn't get all the documentation I needed. I could be completely and totally screwed."

Had I known another form was needed I certainly would have gotten it. I knew that it was not wise to shortchange African or any other bureaucracy when it came to such crucial matters as one's self preservation, but here I was cabled onto the train at the Senegalese border without the right customs form. I certainly couldn't contact Bamako to try to rectify things now.

"Listen," I said, "I didn't make the arrangements in Bamako myself and I'm very sorry I don't have the right form. Is there any way I can make the proper arrangements and get the right form here at the border?"

The Malian shook his head. "No, I'm sorry, this can only be done in Bamako. This is a serious matter. I cannot let you leave Mali without the form."

The man then gave me, Marcel and Yves reason for cardiac arrest and our worst nightmare was realized: he walked to the front of the flatcar in front of the Suzuki and uncoupled it from the rest of the train.

I was in shock but Marcel sputtered to life. "Now wait a minute," he semi-wailed, "you can't stop us from leaving Mali. Our papers are fine. We can't be abandoned here because his papers are out of order".

He was pointing in my direction.

Marcel was losing some of his cool and I could tell that the little Franco-American rapport we had established was floundering on the rocks of my having no customs document. Yves at least kept quiet though I could tell that he too was plenty worried.

This had gone far past serious and I was very shaken. This Malian official seemed bound and determined to respect all the rules, as I supposed he should. If I didn't have the correct form, it certainly wasn't the fault of the customs man. The fact that it wasn't particularly my fault either didn't help me much. And I didn't really blame Marcel in the slightest for trying to save his own neck.

I turned to the Malian customs man.

"Look," I said, "I accept full responsibility for not having the right form but we just can't be cut off from the train and left here. Tell me, how can we get this straightened out so we can go on?"

The Malian looked contemplative and shook his head once more.

"You will have to wait here until we send to Bamako for instructions. We should be able to cable our headquarters tomorrow in the morning. When they reply we'll know better what to do."

He went on. "You may have to leave your car here while you go back to Bamako on the passenger train to get the form, and then return to pick up your car on a later freight train."

This was getting worse, much worse, and I could see Marcel and Yves preparing to enter an altered state of consciousness. There was no way I was going to accept returning all the way to Bamako while our cars, possessions, plus Marcel and Yves cooled their heels on a siding far out in the middle of nowhere on the Mali-Senegal border. Given the weekend, it would probably take until Tuesday to get to Bamako and back — way past the point of acceptability and past the time my family would be arriving by plane in Dakar.

I knew that many, many officials throughout the third world — and the first world for that matter — were always on the lookout for bribes. I wondered two things: one, was this fellow looking for a payoff, and two, should I offer him one?

In all of my time in Mali I had never offered anyone a bribe. I — perhaps naively — didn't believe in them and thought them wrong, and I felt as well that small bribes were just as wrong and corrupting as big ones.

While I was considering my next move, I heard a noise in the distance and my heart sank the rest of the way: it was a train coming from Senegal. The Manantali freight train was here and it did not sound like it intended to stop at the border.

I was running out of time.

"Listen, I simply can't go back to Bamako. It will take too long and these French guys just can't be made to wait here at the border for me until I get back. My family arrives Monday evening by plane in Dakar and I have to be there for them."

I was getting desperate. The Manantali freight was starting to pass on the other track beside us and there was an incredible din. I had to yell to make myself heard. Since I had nothing to lose, I decided to take the plunge.

"Look, I'll do anything to get this straightened out now. I tell you what, I'll leave you 20,000 CFA, my name, passport number, and address in Dakar. You take care of the customs form and send it to me in Dakar and that can be the end of it."

I was giving him a chance to take my money and save face without it appearing to be an overt bribe.

Over the noise of the passing freight train he replied solemnly, "No, monsieur, I do not want your money."

God. I had run into a totally honest man and he really was just doing no more than his job.

The Manantali freight was almost past. Ahead I heard a railroad man's whistle. Our train was ready to depart and we were still uncoupled from it.

My desperation was reaching a new level.

"Please hook us back up. Everything I've told you is true. I thought I had all the right documents but these are all I was given. If you let us continue, I promise to cable my Bamako office the first thing Monday morning. I will have them get the proper form and somehow get a copy of it to you here as quickly as humanly possible. I had no intention of not respecting the rules. I simply must get to Dakar to meet my family."

The passing freight was now disappearing behind us down the tracks. The conductor's whistle blew again.

The honest Malian looked me straight in the eye without saying a word, deep in thought. Slowly he walked to the front of the flatbed and with one hand reached in and reconnected us to the rest of the train. Two seconds later, there was a lurch.

We were off.

I stood on the now moving flatcar hanging onto my car's open door, looking back at the slowing receding figure of my very last Malian official. He stood unmoving in the darkness beside the track, looking back at me.

Mali was behind me. Senegal lay ahead.

Epilogue

I spent my three and a half years in Mali during the early 1980s. Mali had begun its independence in 1961 with a decided Marxist tilt, only to find that this philosophy, when coupled with prolonged drought, was hastening Mali's economic decline along with the lot of its people. Mali was increasingly unable to feed itself, and even the one party state of President and General Moussa Traore had no choice but to begin to change Mali's economic policy and direction.

Though by African standards the early 1980s in Mali was a relatively tranquil period, change was already in the air. Mali, due in part to lessons learned from failed economic policies of the past and its absolute dependence on Western economic assistance, was moving steadily towards a free-enterprise system and the West. Soviet influence in Mali waned.

In 1984 Mali froze public sector salaries for three years and readopted the CFA franc. A number of state-owned enterprises were dismantled, and in the case of the state trading company SOMIEX, sold to private sector investors. After years of donor pressure, including from the U.S., OPAM, the infamous government cereal marketing board that kept city food prices artificially low at the expense of farmers, was finally withdrawing from the business of buying and selling grain. By 1987, Mali had an estimated grain surplus of 150,000 tons which was more than the grain deficit during its worst period of drought. Mali was once more a net exporter of food. Correct policies played a part in creating this surplus as well as one more important fact — adequate rainfall had returned to Mali and the cyclical drought of the 1970's and period of 1983-84 was over, a least for now.

Beginning in 1989, talk of multiparty democracy became increasingly common, spurned on in part through a private, opposition newspaper called *Les Echos* which had become openly critical of Moussa Traore's government. Traore's growing unpopularity was cemented by his abandonment by the French Ambassador, Traore's former confidant, who now urged the adoption of political pluralism. A year later a group of mid and high-level government officials and intellectuals wrote an open

191

letter to the president calling for democracy. In late 1990, a demonstration in favor of multiparty democracy drew some 30,000 people in to the streets of Bamako with little resulting violence.

In late January, 1991, the movement for democracy turned violent when rioters, mainly students, left Bamako with cars smoldering and overturned in the streets, shops burned, and tanks posted at all strategic points of the city. Four rioters were killed. An attempt at staging still another march a few days later led to police beatings and the arrest of one principal democracy leader. Hundreds of students then went on a rampage, sacking stores and burning cars. The government closed the schools indefinitely but this did little to stifle student activism in favor of democracy.

Traore himself was reportedly ready to liberalize the government, but his powerful wife, Mariam, persisted in encouraging military and government hard liners. Strikes and demonstrations continued on through February and March demanding multiparty democracy and freedom of the press.

In mid-March, Bamako students declared a national day of martyrs which resulted in a huge demonstration calling for the resignation of the Minister of Education. Thousands of others joined the students in the streets demanding multiparty democracy. Malian security forces met the demonstrators with machine gun and artillery fire, setting off three days of rioting and looting where government troops killed almost 150 people and injured about a thousand more.

The horror of this three day slaughter finally motivated soldiers to act. Led by Lt. Colonel Amadou Toumani Toure, the rebellious military faction arrested Traore as he was attempting to escape. Some 59 people were killed in the overnight coup including the Minister of Education and several other high officials. Toure's National Reconciliation Council affirmed that "the army will no longer meddle in politics," and within a week named a senior Malian official with the UNDP, Soumano Sacko, to oversee a transitional government until multiparty elections could be held. A new constitution was to be drafted and the military seemed serious about relinquishing power once the planned elections were carried out.

In June, 1992, elections were held as promised and Mali elected its first democratically elected President, Alpha Oumar Konare, who had been a schoolteacher during the troubles with Moussa Traore. President Konare, better known simply as "Alpha OK" by the Malians, made an impressive beginning for a new Mali despite its continued poverty and set out to consolidate a free government dedicated to openness and rule of law. With Moussa Traore coming to trial finally in 1996, Alpha OK opposes the imposition of capital punishment saying, "I hope that Moussa Traore and his friends live as long as possible so that they may see democracy flourish in Mali."

Alpha OK has carried out a privatization program and other free market reforms and has the economy growing at a 6% clip. The success of the reforms has recently been recognized with a $91 million loan from the IMF. He further settled a serious Touareg rebellion that had been raging in Mali's far north, culminating in March, 1996, with the signing of a peace treaty with the Tuaregs. The event was solemnized with a huge bonfire of some 3,000 weapons at Timbuktu while 10,000 people roared their approval — thus symbolizing the start of a new and hopeful day in Mali's history.

Several months after leaving Mali for good and settling in Dakar, I and my family took our required second "Home Leave" back to Texas. Joy was pregnant once again with what would turn out to be our second daughter, and I underwent knee surgery to repair the effects of half a lifetime of sports wear and tear. As the vacation approached its end and we prepared to return to Dakar, we received a telephone call from our old Mali friend Pat of softball fame. He was calling from Arizona and he was crying. He choked out his news: Mickey was dead.

Pat told the story as best he could. Mickey had returned to Bamako after a short stay with his mother in Geneva. Back in Mali and after a particularly contentious episode with the Malian director of *'Operation Haute Vallee'* where he worked, Mickey had fallen ill. The symptoms pointed to malaria and Mickey — as an AID contractor — had sought treatment at the U.S. Embassy medical unit. He was given a large dose of the drug Aralen which one normally took in small quantities to avoid malaria, and in larger quantities as treatment if one contracted the disease.

Mickey's condition had worsened and Ellie got very worried. She contacted the Paris office of Mickey's firm to request they medevac Mickey to Paris by special plane, but his employer had concluded somehow that Mickey was not ill enough to warrant such expensive and special treatment. Mickey's condition continued to worsen. Finally, the U.S. Embassy health unit decided on its own to medevac Mickey. But it was a Tuesday morning and the next direct flight to Paris was not until Thursday night. The next best way to Paris was via Dakar so Mickey was finally flown out of Bamako to Dakar on Air Afrique. Once in Dakar, Mickey's condition had deteriorated to the point that Air Afrique had at first refused to put him on its Paris flight for fear that he would die during the trip.

The U.S. Embassy doctor in Dakar — a friend of ours and a highly competent physician — had sprung into action and though he didn't know Mickey at all, moved heaven and earth to convince Air Afrique to accept Mickey, and finally having accomplished that, to have an ambulance meet the plane in Paris and have Mickey admitted to the highly regarded

American Hospital in Paris. Mickey was in a near coma by the time he was allowed to leave Dakar, but somehow was able to sit up from his litter and write a check to the airline for his airfare just before departure.

Mickey was admitted to the American Hospital and was soon joined by Ellie who by now had taken the Thursday night Paris flight from Bamako. But is was too late for Mickey. Though the official diagnosis was now hepatitis instead of malaria, the damage done to Mickey's liver was too great. The time that it had taken to get him to a decent medical facility had simply been too long. Mickey died without ever regaining consciousness. Ellie woke from a dream in her hotel room knowing that Mickey was gone — soon confirmed by a call from the hospital.

Devastated, Joy and I made plans to fly to Geneva for the funeral, joined there by Pat and Roberta and another close friend of Mickey's from work. His mother, whose husband had died the year before, described Mickey's last recent trip to Geneva. He had walked around his mother's apartment staring at the beautiful paintings on the wall and shaking his head, telling his mother, "I'll never see these paintings again."

The sad story ultimately had a positive turn. Though everyone was grief-stricken over Mickey's death, the immediate worry had to be Ellie and Roya. They certainly wouldn't want to remain in Bamako. Yet returning to Iran was out the question and likewise being permitted entry into the U.S. was similarly impossible given their status as Iranian citizens and passport holders.

Ellie, who was holding herself together about as well as could be expected, returned to Bamako to gather her possessions and life together as best she could, while all her friends sprung into action. Ambassador Borg, still in Bamako, contacted the State Department in Washington about possible special provisions for Ellie and Roya's admission into the U.S. — after all, Mickey had been working on a project financed by the U.S. Government. David Wilson, also a friend of Mickey's, wrote letters to Senators and Congressmen, as did I and others.

Back in Dakar, Joy and I heard the good news. Ellie and Roya had been granted political asylum in the U.S. We found later that Ellie had had a very key ally in the State Department's asylum decision — an American politician named George Bush — who had been a friend of Mickey's father when both had been Ambassadors to the United Nations for their respective countries. Ellie and Roya settled in Washington, D.C. while Ellie looked for work and began a two year process to be granted status as a permanent resident of the U.S.

Meanwhile in Dakar, I convinced my boss Vito to let me return to Bamako to work further on Manantali resettlement. Joy went with me and caught up with Barbara as Jerry took up the final stages of the detailed resettlement design that I knew was now poor Jerry's main work task and cross to bear. I contributed the maximum I could in the week allotted to me and then returned to my own regular duties in Dakar. Jerry and I at least were able to catch up with each others' lives and exchange stories about Mickey.

Manantali resettlement began actual implementation in 1984 following signature of a formal agreement with the Government of Mali. Implementation contracts were signed, advisors were hired, detailed preliminary studies were carried out and completed, and the Malian Government gave further attention to the staffing of its Resettlement Project Unit.

The dam was completed by 1985 and the reservoir began filling. Half of the Manantali area villagers — beginning with those first affected by the rising water levels — were supposed to have been moved to their new homes by mid-1986, and though their were some delays, particularly in clearing agricultural fields, construction of new villages sites, and provision of building materials, essentially the goal of resettling half the villagers by mid-1986 was successfully achieved.

Beginning in June of 1986, the first villagers began moving to their new sites, though only about half of the required houses were finished and mud bricks were in short supply. Daily, trucks moved people and their goods to the new sites, and cattle walked to the new resettlement areas when distance made this feasible. At the end of 1986, about 50% had been successfully moved, and 1987 was to see the movement and reinstallation of almost all of the remaining Manantali area villagers.

Distribution of farm land in the new sites had proven to be an important resettlement implementation issue. Jerry, I, and the Malian Resettlement Project Unit had assumed that the villagers' customary system for parceling our land would be applied in the new sites. Yet by 1985, villagers were asking project planners about how they planned to distribute agricultural parcels. Everyone was understandably worried about the inevitable inequalities of land distribution no matter who made the decision. The problem was ultimately solved to most villagers' satisfaction by use of a blind land distribution lottery system.

Another of our original plans — to amalgamate villages into resettled larger units — was also dropped. Villagers, who had originally thought the plan a good idea, soon began to worry about who would govern and lead the new larger villages, realizing that power would be drastically altered once previously autonomous units were formed. The amalgamated village idea was soon altered in favor of separate village units.

Actual movement of villagers to their new sites was completed by late 1987, but the accompanying work to complete construction of houses, granaries, chicken coops, and so forth was to continue for several more years. As the design had come to represent, some of the actual construction was provided by the project, some by the villagers themselves.

While a majority of the resettling villagers chose to locate their new villages downstream from the Manantali dam and seemed to reestablish themselves better and faster than the villagers who remained upstream, it is projected that availability of adequate agricultural land for the downstream villagers may eventually develop into more of a problem than for the upstream zone.

The question of land availability has already begun to be a problem in some new villages as there is insufficient agricultural land to permit villagers to follow their traditional fallow/crop rotation system. This in turn has led to overly intense cultivation of the same land season after season, inevitably leading to decreased yields and possibly pointing to future squabbles over sufficient land availability for cultivation. Despite potential future problems of this kind, agricultural production was reestablished at most of the new village sites by 1988 which was earlier than expected by project implementors, with better-than-average yields achieved thanks in part to abundant rainfall during the crucial time period immediately following resettlement. Some years after the villagers were resettled in their new villages, fruit production of mangoes, papaya, guava, and dates was still not fully reestablished at the levels of the old sites, as new tree plantings were very susceptible to being eaten by cows, goats and sheep.

Not unexpectedly, the construction of the dam resulted in an end to the former isolation of the zone, with formal marketplaces now established, especially the vibrant daily market at Manantali village. Also significantly, regular outlets for local agricultural and artisan production developed permitting individuals to more regularly market their produce rather than rely as before on the erratic arrival of the occasional trader. The availability of cash from wages during dam construction and for a while afterwards also changed things, allowing some villagers to respond to the new economic activity by selling a variety of goods like foodstuffs, charcoal and game. As time passed after dam completion, cash available from wages dried up and there were few development activities to absorb the available excess labor.

Though in as complex and controversial an undertaking as forced resettlement, chaos often will reign and a host of controversial issues will arise, the project was completed with the 12,000 Malinke villagers resettled into their new sites. One U.S. anthropologist who worked as a project monitoring and evaluation specialist on the Manantali project wrote in 1994 that, "It is possible to make the argument that the Manantali resettlement project was the most successful, large-scale involuntary resettlement project ever completed in a developing country. I attribute this to a very sound design that sought to apply many of the lessons that had been learned during less successful resettlements, and to the extraordinary hard work and commitment to making the project successful by people in the Malian Resettlement Project Unit like Djibril Diallo, Mamadou Sidibe, Yacouba Coulibaly, Robert Dembele, as well as many others."